100 OREGON HIKING TRAILS

By DON & ROBERTA LOWE

THE TOUCHSTONE PRESS
P. O. BOX 401
PORTLAND, OREGON
97207

Library of Congress Catalog
Card No. 75—80014

Maps Courtesy of
U.S. Geological Survey

preface

HOW TO USE THIS BOOK

Welcome to the outdoors! Whether you want to take a relaxed stroll, a rigorous backpack trip or perhaps something in between, you will be able to find many hikes to suit your style from the trails described in this book. This is a field book, and you are encouraged to use it throughout the entire year since every season has certain unique features which cannot be enjoyed during other times.

In the spring there are pungent odors on the first dry and warm days, new leaves unfolding to the sunlight, brilliant wild flowers in a myriad of colors, and the many sparkling snow patches rapidly melting into oblivion. The cool, clear atmosphere of fall lends a feeling of exhilaration which is heightened by the spectacular display of the red vine maple, the yellow alder and larch and, east of the Cascades, the beautiful gold of the aspen. Also to be observed are the hundreds of different kinds of mushrooms which at this time of year begin thrusting their heads through the soil. In the hush of winter, after the first snowfall, you can observe the tracks of all those animals you suspected were in the forest but may never actually have seen. Of course, the summer months are best for camping, swimming, and backpacking into the high country.

Described in this book are 100 different hikes, 96 in Oregon and four on the northern side of the Columbia River Gorge in the State of Washington. The trails are grouped into six geographic sections for ease of identification. These sections are: Northern Oregon Coast, Columbia River Gorge, Northern Oregon, Central Oregon, Southern Oregon, and Northeastern Oregon. A map of Oregon showing the major cities and highways as well as the section boundaries follows the Table of Contents, which lists the trails in the order they appear. At the beginning of each section is a map showing the location of the trails within that section, as well as highways, relevant side roads, cities, towns, and certain physiographic features in greater detail than the large map at the beginning of the book. Photographs representative of the region and a one-page introduction describing that particular part of the state will be found at the beginning of each section.

The individual trails are presented in a two-page format consisting of a topographic map, text describing the hike and one or more photographs typical of the views along the trail. Accompanying the text is data pertinent to the hike.

Hiking time given is one-way and is from the beginning point to the destination as identified by the farthest mile number on the map. In four cases, loop trip times are shown since these trails are customarily hiked without returning along the same route. The time is determined from the basic calculation of two miles per hour, with allowance for steepness and rest stops. At altitudes above 6,000 feet, additional time is allowed since it is assumed that most Oregon hikers will not be acclimated to such heights. Naturally, the time it takes any one individual to make a specific hike may vary from that shown, but after a few trips you will be able to tell whether to add or subtract from the times listed.

Hiking distance is measured one-way only so that it will correlate with the suggested hiking times. To avoid confusion, mileages are not given for *optional* loop trips.

Elevation gain is listed as a total footage increment and is not necessarily just the difference between your lowest and highest altitude. Many hikes have an appreciable loss of altitude which is subsequently regained and, if ignored, would result in an understatement of the amount of climbing you actually have to do. Significant elevation loss is also shown.

The high point is the highest elevation that is reached on the trip, and is either a specific bench mark altitude or an interpolation of contour line elevations.

A hike identified as a one-day trip is usually either very short or lacks suitable campsites. A trip classified as one-day or backpack (for which you carry overnight camping equipment) means that the hike can normally be done in one day but that because of length, scenic attractions, or the availability of good campsites, you may prefer to camp overnight. Those trails designated for backpack only normally are too long for the average hiker to do in one day. Very long trips with no water or campsites are not included in this book.

The length of time the trails are open will vary from one year to another depending upon the depth of the snowpack and the prevailing temperature. If you have doubts about a particular area, check with the forest ranger station nearest the trail, the district forest service office, or some other reliable source.

The text for each trail is divided into three general parts. The first paragraph attempts to describe briefly special attractions such as panoramic views, lakes, flowers and other features of particular interest.

The second section provides information on driving directions to the start of the trail. These instructions are given for all commonly used approaches and do not presuppose that everyone will start from a major metropolitan area. Smaller towns that are mentioned can be located on the individual section maps if not on standard road maps. The remainder of the text is devoted to a detailed description of the trail route including possible side trips and points of interest along the way with specific emphasis on the avoidance of wrong turns, unmarked trails, and other problems the hiker may encounter. Comment also is made on the lack of water, extreme steepness or exposure, and other special precautions which should be observed.

No attempt has been made to grade the trails according to difficulty, since this would necessitate a subjective evaluation which might not fit each individual's concept of an easy or hard hike. In addition, weather conditions may increase considerably the difficulty of a trail, or perhaps a hiker who usually considers a twelve mile hike exhilarating may have an off day and be exhausted by a five mile walk. Elevation gain is a major factor in the determination of how strenuous a trip will be. After a few times out you will be able to grade the trails for yourself by comparing the mileage, elevation gain, and taking other factors into consideration such as the weather and how you feel on a specific day.

Each photograph in this book was taken specifically to illustrate this volume and all were acquired within eighteen months preceding the date of publication. In the main, the pictures are intended to provide the hiker with views typical of what can be seen along the trail. In some cases, aerial photographs were taken to illustrate a geographic area, which for one reason or another could not be shown best from a terrestrial vantage point. Some photographs of trailside minutia have been provided for variety.

The maps for each trail are enlarged or reduced sections of topographic maps produced by the U.S. Geological Survey. The items in red are those which are particularly important in helping you find, stay on, and enjoy the trail. Some features were already on the original map, while others have been added to enable you to get the most benefit from the book and the hike. You are urged to read the text carefully and simultaneously follow the map.

Despite their foreboding appearance, topographic maps are simple in theory and with practice you will be able to visualize the terrain covered by a trail before you arrive in the area. Through interpretation of these maps you will be able to determine to some extent beforehand the difficulty of the trail and feasibility of reaching a lake or peak off the trail which you may wish to visit, to make a loop trip not described in the text or just to derive more enjoyment from each trail. Also, in case you ever become confused, being able to read a topographic map will make it easier for you to orient yourself.

All those lines that seem to wiggle around on the map are contour lines connecting points of equal elevation. The space between any two contour lines is called a contour interval and is a measure of vertical distance. Since the number of feet in each interval remains constant for any one map, the spacing of the contour lines will be the key to the slope of the ground. The closer the contour lines the steeper the terrain. How steep depends on the magnitude of the contour interval which, in this book, is usually 80 feet, but may be 40 feet — or even 10 feet. You can calculate the interval for a map by finding the difference between any two consecutive figures appearing along every fifth contour line and then dividing by five. Keep the contour interval in mind when you study each map because terrain that appears steep on a map with 80-foot contour intervals is far steeper than terrain marked by 40-foot contour intervals spaced the same distance apart on a map of the same scale. *NOTE* — Some of the trails in this book required the combining of two or more maps of dissimilar scales.

Topographic maps also show lakes, rivers, creeks, and the works of man such as roads, railroads, buildings, clearcuts, and other relevant features. Unshaded areas are regions of little or no vegetation. Figures either along the contour lines, at the summits of peaks, or elsewhere mark elevations above mean sea level. Original topographic maps have a green overprint depicting areas with plant cover. These areas appear in this book as a medium to dark grey shade depending on the density of the green ink used on the original map. The scales of the maps (the ratio of any unit of distance on the map to the equivalent unit on the ground) vary, but the most common are 1 to 62,500, called 15-minute series and usually has an 80-foot contour interval, and 1 to 27,500, termed a 7.5-minute series and normally has a 40-foot contour interval. All maps in the book are north oriented.

The individual topographic maps usually cover an area considerably greater than the region traversed by the trail. If you wish to purchase copies of the original topographic maps from which those in this book have been reproduced, the map name, identifying number, scale, and year of publication is provided. If more than one map was used to show a specific trail, you will find the data listed for each map. U.S.G.S. topographic maps are sold through selected retail outlets in major cities, or you can purchase them from the U.S. Government by sending $0.50 and the identifying information for each map to: Distribution Section, Geological Survey, Federal Center, Denver, Colorado 80225. Be sure to include your Zip Code.

The Skyline Trail which follows the Cascades through Oregon has been re-designated No. 2000, but in some places older signs will show other numbers. Also, in certain places some confusion may exist as certain portions of the Pacific Crest Trail system are being re-routed. The mileages shown may not always agree with those on the trail signs. Mileages shown on the maps are taken from known points or have been interpolated from specific fixes and U.S. Forest Service logs. Frequently you will see trails on the topographic maps which are not overlayed in red. This is because they either have no relevance to the trail being described or are no longer maintained. However, some trails, although now abandoned, have been included on the map because of their good condition. Campsites which are marked with open triangles may or may not be improved and water is not necessarily available at these locations. Important sources of water not obvious from the topographic map are identified by the word "water" or "spring."

Hiking and backpacking techniques are not discussed here because there are many fine books available which cover this subject very thoroughly. However, for those inexperienced hikers who intend to use this book for one-day trips only, there are a few points which should be mentioned for your enjoyment as well as your safety. Although many of these 100 trails can be done in tennis shoes, a good hiking boot with lug soles will give you more traction and more foot support. Most of these trips are in mountainous country where the weather can deteriorate very quickly. It is always wise to carry a wool hat, gloves, a sweater, and a windbreaker in your pack. Also, if one of your party is injured or becomes ill on the trail and must wait for help, these extra clothes will keep him more comfortable. A flashlight should also be carried since groping your way down a dark trail may be dangerous. Halozone water purifying tablets and a first aid kit should also be standard equipment in your pack.

Although many hikers may snicker, a man's large umbrella is a wonderful companion in wet weather. Surprisingly, your arm won't get tired holding one up and it will keep you dry. It is a particular boon if you are wearing glasses. Rain clothes, while desirable for wearing around camp and walking on the level, will get you as wet from perspiration when climbing as the rain would if no rain clothes had been worn. However, an umbrella keeps off the rain and you can wear lighter clothing while climbing, thereby keeping both cool and dry.

Although information is given in the description of trails where water is either in short supply or not available at all, it is always a good practice to leave home with a plastic bottle full of tap water. Lastly, be sure to build fires only in prepared areas and make sure they are out when you leave camp. DON'T LITTER — KEEP OREGON GREEN AND CLEAN to insure the survival of the wilderness for everyone to enjoy.

As noted elsewhere, the authors hiked each of the trails in this book in 1967-68 to insure that the most accurate and up-to-date trail information was available to those who use the book. However, trails change or are changed, either because of rock falls, washouts, and other natural causes, or because the officials who maintain the trails change to alternate routes. It is the intention of the authors to revise this volume every four to five years. If you have found this book helpful to you, and you wish to assist the authors in this updating process, you are invited to send changes or irregularities noted on your hikes to the authors in care of Touchstone Press, P.O. Box 401, Portland, Oregon 97207.

D. L.
R. L.

contents

legend

●	Starting Point
– – – –	Trail
·········	Obscure Trail
△	Campsite
■ ◣	Building or Remains
3.5	Mileage
No.16	Trail No.
S-37	Road No.
	Bridge
═══	Access Road

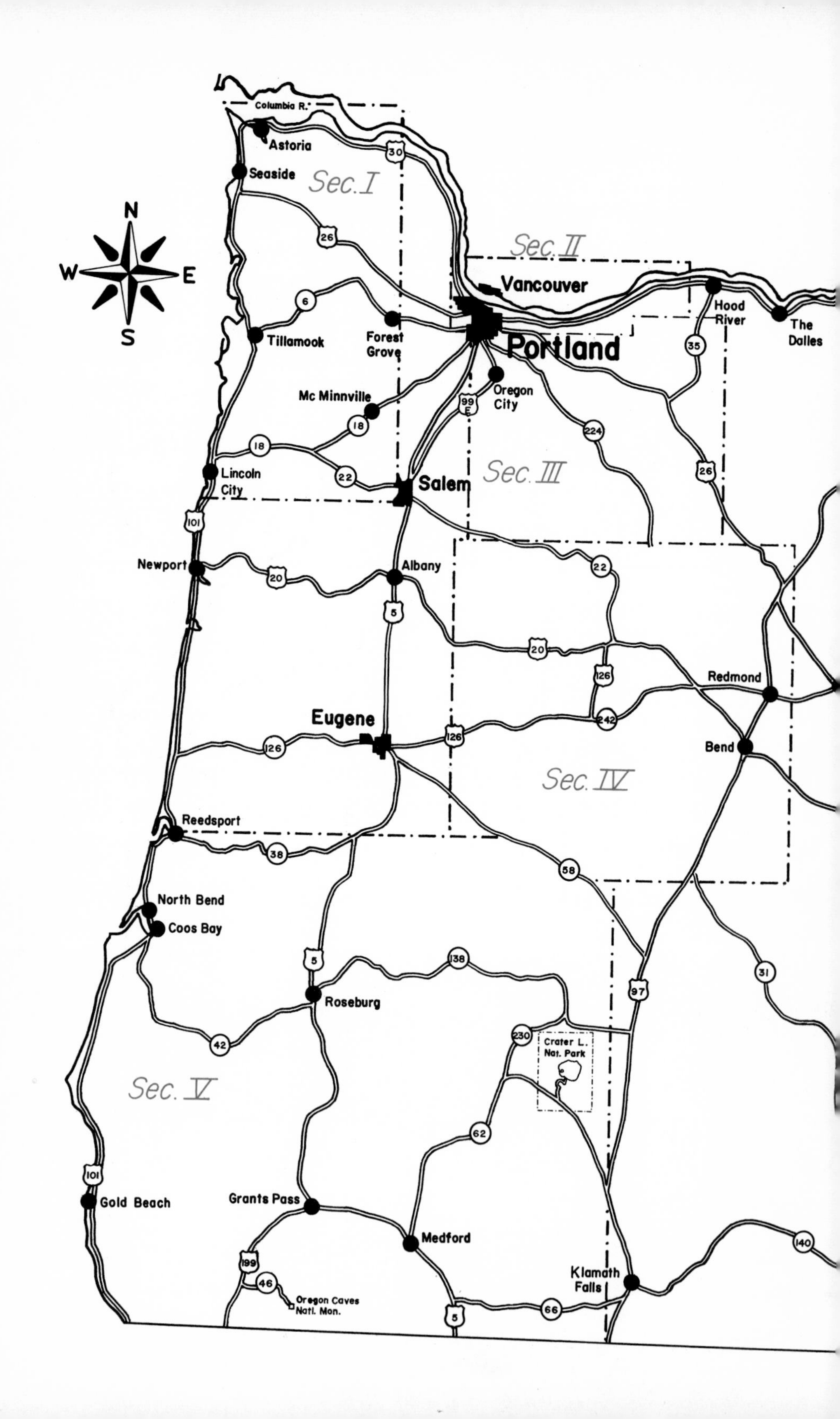

Columbia R.
Astoria
30
Seaside
Sec. I
N
W
E
S
26
Sec. II
Vancouver
6
Forest Grove
Tillamook
Portland
Hood River
The Dalles
35
Oregon City
Mc Minnville
99 E
18
224
18
22
Lincoln City
Salem
Sec. III
26
101
Newport
20
Albany
22
5
20
126
Redmond
Eugene
242
126
126
Bend
Sec. IV
Reedsport
38
58
North Bend
Coos Bay
5
138
Roseburg
97
31
42
230
Crater L. Nat. Park
Sec. V
62
101
Gold Beach
Grants Pass
Medford
140
199
46
Klamath Falls
Oregon Caves Natl. Mon.
66
5

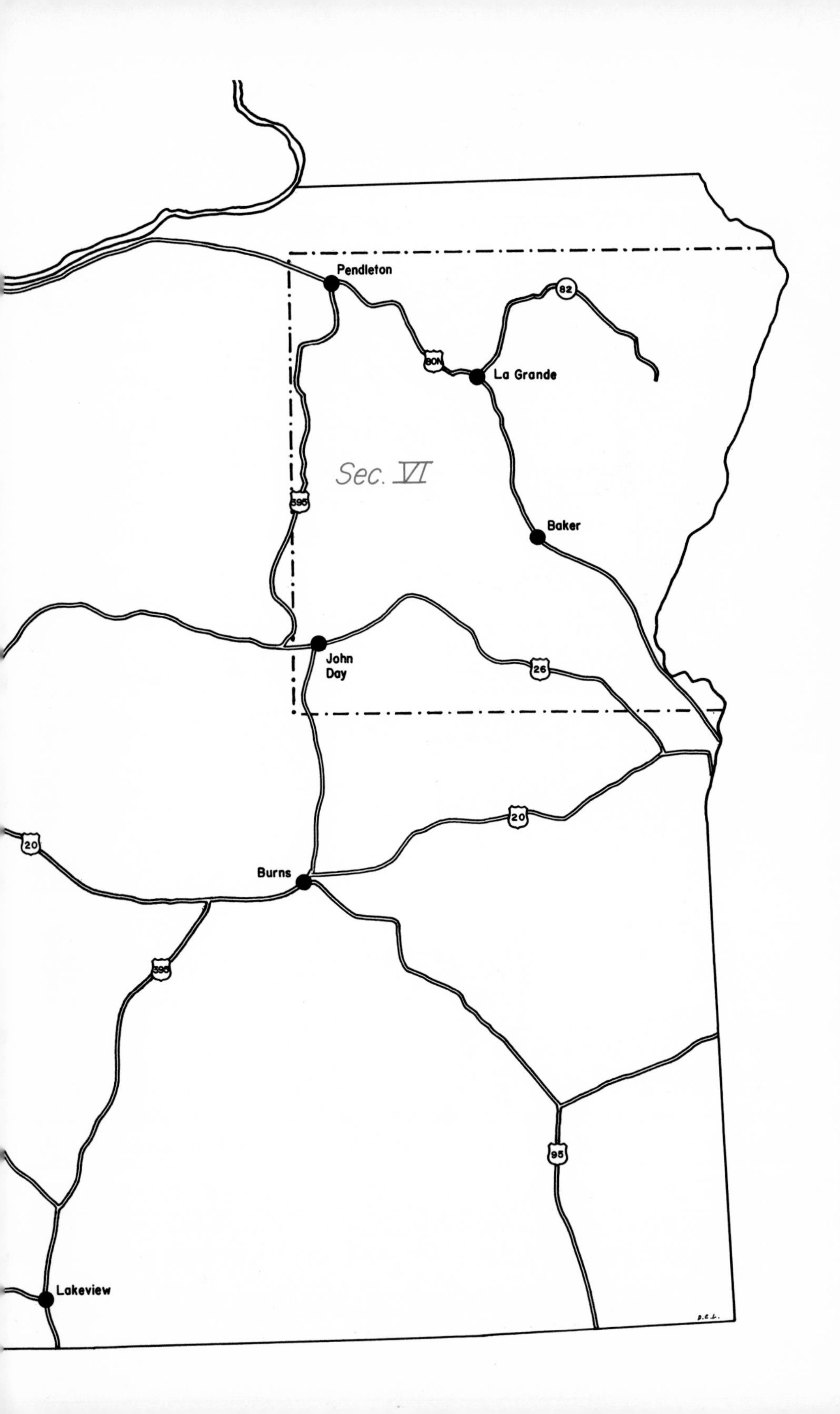
Pendleton
82
80N
La Grande
Sec. VI
395
Baker
John
Day
26
20
20
Burns
395
95
Lakeview
D.C.L.

SECTION I — NORTHERN OREGON COAST

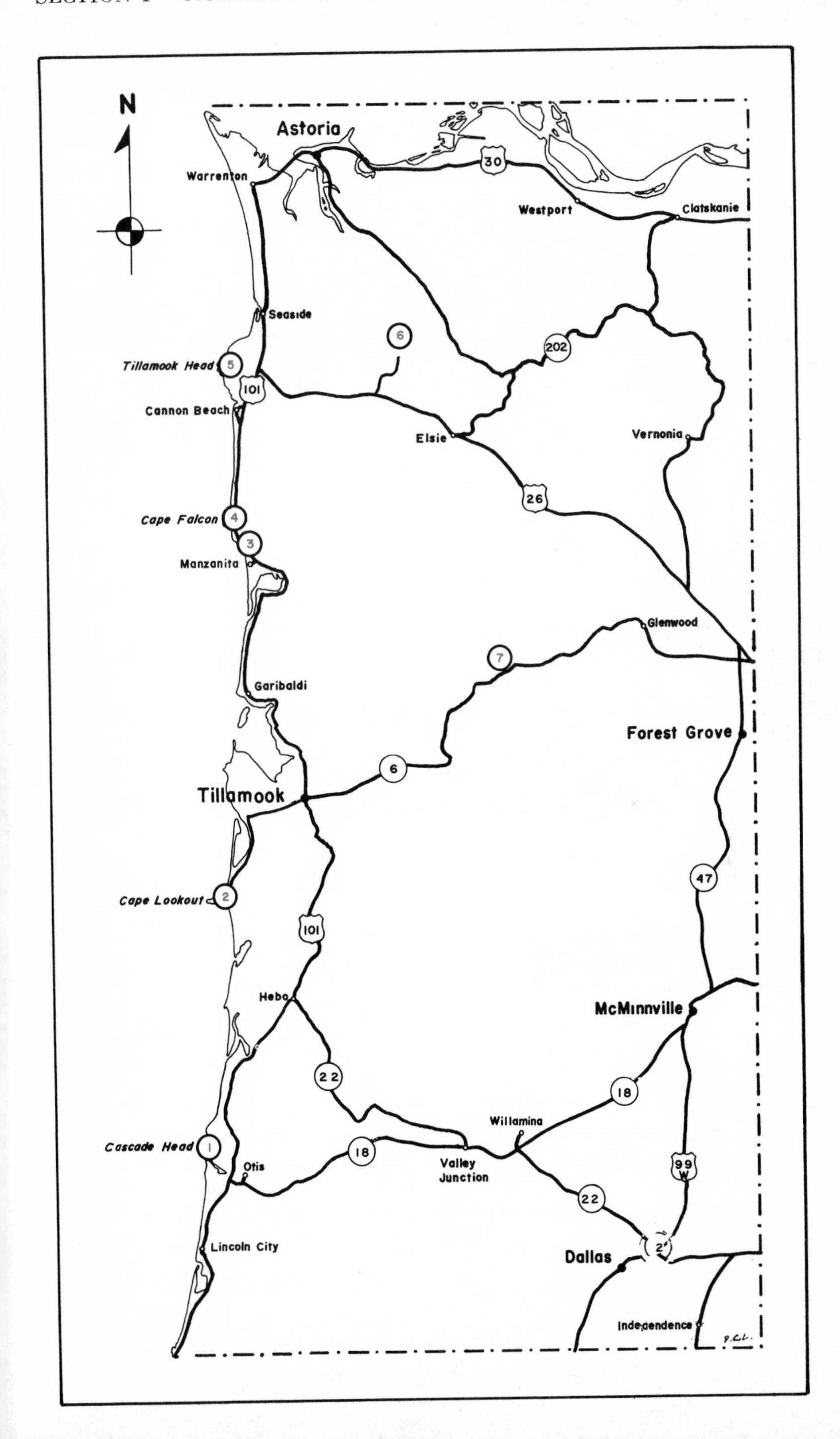

Many persons say that Oregon possesses the most beautiful coastline in the world. Its sculptured cliffs, headlands, arches, and the heavily-timbered foothills of the Coast Range form an ever-contrasting backdrop for the Pacific Ocean.

In some areas along the coast a calm sea caresses lengthy stretches of sandy beach; elsewhere immense waves explode against massive rocks. During a storm, the sound of the pounding surf can be heard for a considerable distance inland.

Five of the seven trails in this section are located between the towns of Seaside and Lincoln City. They offer a good cross section of Oregon's coastline. The two remaining trails, Saddle Mountain and Kings Mountain, are somewhat inland, near the center of the Coast Range. From the summit of the former you can see the silver streak of the ocean and the city of Astoria at the mouth of the Columbia River.

Kings Mountain is of particular interest since it lies in the heart of the Tillamook Burn, an area covered by three enormous forest fires which left a total of 411,000 acres of destruction. The first fire erupted August 14, 1933, in a private logging operation. The weather was very hot and extraordinarily dry, and the already dangerous fire hazard was further worsened by a high east wind which sometimes blows into western Oregon from the deserts east of the Cascades. At that time fire-fighting techniques were unsophisticated, and the fire was not contained until it killed almost 13 billion board feet of timber.

Subsequent to the first fire, two other major conflagrations occurred, one in 1939 and the other in 1945. (A fire that is minor by comparison burned 20,000 acres in the same general area in 1951.) Since the early 1950's the U.S. Forest Service and private groups have been reforesting the area. Although substantial progress has been made in some areas, "The Burn" looks much like it did just after World War II, except that most of the snags have been removed by salvage logging operations. From the top of Kings Mountain almost the whole area covered by these fires can be seen, an example of the immensity of the destruction capable of being wrought by the carelessness of man.

Since most of the coast trails are situated at or near sea level, they usually can be hiked throughout the entire year. In fact, some of the most pleasant weather occurs during the winter months when the rest of the state is cold and wet. There are no backpack trips along the coast, but many excellent state parks afford good places for overnight camping. These parks are usually very crowded in the middle of summer, but if you make use of them in the early spring or fall, ample camping space will not be hard to find. Only a few of the state parks are kept open during the winter months.

A windbreaker is a useful garment on the coastal trails most of the time, and heavier clothing often is comfortable.

You will have very little elevation gain on the coastal trails. Saddle and Kings Mountain are the exception with Kings Mountain being the more difficult, demanding stamina and some route-finding ability.

Despite the heavy vegetation along the coast, most of the trails are well-maintained, and all have splendid views from many vantage points. Cascade Head is particularly pleasant during the spring when tall grass covers the many acres of open hillside. This area has been purchased by a private conservation group and will be kept in its original condition without buildings or other encroachments.

1 CASCADE HEAD NORTHERN OREGON COAST

One day trip
Distance: 2 miles one way
Elevation gain: 440 feet, loss 160 feet
High point: 600 feet
Allow 1½ hours one way
Open all year
Topographic map:
U.S.G.S. Hebo, Oreg.
N4500-W12345/15
1955

A panorama of ocean headlands to the north and south, and of the Salmon River Valley to the southeast awaits you from the top of Cascade Head. The open slopes of the headlands are spectacular, also.

Three hundred acres around Cascade Head were purchased by Nature Conservancy early in 1967, thus assuring preservation of the area in its wild state. Forest Service land borders the Head on the north and access from the east is via easements through private land.

Take U.S. Highway 101 to the Three Rocks Road, located just north of the Salmon River, and one mile north of the junction of highways 18 and 101. Turn west and follow this road for 2.3 miles, then turn right onto the Lower Salmon River Road. Travel for 0.4 of a mile to the trail head. The entrance is well marked with wood carved signs and a stile to impede all but foot traffic.

The trail climbs through deciduous woods for about one-fourth mile before coming to the edge of a meadow. Turn north and follow along the fence on the right, which returns again to the woods. After going through a gate, you climb in a northerly direction for about one-half mile, where the trail levels off. Then continue through the forest to the west for an additional one-half mile, crossing several small streams. There the trail leaves the woods and contours along expansive grassy headlands, continuing along the hillside until reaching a junction of four fences. At that point, proceed downhill along the fence line which borders the edge of the cliff. Crawl under the fence where it turns to the south and climb up the final 100 yards to the top of the Head.

Cascade Head

Cascade Head — Cape Lookout in background

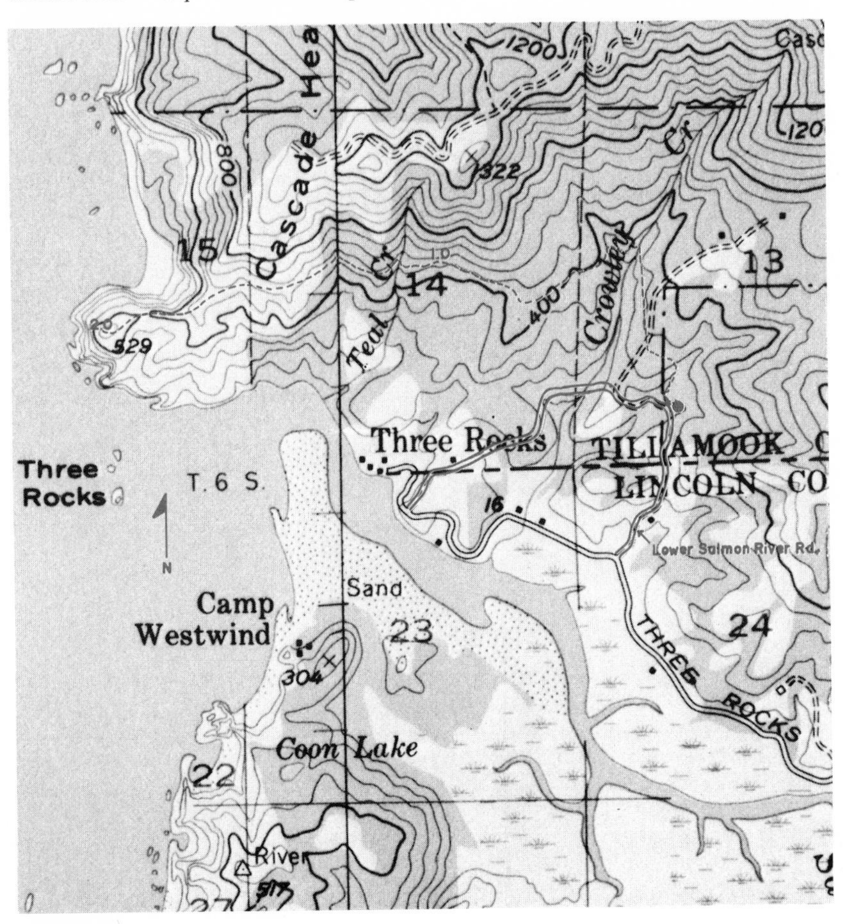

2 CAPE LOOKOUT
NORTHERN OREGON COAST

One day trip
Distance: 2½ miles one way
Elevation gain: 300 feet, loss 770 feet
High point: 830 feet
Allow 1½ to 2 hours one way
Open all year
Topographic map:
U.S.G.S. Tillamook, Oreg.
N4515-12345/15
1955

Westernmost tip of Cape Lookout

Cape Lookout is a thin peninsula that juts into the sea southwest of the city of Tillamook. The trail to the end of the cape was much longer before the construction of a road which passes over the eastern end of the strip of land joining Cape Lookout State Park with the town of Sandlake.

On August 1, 1943, an Army Air Force four-engined aircraft crashed near the present trail head, and much of the wreckage can still be found. A commemorative plaque listing the names of the deceased and the lone survivor has been placed on a rock near the site.

To get to the trail, drive west from Tillamook on the road to Cape Meares. Just after crossing the Tillamook River turn south and drive toward Cape Lookout State Park. Four-tenths of a mile north of the park turn left on a paved road and continue south for 2.8 miles to the crest of the Cape. Turn right and proceed 0.1 mile to a gravel yard where there is ample parking.

The trail starts on the west end of the gravel yard and contours along the south side of the Cape through heavy timber. At one-fourth mile the plaque may be seen on the right, about head high. For some distance beyond the plaque large pieces of wreckage still remain entangled in the dense undergrowth. At 1.2 miles there is a short side trail leading to a viewpoint high above a small bay. The mournful tone of the buoy off the west end of the Cape can be heard from here as well as from many points along the trail, especially if the wind is from the west.

From the view point to the end of the Cape the trail frequently alternates between tunnel-like vegetation, so thick in places that you must almost crawl to get through, and narrow ledges that drop precipitously to the sea several hundred feet below.

From the westernmost tip of the Cape you can see the warning buoy about one-half mile off shore. To the south is the town of Tierra Del Mar and the bulk of Cape Kiwanda, while to the north lies the broad expanse of Netarts Bay and the Three Arch Rocks off Maxwell Point.

Cape Lookout

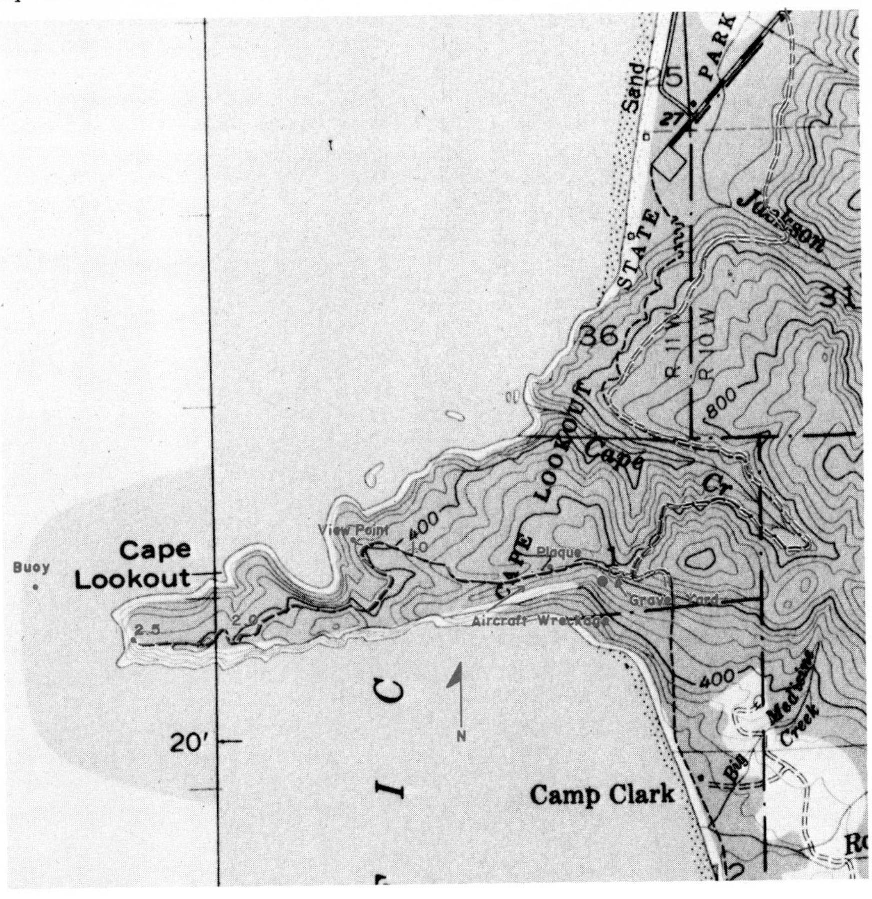

3 NEAHKAHNIE MOUNTAIN NORTHERN OREGON COAST

One day trip
Distance: 1 mile one way
Elevation gain: 1,111 feet
High point: 1,631 feet
Allow 1 hour one way
Usually open all year
Topographic map:
U.S.G.S. Nehalem, Oreg.
N4530-W12345/15
1955

Manzanita and Nehalem Bay

Nehalem Bay and the beaches to the south are the predominant views from the summit of Neahkahnie Mountain. The golf course and houses almost 1,600 feet below look like small models and give the impression of an aerial view.

The hike to the summit is short and is not difficult. However, since there is no water available on the trail, you should carry an adequate supply.

Take U.S. Highway 101 to a gravel road marked by a sign pointing to Neahkahnie Mountain Trail, located 2.6 miles south of Short Sand Beach parking area and just north of the Neahkahnie Golf Course. Turn east on the gravel road and proceed 0.4 mile to the trail head, which also is identified by a sign.

The first half of the trail is composed of many switchbacks angling up the brush-covered south slope of the mountain. At one-half mile the trail enters a wooded area contouring via switchbacks up the mountain's eastern slope. Here there is a junction with an access road leading to the old television relay station on the east peak. Turn left (west) onto the road, which runs along the ridge, and be sure to take note of where the trail joins the road so you won't miss the trail on the return trip. Continue west keeping to the left where the road forks. A short distance beyond is the television relay station. Twenty-five feet east of the building and to the north, drop down to a trail which runs past the building to the narrow summit ridge. The best views are to be found on the west peak.

Summit of Neahkahnie Mountain

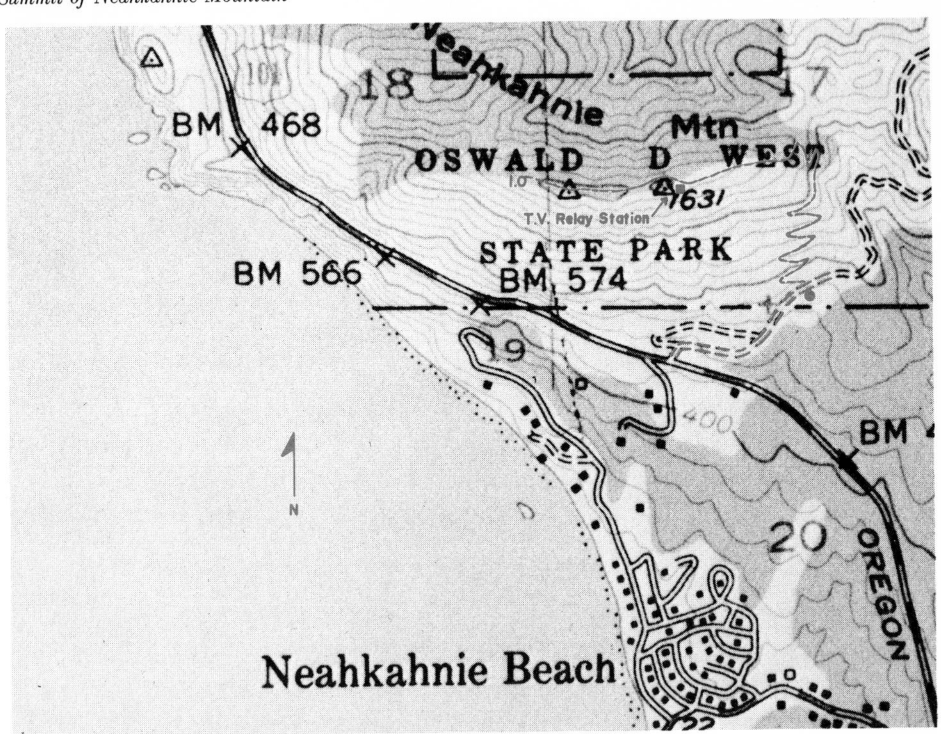

4 CAPE FALCON NORTHERN OREGON COAST

One day trip
Distance: 2 miles one way
Elevation gain: 400 feet, loss 100 feet
High point: 300 feet
Allow 1 to 1½ hours one way
Usually open all year
Topographic map:
U.S.G.S. Cannon Beach, Oreg.
N4545-W12345/15
1955

Cliffs, coves, dense rain forest, and a panoramic view of Smuggler Cove and Short Sand Beach highlight this easy trail. For those who wish to spend some time here, overnight camping facilities are provided near the beach. Water and fire wood are available.

Drive on U.S. Highway 101 to Oswald West State Park, located approximately half way between the towns of Seaside and Tillamook. You may park on either side of the bridge spanning Short Sand Creek.

There are two possible starting points for the hike. The first begins on the southeastern end of the bridge adjacent to a drinking fountain. It passes under the bridge and descends gradually for about one-quarter mile to the camping and picnic area just above the beach on a low bluff. From here it turns north and joins the other trail a short distance beyond.

The second trail is less used and offers more solitude. It is like being in a primeval forest because the huge trees obscure most of the sunlight, creating a lush park-like atmosphere that is complemented by the meandering trail. It leaves the parking area beyond the northwest end of the bridge at a sign pointing to Falcon Point. After about one-third mile of nearly level travel it joins with the other trail above Short Sand Beach.

From the junction, the trail leads first north, then curves to the west, contours in and out of several wooded ravines, and occasionally offers beautiful views of the ocean and Smuggler Cove.

At 1.5 miles a short side trail to the left leads through heavy undergrowth to a view point, where you will get an unobstructed view of Neahkahnie Mountain to the south. The rugged cliffs of Cape Falcon also can be seen immediately to the north.

The main trail continues for about one-third mile to its termination at a high point on the edge of a cliff overlooking a small bay and Falcon Rock, about three-fourths mile offshore.

Cape Falcon

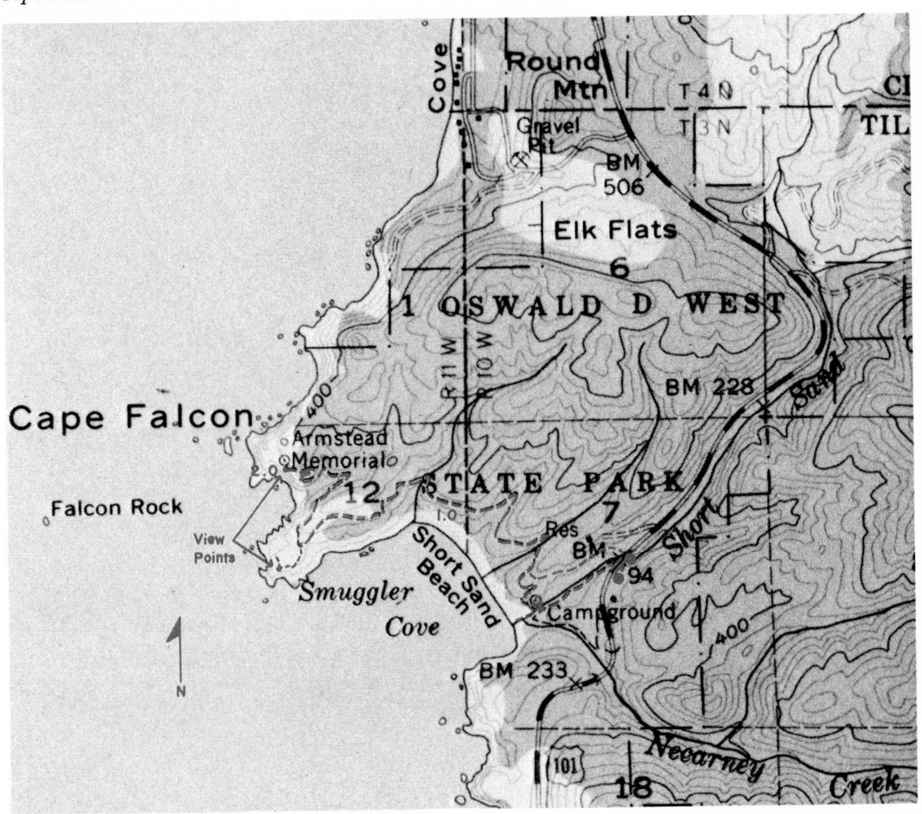
Round
Mtn
Cove
T 4 N
T 3 N
Gravel
Pit
BM
506
Elk Flats
6
1 OSWALD D WEST
R 11 W
R 10 W
BM 228
Sand
Cape Falcon
Armstead
Memorial
12 STATE PARK
7
Falcon Rock
View
Points
Res
BM
94
Short
Short Sand
Beach
Smuggler
Cove
Campground
400
BM 233
N
101
Necarney
Creek
18

5 TILLAMOOK HEAD NORTHERN OREGON COAST

One day trip
Distance: 6 miles one way
Elevation gain: 1,190 feet, loss 1,230 feet
High point: 1,200 feet
Allow 3 hours one way
Usually open all year
Topographic map:
U.S.G.S. Cannon Beach, Oreg.
N4545-W12345/15
1955

The trail along Tillamook Head traverses a cape jutting out into the sea between the towns of Seaside and Cannon Beach near Ecola State Park. If car shuttling is available, a one-way trip can be made from either direction with easy access on paved roads to both ends of the trail.

The hike over the Head is not difficult, with only a moderate elevation gain. However, several of the viewpoints, especially those near Indian Beach, consist of overhanging grass cornices with no guard rails. You should keep well back from the edge at these points.

The southern terminus of the trail is at Indian Beach in Ecola State Park. Take U.S. Highway 101 to Cannon Beach and follow the signs to Ecola State Park. From the picnic area at the park, take the road to the right and drive to Indian Beach. The trail starts at a foot bridge crossing Indian Creek next to a dirt road a short distance north of the Indian Beach picnic area.

To reach the northern end of the trail, drive on U.S. Highway 101 to the southern edge of Seaside and turn west at the sign pointing to the beach and hospital. Cross the Necanicum River, proceed past the golf course, and turn left on South Edgewood Road. Drive south for 1.3 miles to the end of the pavement. The trail begins on the south side of the road at a sign pointing to Ecola Park.

When starting the hike from the north, you will find that at about one-fourth of a mile the trail crosses a road and re-enters the woods 50 feet to the left.

After a number of switchbacks, you will see a small cairn which marks a short path to the left that leads to a log bench. Here you have a good view of Seaside and the long stretch of beach to the north. Beyond the switchbacks, follow a road for about 200 yards to the top of a logging cut where it enters a beautiful park-like forest.

The trail contours along the west side of another logging area and drops down through the woods to several viewpoints from which Haystack Rock and Cannon Beach can be seen. Additional viewpoints offer broad seascapes including the now-abandoned Tillamook Rock Lighthouse on an island one mile off the coast.

At four miles you will find a picnic ground with tables and fire places. Beyond the picnic area turn left on a gravel road and right again after 50 yards at the second post marker. The trail re-enters the woods between two large stumps and begins a steady descent via switchbacks all the way to Indian Beach. Along this part of the trail are several areas with good views of the lighthouse.

Tillamook Head

Trail near top of Tillamook Head

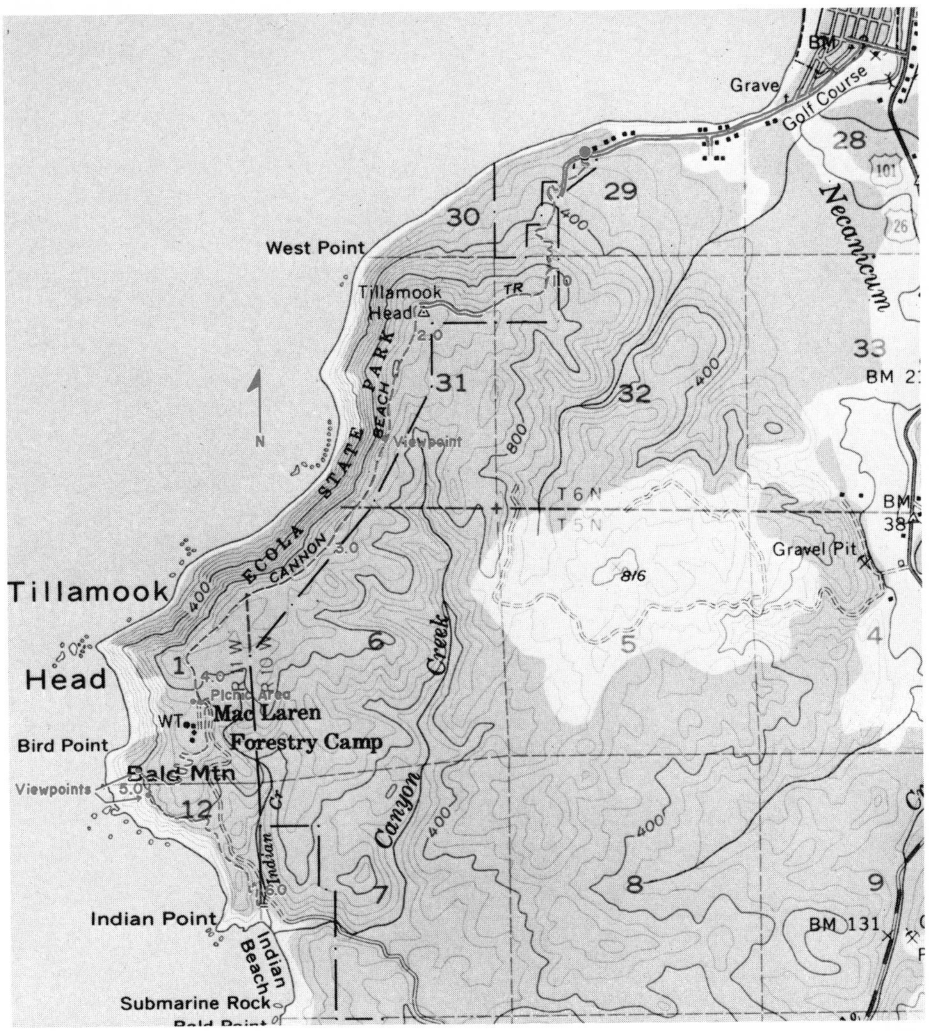

6 SADDLE MOUNTAIN NORTHERN OREGON COAST

One day trip
Distance: 3 miles one way
Elevation gain: 1,663 feet
High point: 3,283 feet
Allow 1½ to 2 hours one way
Usually open March through December
Topographic map:
U.S.G.S. Saddle Mountain, Oreg.
N4545-W12330/15
1955

Saddle Mountain is the highest peak in the northern portion of the Oregon Coast Range. The hike to its summit affords splendid views of the ocean, the mouth of the Columbia River and the city of Astoria to the northwest. Far in the distance to the east are the snowcapped peaks of Mt. Rainier, Mt. Saint Helens, Mt. Adams, Mt. Hood, and Mt. Jefferson.

Drive on U.S. Highway 26 to the turnoff to Saddle Mountain State Park, 14 miles east of the town of Seaside. Proceed for 7.2 miles along this road to the parking area adjacent to the campground. The trail starts on the southeast side of the parking lot and is well-marked. Be sure to carry adequate water which may be obtained in the picnic grounds, as none is available beyond this point.

The trail begins as a gentle grade through dark woods. At 0.3 mile a path to the right leads one-fourth mile to the top of a large rock about 200 feet above the trail from which point a good view may be obtained. The trail continues to the east for one-half mile and then switchbacks up the south side of the mountain. It progresses alternately through woods and along rocky slopes. Various formations such as a volcanic dike and other geologic phenomena may be observed. There is a good view to the southeast of the Lewis and Clark River Valley and Humbug Mountain.

At 2.5 miles, the first saddle is reached. Just beyond this depression you will have your first view of the ocean and of the summit of Saddle Mountain. Proceed through a small section of woods and down steeply to the second saddle. From here the trail switchbacks up the grass, rock, and brush-covered slopes past the foundation of an old building and up to the now-abandoned summit lookout cabin, from which the 1933 Tillamook Burn was first reported. The building is open and affords a good place to take shelter from the strong winds that often occur here. An added attraction during the spring months is the wildflowers which adorn the upper slopes of the mountain.

Saddle Mountain

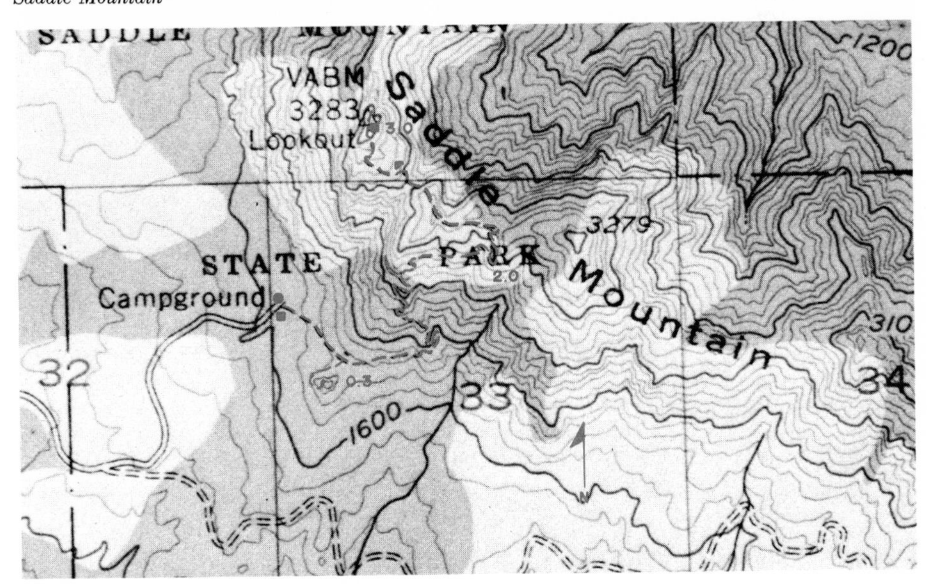

7 KINGS MOUNTAIN OREGON COAST RANGE

One day trip
Distance: 2½ miles one way
Elevation gain: 2,456 feet
High point: 3,226 feet
Allow 2 to 3 hours one way
Usually open March through December
Topographic map:
U.S.G.S. Enright, Oreg.
N4530-W12330/15
1955

This peak is located almost in the center of the Tillamook Burn and offers the hiker most compelling evidence of the damage of a monstrous forest fire. With the exception of a few distant wooded mountain tops, all that one can see is peak after peak completely devoid of timber. The summit of Kings Mountain is covered with a forest of burned snags, both fallen and standing, and it is almost possible to climb the last thousand feet by literally log-walking.

Drive on the Wilson River Highway (Oregon No. 6), east of Lee's Camp junction to an unmarked logging road on the north side of the highway, one-half mile west of the 26 mile post. (The mile posts start at Tillamook and measure the mileage east of that city.) The logging road is about 60 feet west of a low broken stone wall next to dark green six-foot high post, the first tree behind which has been sprayed with an orange paint band. You may park on the highway shoulder, as the logging road is now impassable since young trees are growing in the roadbed.

The trail begins behind the green post and follows the logging road next to a small stream. Carefully follow the orange paint marks on the trees, stumps, and snags as these, in many places, constitute the only evidence of the trail. Continue to follow the road through a clearing and up a steep slope to an open grassy area where it turns gradually left and then right to a clearing. A short distance beyond the clearing the trail leaves the road and drops down to the left, crossing a usually dry stream bed. Climb up a steep bank to a post marked with orange paint. Turn right and again climb steeply to another logging road, turning left and following it to a level area. At this point, turn sharply right and proceed straight uphill to a small ridge and yet another logging road. Turn left and traverse the slope for 50 yards, then turn right and follow the orange paint markings to the saddle, 1,000 feet below the summit ridge. Turn left on the ridge and follow the western skyline through an extensive forest of dead snags to the top of the mountain.

On a clear day, you can see from the Tillamook Valley on the coast to the Cascade Mountains, with Mt. Saint Helens, Mt. Adams, and Mt. Hood dominating the eastern skyline.

Summit of Kings Mountain from the saddle

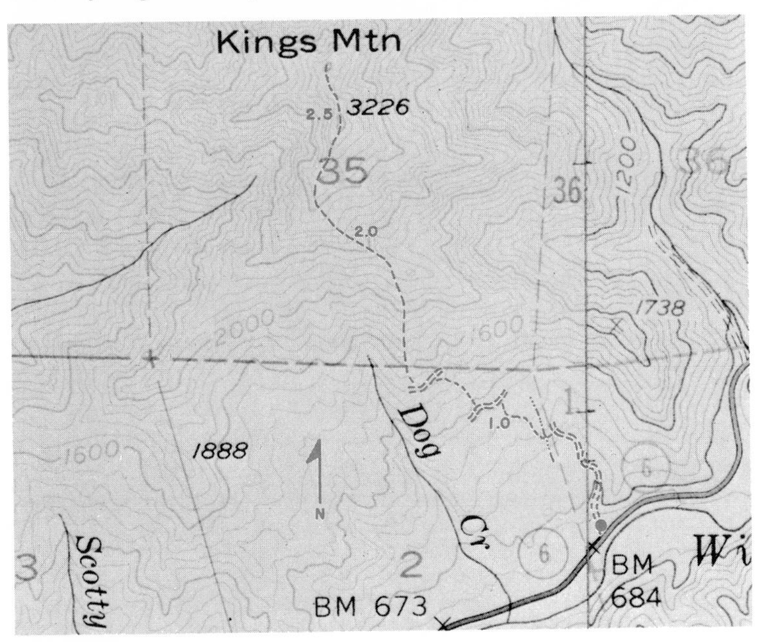

SECTION II — COLUMBIA RIVER GORGE

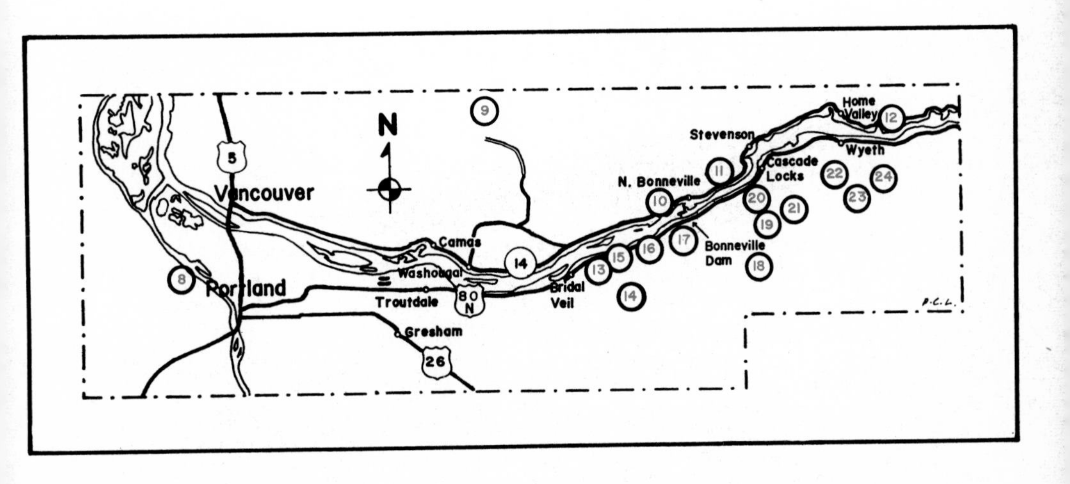

COLUMBIA RIVER GORGE

Geographically, the Columbia River Gorge extends from the town of Troutdale, near Portland, east to The Dalles, a distance of about 55 air miles. In addition to being one of Oregon's most famous scenic attractions, this area serves as an outdoor laboratory with individuals and groups frequently visiting it to study the many fine geologic formations. In contrast to the more violent origins of the volcanic peaks such as Mt. Hood and Mt. Jefferson, the Gorge area was formed by the gradual uplift and erosion of the numerous layers of Columbia River basalt which had been deposited over many thousands of years. As the surrounding region rose, the Columbia eroded through the rocks along its banks thus constantly maintaining its almost sea level elevation.

Because of various physical factors, the Oregon and Washington sides of the Gorge differ markedly in their geomorphology and ground cover. The Oregon portion consists of high cliffs and deep canyons running perpendicular to the Columbia River. The altitude of the Oregon side varies from about 600 to 700 feet at the west end to a high point of almost 5,000 feet near the eastern boundary, with an average elevation range of between 3,500 and 4,000 feet. The western half is covered with extremely lush vegetation and many waterfalls plunge over the cliffs in spectacular cataracts. However, as you travel east the aridity increases, forests become less dense and waterfalls scarce.

The mountains on the Washington side of the Columbia River are neither as rugged nor as well-timbered as those in Oregon, although several major peaks on the edge of the Gorge rise as high as 2,500 to 3,500 feet. Several landslides have occurred, one of which blocked the Columbia River near the legendary Bridge of the Gods, a span which the Indians believe joined what is now Oregon and Washington. Years ago a fire called the Yacolt Burn swept through the southwestern Washington Cascade Mountains and its destruction is obvious from the many denuded hills and burned snags.

All the trails in this section are west of Hood River and none are in the arid region. Because of the physical nature of the Gorge, most of the hikes necessitate a great deal of climbing. However, you will be rewarded with excellent views on the more strenuous trips. Since the hikes begin at near sea level, lower portions of the trails are open almost all year so you can hike as far as you wish or the snow conditions permit. Remember, though, that during the winter months the Gorge can be extremely cold, wet, and windy, so either wear or carry adequate protection. The higher regions are usually open by the beginning of June, although patches of snow remain later in shaded areas.

Although all the trips in this section are unusually scenic, two merit special mention. One is Eagle Creek, an almost level trail that climbs only slightly through a narrow valley. The trail passes deep pools and high gorges, and at six miles, travels behind waterfalls through a man-made tunnel. Dog Mountain, the other trail, is covered with balsam and in the spring the large yellow blooms from these plants completely cover the hillside, a sight well worth the climb.

The 5,000-foot trail to the summit of Mt. Defiance is used by many mountain climbers as a pre-climbing season conditioner, although some feel that you should reverse the procedure and climb a major peak to train for Mt. Defiance.

Residents of the Portland metropolitan area are fortunate to have such an extensive hiking area less than an hour's drive. Bonus trails are in Forest Park, which although not part of the Gorge proper, are only a few minutes drive from downtown Portland.

8 FOREST PARK
COLUMBIA RIVER GORGE (Portland)

One day trip
Distance: 7.6 miles one way
Elevation gain: 900 feet, loss 500 feet
High point: 975 feet
Allow 4 to 5 hours one way
Usually open all year round
Topographic maps:
U.S.G.S. Portland, Oreg.,-Wash.
N4530-W12237.5/7.5
1961
U.S.G.S. Linnton, Oreg.
N4530-W12245/7.5
1961

In less than a 10-minute drive from downtown Portland you can be in Forest and Macleay Parks, where it takes many hours to explore all of the trails within their boundaries. The slopes along Balch Creek are in the area commonly referred to as Lower Macleay Park and Upper Macleay Park includes the trails above Cornell Road. However, the trail described here is primarily in Forest Park and travels along slopes of second growth timber several hundred feet above the Willamette River to Rocking Chair Dam.

Drive to the end of Upshur Street in northwest Portland. (The streets are named in alphabetical order north from West Burnside.) Turn left on the unpaved portion and pass under the Thurman Street Bridge to the parking area. City buses are routed up Thurman Street and also offer access to the park. A sign just past the Forest Park headquarters building at the beginning of Balch Creek Canyon reads Forest Park, Lower Macleay Trail — Cornell Road 1.3 miles, N.W. 53rd Drive 4.6 miles and Rocking Chair Dam 7.6 miles.

After 200 yards, cross a bridge and follow Balch Creek for one-fourth mile before crossing two more bridges. Continue another quarter mile to a large, roofless stone building. Turn right onto the trail that leads upslope from the end of the structure. The trail climbs gradually above the canyon floor and after about one-half mile contours above the west side of a meadow. Cross a road and re-enter the woods at the north end of the clearing.

Continue through the woods for one-fourth mile to a junction. Take the upslope trail (that does not have a log across it) to the left. The trail on the right descends for a short distance before ending on N.W. Aspen Avenue. You are now on the Ditch Trail that winds through the woods for 2.5 miles to the junction with the Ridge Trail, which goes left to Inspiration Point with a fine view of Portland, and right to N.W. Leif Erikson Drive. (Periodically trails to N.W. 53rd Drive lead off upslope to the left).

Continue on the Ditch Trail following the sign pointing to Rocking Chair Dam. One-half mile later, the trail meets N.W. 53rd Drive and the Ditch Trail becomes Cleator Trail. Hike along the Cleator Trail for 1.5 miles, passing the Bee Trail, and go through a gate. Shortly thereafter follow a road to your right through cement posts and pass through a second gate. Cross a small open area and re-enter the woods where the trail is marked by a white post. The trail drops down to a picnic area equipped with a shelter, tables, fire grates, and outbuildings. Descend for three-fourths mile to the small reservoir behind Rocking Chair Dam. If you wish, you can return along Leif Erikson Drive which winds in and out of small canyons and affords views of Swan Island and the industrial areas along the Willamette River. There are steps on the northeast end of the Thurman Street Bridge which descend into Balch Canyon at the park headquarters.

Be sure to carry water as none of the creek water in the park can be considered safe for human consumption.

Trail in Forest Park

9 SILVER STAR MOUNTAIN COLUMBIA RIVER GORGE (Washington)

One day trip
Distance: 3.5 miles one way
Elevation gain: 2,100 feet
High point: 4,390 feet
Allow 2 hours one way
Usually open June through November
Topographic maps:
U.S.G.S. Camas, Wash.-Oreg.
N4530-W12215/15
1954
U.S.G.S. Bridal Veil, Wash.-Oreg.
N4530-W12200/15
1954

Summit of Silver Star Mountain

Silver Star Mountain is the highest point on an east-west ridge a few miles northeast of Camas, Washington in an area known as the Yacolt Burn. With the exception of the last one-half mile, the trail to the summit follows a steep roadbed, impassable to most types of wheeled vehicles. From the lookout cabin there are impressive views of Mt. Saint Helens and Mt. Adams as well as the cities of Vancouver, Washington and Portland, Oregon.

NOTE: this trail may be closed during periods of extreme fire danger.

Drive on Washington Highway 14 to the town of Washougal, Washington. Proceed north on Washington 120 for 6.7 miles and turn left at the sign pointing to Bear Prairie, one mile. Drive on the Bear Prairie road for 3.3 miles to the Skamania County line. Turn left onto the Larch Mountain road. Three-tenths of a mile north of the Larch Mountain road junction, turn right on the Skamania Mines Road, No. VN-W-1240, and follow it for 8.5 miles past several side roads marked with other numbers to a saddle where the main road begins to descend and where there are several radiating spur roads. You may park in the ample turnout area at the saddle.

The trail (road) leads north up a steep incline for the first mile, then levels out somewhat for the remaining distance. The lookout cabin comes into view before you pass under a large cliff on the right, known as Pyramid Rock. About one-half mile below the lookout there is a saddle where the road turns left. Leave the road at this point and contour to the ridge crest on the right where a faint trail may be found. Proceed on this trail directly up the ridge to the summit. An interesting side trip can be made by following a sign pointing to trail No. 174.1 which leads south for one mile to several Indian pits.

No water is available during the summer months so you are advised to carry a canteen.

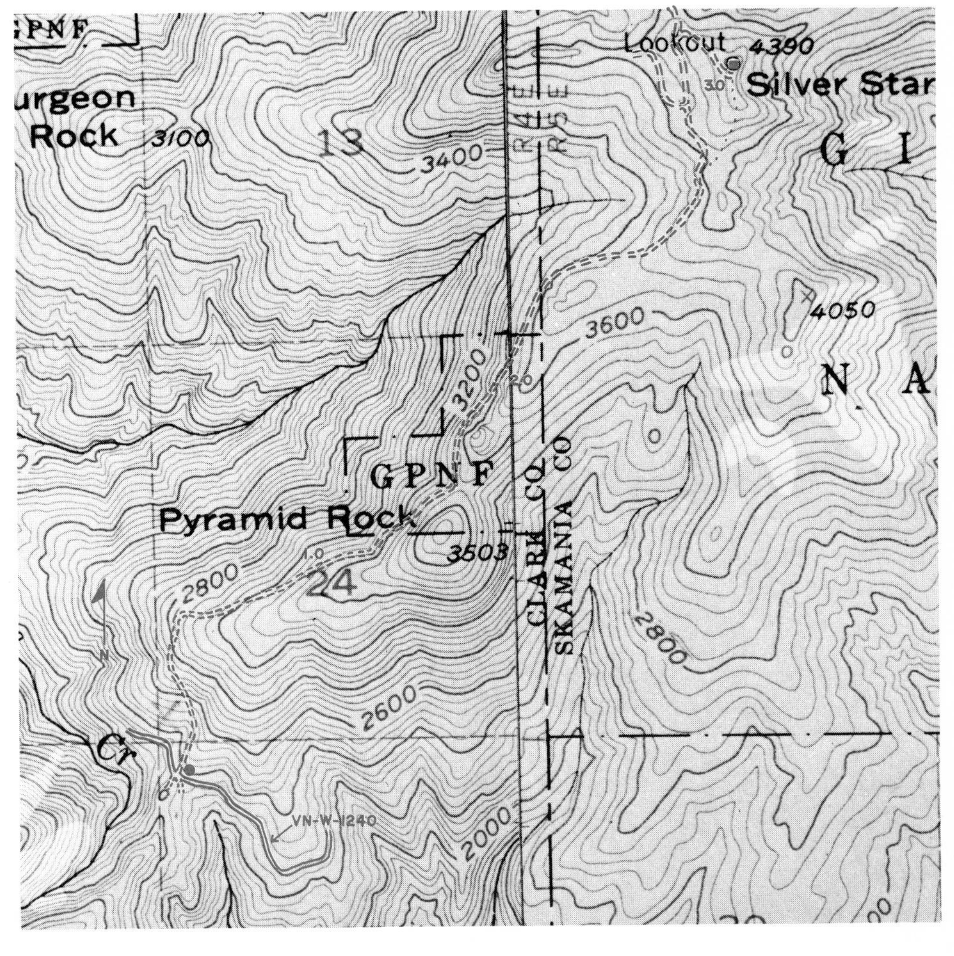
GPNF
urgeon
Rock
3100
13
3400
Lookout
4390
Silver Star
G I
4050
3600
N A
3200
GPNF
Pyramid Rock
3503
CLARK CO
SKAMANIA CO
2800
24
2800
2600
Cr
VN-W-1240
2000

10 HAMILTON MOUNTAIN COLUMBIA RIVER GORGE (Washington)

One day trip
Distance: 4 miles one way
Elevation gain: 2,050 feet
High point: 2,445 feet
Allow 2½ to 3 hours one way
Usually open April through November
Topographic map:
U.S.G.S. Bridal Veil, Wash.-Oreg.
N4530-W12200/15
1954

The Hamilton Mountain trail is the most popular on the Washington side of the Columbia River Gorge. It was improved in 1967 and in some places relocated to afford a more scenic and more direct route to the summit. By actual count, there are 72 switchbacks between Rodney Falls and the top.

Drive on Washington Highway 14 to Beacon Rock State Park. Turn north opposite Beacon Rock onto a paved road leading to the camping and picnic area and proceed 0.3 mile to the parking lot adjacent to the picnic area. The trail starts at the east end of the picnic grounds. A sign here reads Hamilton Mt. 4 miles, Rodney Falls 1¼ miles and Hardy Falls 1¼ miles.

At the beginning, the grade is quite gradual. Just before reaching a powerline the trail divides. To avoid confusion, take the fork to the right which offers the most direct route. Upon reaching the woods, you will cross two small creeks on footbridges. Just beyond the second bridge there are two separate paths leading to the right. The upper path goes a very short distance to a viewpoint overlooking Hardy Falls, while the lower trail, equally short, provides a splendid view of Rodney Falls. On the west side of the bridge at the base of Rodney Falls is a short path to the edge of the cataract which is attained by passing through a small crawlway.

Beyond Rodney Falls the trail begins to climb steeply. About one-fourth mile above the falls it forks. Keep to the right, as the left fork is a section of the old trail and is no longer maintained. At the top of the first series of switchbacks a side trail leads to the right about 100 yards where the full expanse of the Columbia Gorge may be seen.

For the next two miles the trail climbs steadily in switchbacks until it emerges on the north-south summit ridge. Here a small clearing offers a fine place to admire the Oregon side of the gorge. This is especially interesting if you are contemplating a trip on any of the many trails leading into the mountains from the south shore of the Columbia River.

As an added attraction, the 600-foot monolith of Beacon Rock, across the highway from Hamilton Mountain, can easily be climbed via a series of stairways leading to its summit.

Snag on Hamilton Mountain

Bridge at Rodney Falls

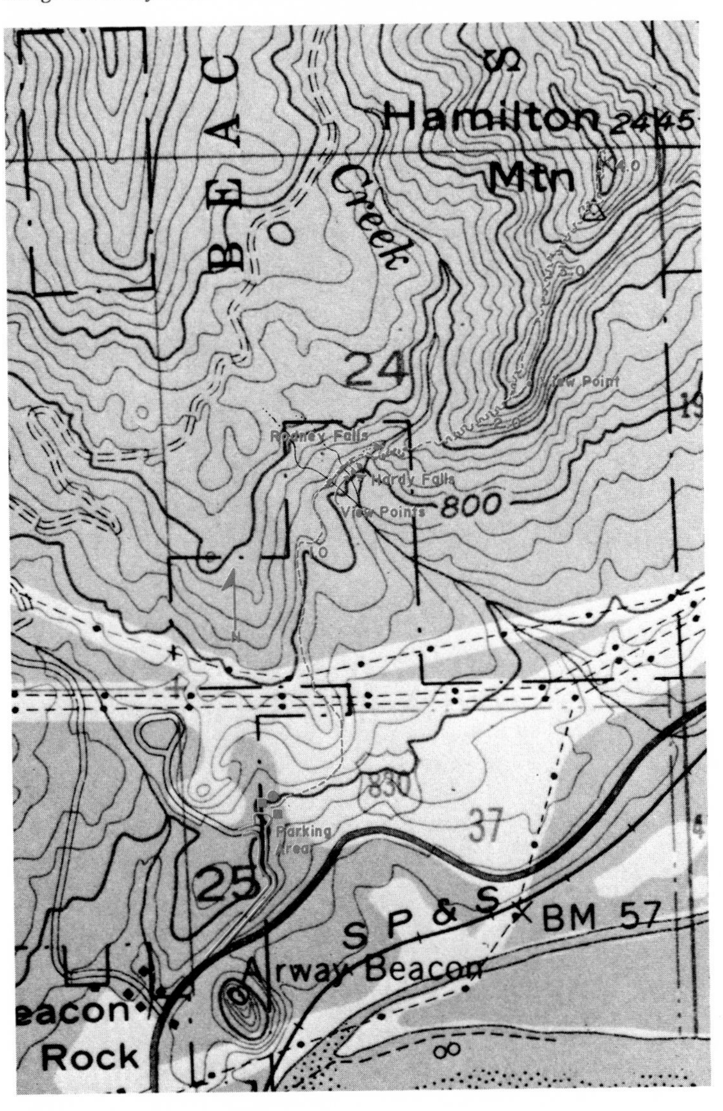

11 TABLE MOUNTAIN COLUMBIA RIVER GORGE (Washington)

One day trip
Distance: 3 miles one way
Elevation gain: 2,830 feet
High point: 3,420 feet
Allow 3 to 4 hours one way
Usually open mid-April through November
Topographic map:
U.S.G.S. Bonneville Dam, Oreg.-Wash.
N4530-W12145/15
1957

At one time this flat-topped peak, located just to the north of Bonneville Dam, was responsible for altering the course of the Columbia River. The southern portion of Table Mountain and Greenleaf Peak, its neighbor to the east, broke away from the main part of the ridge. The huge slide dropped several miles into the valley below and constricted the river channel from a point just east of the Bridge of the Gods west to the town of North Bonneville. Even today, large earth slides may be observed after heavy rains and rockfall is a constant hazard below the main cliffs.

The trail to the summit is not well maintained, and usually involves some road walking. However, the view of the Oregon side of the Columbia River Gorge and of Bonneville Dam are worth the effort. The loop trip described below should be attempted with some care as the return route is not well marked and you will be wise to reserve some extra time to back-track if you lose the trail.

Proceed on Washington Highway 14 to the east end of North Bonneville. Turn north on N.W. Moffitts Springs Road, marked by a large sign pointing to Bonneville Hot Springs. Drive to the end of the improved road across a small bridge. Continue on an unimproved road for a short distance until there is a fork. Keep right, drive under the powerlines, and continue steeply uphill to the north until Carpenters Lake is reached. It is best to leave your car here as the road beyond is usually in very poor condition with little room to park on its shoulders.

Walk up the road that turns south (left) until a fork is reached. Keep to the right. Eight-tenths of a mile north of the lake a small spur road goes to the right 100 yards to a viewpoint where the sheer south-eastern face of the mountain and a rock formation known as the Rabbit Ears can be seen. Continue up the main road to its end.

The trail proper begins here and is marked by red paint on the trees. It climbs very steeply with no switchbacks and finally tops out on the crest of a rocky ridge. At this point, contour left through dense bush following the red paint marks to the base of the summit pyramid. Climb straight up the ridge crest avoiding the exposed edge of the cliff face as much as possible. From the summit, walk to the right a short distance to a viewpoint affording a panorama to the east.

If you wish to return via the southwest ridge, proceed west across the summit past a grove of trees to the point where the trail leads down in switchbacks through very loose rock. At the base of the rocky portion there is a cairn marking the trail as it enters the woods. Continue down through the woods past an open clearing. South of the clearing the trail again drops steeply to a level area. Here a white sign on a tree marks the summit trail. Cross a small stream on the other side of which a sign marks the location of Porcupine Camp. Turn right and recross the stream. Then turn left and follow an overgrown logging road to a slide area at the end of the road. From here contour sharply left for about 200 yards to the main logging road, where you will head south (right) to get back to your car.

Looking southeast from Table Mountain

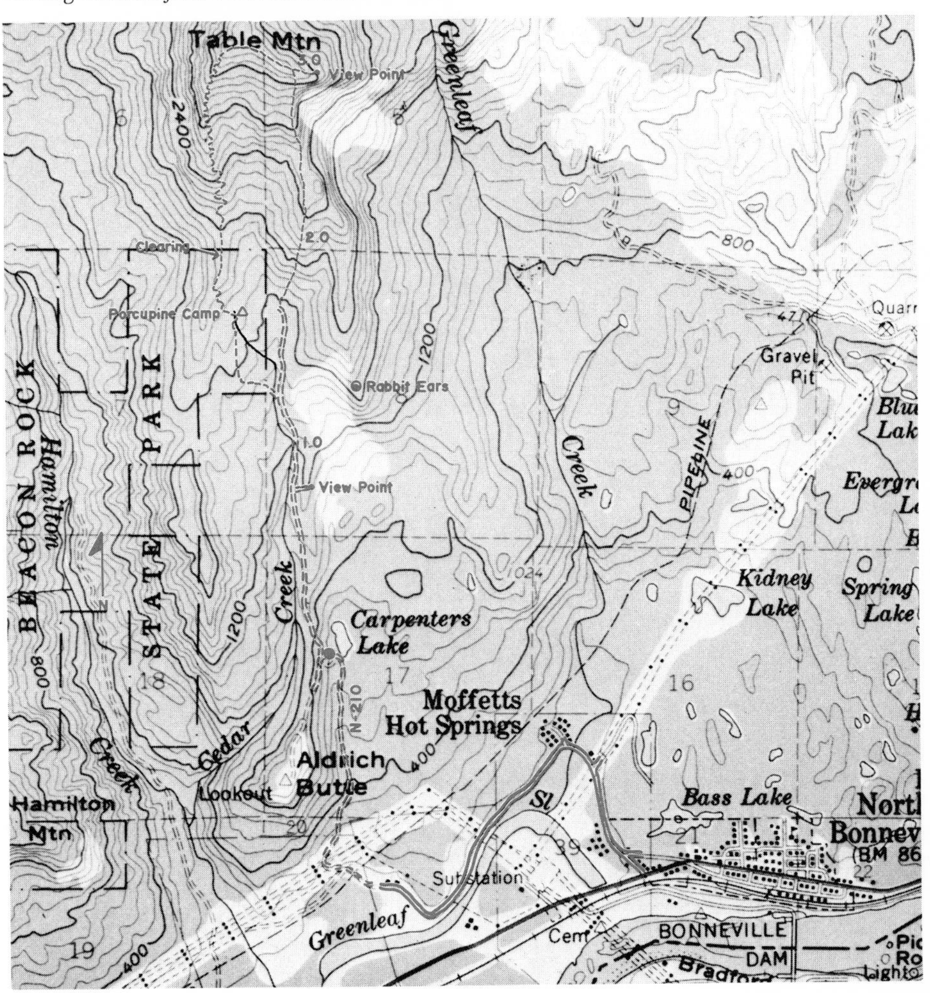

12 DOG MOUNTAIN COLUMBIA RIVER GORGE (Washington)

One day trip
Distance: 2.5 miles one way
Elevation gain: 2,390 feet
High point: 2,500 feet
Allow 2 to 3 hours one way
Usually open March through mid-December
Topographic map:
U.S.G.S. Hood River, Oreg.-Wash.
N4530-W12130/15
1957

During the month of May and June, the grassy slopes on the upper part of Dog Mountain turn a vivid yellow and blue from blossoming balsam weed and lupine. The trail to these slopes follows the southernmost portion of the Cascade Crest Trail system which continues on through the entire length of the State of Washington to the Canadian Border. The trail is short but quite steep; you should carry water since the only spring is located quite far down the mountain and may dry up during a prolonged hot spell.

Take Washington 14 to the Crest Trail Inn, located between Carson and Cook, Washington. The trail, No. 2000, begins at the east end of the large parking area and is marked by a sign giving mileage information to points as far as White Pass, 116 miles to the north.

Follow the gravel road to the east of the sign past a water tank to a point about 200 yards from the parking area where another sign points to the left as the trail

Dog Mountain

enters the woods. From here it climbs about 800 feet in switchbacks until joining a logging road in a small meadow.

Continue north along the old roadbed which climbs steeply for some distance. At one mile a sign points to the right about 50 yards to a small spring which is the only source of drinking water.

One-third of a mile above the spring the trail leaves the logging road turning eastward (right) through second growth timber and a burned-over area. Upon entering a deeper forest, the trail climbs steeply in several switchbacks and emerges onto a grassy slope contouring over to the site of the former Forest Service fire lookout cabin.

From this vantage point much of the eastern part of the Columbia Gorge can be seen, with Mt. Defiance dominating the Oregon Skyline. You can get a good view of Mt. Hood and Mt. Adams by climbing the grassy hillside an additional 500 feet to the south peak of Dog Mountain.

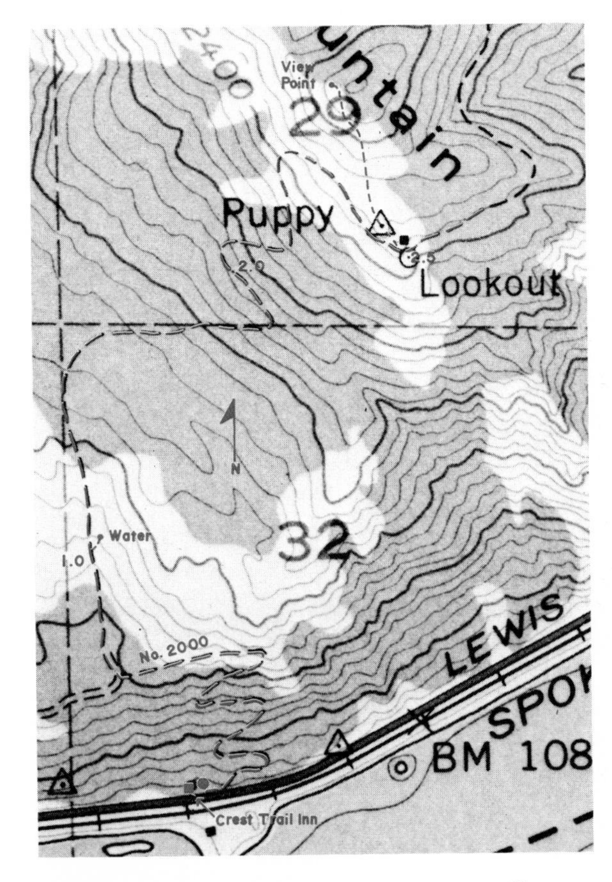

13 ANGELS REST COLUMBIA RIVER GORGE

One day trip
Distance: 1.5 miles one way
Elevation gain: 1,460 feet
High point: 1,600 feet
Allow 1 to 1½ hours one way
Usually open March through December
Topographic map:
U.S.G.S. Bridal Veil, Wash.-Oreg.
N4530-W12200/15
1954

Angels Rest is easy to distinguish from the Columbia River Highway as its appearance resembles that of a fort protruding from timber-covered ridges at the 1,600 foot level above the town of Bridal Veil. For persons living in or near Portland, it is a good trip if you do not want to spend the entire day in the woods. The mesa is high enough to permit a good view of Portland and Vancouver, but the terrain to the south is obscured by the rim of the Gorge which rises somewhat higher than Angels Rest itself.

Drive on U.S. Highway 80N and turn off at the Bridal Veil junction about 10 miles east of Troutdale. Proceed through Bridal Veil to the junction of the Old Scenic Highway and park your car either in the gravel triangle at the junction or alongside the road. The trail starts on the south side of the old highway about 100 yards east of the junction. It is not marked but is easy to see as it begins at a point just a few feet to the west of an unimproved side road.

The trail starts out at a moderate grade in switchbacks. At one-fourth mile the trail crosses a rockslide and then follows the edge of a ridge above Coopey Falls. Just before coming to the falls, the trail branches, but either branch can be taken as they again become one trail a short distance later. A good view of the falls can be had from the left branch.

You will cross Coopey Creek on a log bridge above the falls, then climb to the south on the east side of Coopey Creek Canyon. After traversing several switchbacks, you will come to a point where Angels Rest is in view. Here, on the north side of the bluff, you will see the "eye," a formation created by rocks breaking away and shaping a hole resembling an eye socket. The trail continues climbing in switchbacks until it contours around a slab rock slope just below Angels Rest. When you reach the ridge crest, proceed north to the head of the bluff where the best views are to be found.

Columbia River from Angels Rest

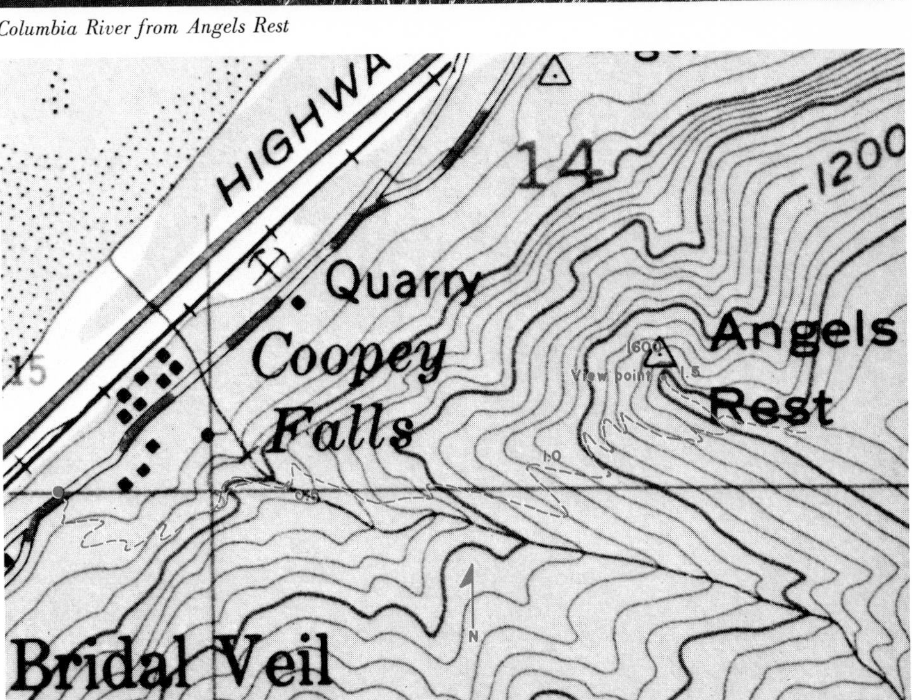

14 LARCH MOUNTAIN COLUMBIA RIVER GORGE

One day trip or backpack
Distance: 6.5 miles one way
Elevation gain: 4,013 feet
High point: 4,045 feet
Allow 4 hours one way
Usually open late May through November
Topographic map:
U.S.G.S. Bridal Veil, Wash.-Oreg.
N4530-W12200/15
1954

Four large water falls, long stretches of trail that follow cascading Multnomah Creek, and a panoramic view from Sherrard Point are but a few of the many attractions of the Larch Mountain Trail. This locale is unique since, with the exception of the winter months, the top of Larch Mountain can be reached by automobile. Therefore, you have the option of either hiking from the bottom to the top or the reverse, as well as making the round trip. Except for the first 1,000 feet, the trail has a moderate grade and the lower half has several campsites.

Drive on U.S. Highway 80N or the Old Scenic Highway to the Multnomah Falls parking lot near the western end of the Columbia River Gorge.

The trail, No. 441, begins on the east side of the lodge and is marked by a sign that reads Larch Mountain 6½ miles. The first few hundred yards, which lead to the concrete bridge above lower Multnomah Falls have been paved. Beyond the bridge, the trail turns left and climbs in a series of switchbacks to a point near the top of the upper or main falls. Just before reaching Multnomah Creek, a way trail leads a short distance to the right to the edge of the falls where you can look down to the Multnomah Falls Lodge and the Columbia River, about 700 feet below.

Multnomah Creek is crossed on a stone bridge and a few yards beyond is the junction of the Perdition Trail, No. 421, to Wahkeena Falls. Turn left and follow along the west side of Multnomah Creek past the two upper falls and over a steel foot bridge crossing the creek at the two-mile point. At 2.5 miles the route divides into a high-water and a low-water trail. Unless it is late summer, take the high-water trail, which climbs above the creek in switchbacks and rejoins it a short distance later.

At three miles, you will cross the access road to Multnomah Basin and continue into the woods on the other side. Then, as you proceed up the trail, you will have to cross a side stream and Multnomah Creek without footbridges. (These crossings normally present no problem. However, in periods of high water caution should be observed.)

At five miles is the site of Spring Camp which once contained a shelter cabin. Good campsites can be found here in open woods. Just above the camp the trail crosses an access road to an abandoned rock quarry and proceeds into the woods on the opposite side. It is marked here by a concrete post and several signs.

The final 1.5 miles follow the crest of the north ridge of Larch Mountain, reaching the top at the abandoned lookout tower. A special cabin near the tower is provided for winter use by hikers and cross-country skiers seeking shelter from inclement weather.

The best view from the top of the mountain is from Sherrard Point, a one-quarter mile hike northeast from the lookout tower.

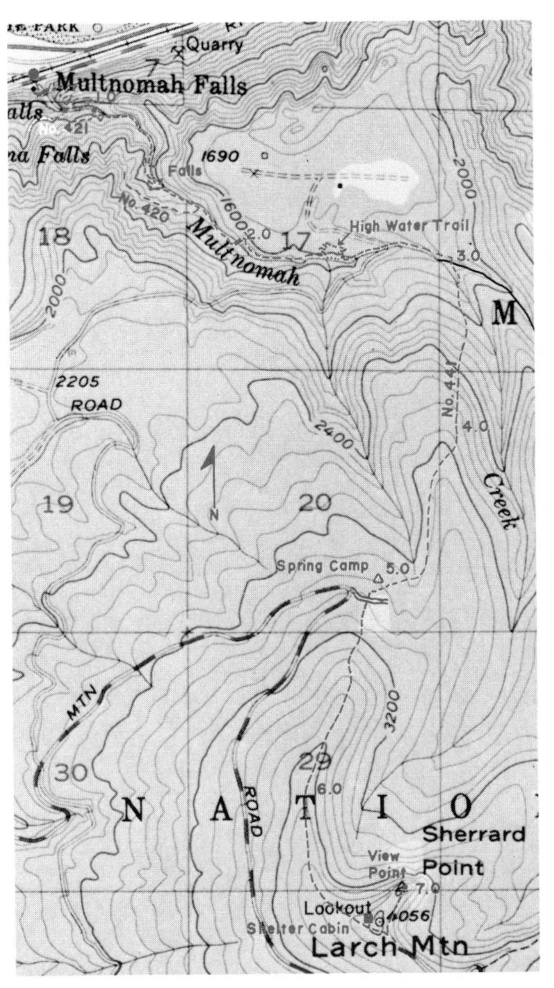

Upper Falls, Larch Mountain Trail

15 MULTNOMAH-WAHKEENA FALLS LOOP COLUMBIA RIVER GORGE

One day trip
Distance: 3.5 miles round trip
Elevation gain: 1,000 feet
High point: 800 feet
Allow 1½ to 2 hours round trip
Usually open all year
Topographic map:
U.S.G.S. Bridal Veil, Wash.-Oreg.
N4530-W12200/15
1954

The hike from Multnomah Falls to Wahkeena Falls and return via the Perdition Trail is quite short, but very scenic with several splendid views of Multnomah Falls, the Columbia River, and Archer Falls to the west of Archer Mountain on the Washington side of the Gorge. This is a fine trail on which to take the entire family, young and old. However, small children should be watched closely at the view points even though these spots are well fenced.

Take U.S. Highway 80N or the Old Columbia River Scenic Highway to the Multnomah Falls parking lot. The trail, No. 441, begins on the east side of Multnomah Falls Lodge and is identified by a large wood carved map of the area and a nearby sign reading Larch Mountain 6½ miles, Wahkeena Trail 1½ miles, and the Perdition Trail 1 mile.

Proceed along the paved portion of the trail which ends on the east side of the bridge spanning Lower Multnomah Falls. Turn sharply left and climb via several switchbacks to the top of the ridge above Multnomah Creek. Follow the trail down to the creek near which a short side trail to the right leads to a view point at the top of Multnomah Falls. Cross the creek and walk about 50 feet beyond the stone bridge to the junction of the Perdition Trail, No. 421. Here the trail turns right and follows Multnomah Creek to a view point overlooking the main falls. Beyond this point for a distance of about one-fourth mile there are several bluffs which permit good views of Bonneville Dam, the Columbia River, and Multnomah Falls Lodge directly below. A noteworthy feature of this part of the trail is the many wooden stairways that traverse up and down the steeper slopes. These have been provided to prevent erosion which would result from the heavy usage the trail receives.

Beyond the view points, the trail descends via an east-west ridge. Just before coming to Wahkeena Falls, the trail forks. Take the right fork and cross Wahkeena Creek on a stone bridge below Wahkeena Falls. A rock avalanche in the mid-1960's on the east side of the falls destroyed some of the natural beauty of the area and the stream is now forced to flow underneath a large quantity of rock in its path.

Beyond the falls, the trail switchbacks to the Wahkeena Falls parking lot. The one-mile return trail to Multnomah Falls starts on the east side of the picnic area and contours above the Scenic Highway to the base of a large cliff about 150 yards west of Multnomah Falls Lodge.

Wahkeena Falls

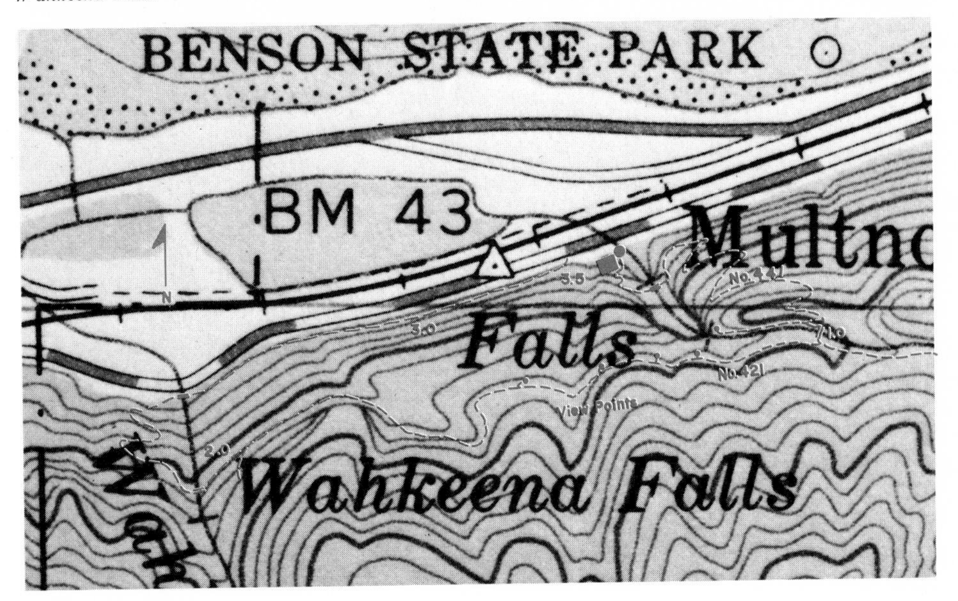

16 HORSETAIL FALLS— ONEONTA GORGE LOOP COLUMBIA RIVER GORGE

One-half day trip
Distance: 2 miles round trip
Elevation gain: 400 feet
High point: 480 feet
Allow 1½ to 2 hours round trip
Usually open all year
Topographic map:
U.S.G.S. Bridal Veil, Wash.-Oreg.
N4530-W12200/15
1954

This short loop trip of only two miles can be made by the entire family and, with the exception of a few snowy days during the winter months, it is open all year. Highlights of the trip are a walk behind Upper Horsetail Falls and a beautiful view of Oneonta Gorge from above.

Drive the Old Scenic Columbia River Highway to the Horsetail Falls parking lot, two miles east of Multnomah Falls. The trail, No. 438, begins on the east end of the parking area behind a sign reading Upper Falls ½ mile, Oneonta Creek ¾ mile, Oneonta Creek Trail 1 mile, and Old Columbia River Highway 1½ miles.

The trail climbs in switchbacks for several hundred feet, then passes behind Upper Horsetail Falls, where the water cascades from a narrow moss-covered cleft in a volcanic cliff, landing in a pool below the trail. Beyond the falls the trail circles around a bluff and then turns south for a short distance until coming out on a view-

Oneonta Gorge

point overlooking the entire length of Oneonta Gorge from high above Oneonta Falls. This deep canyon was formed as Oneonta Creek gradually eroded through a weak area in the basalt north of the falls. The stream bed below is almost level, and in periods of low water it is possible to walk from the highway bridge at the mouth of the stream back along the entire length of the canyon to the bottom of Oneonta Falls.

Just west of the bridge across the creek you will reach the Oneonta Gorge Trail, No. 424. Turn right and follow it to the north and west for one-half mile descending very gradually until you reach the Old Columbia River Highway.

Near the highway, the trail forks. Take the right-hand fork which meets the highway several hundred yards to the east of the left fork. Walk east on the highway for about one-half mile to the Horsetail Falls parking lot.

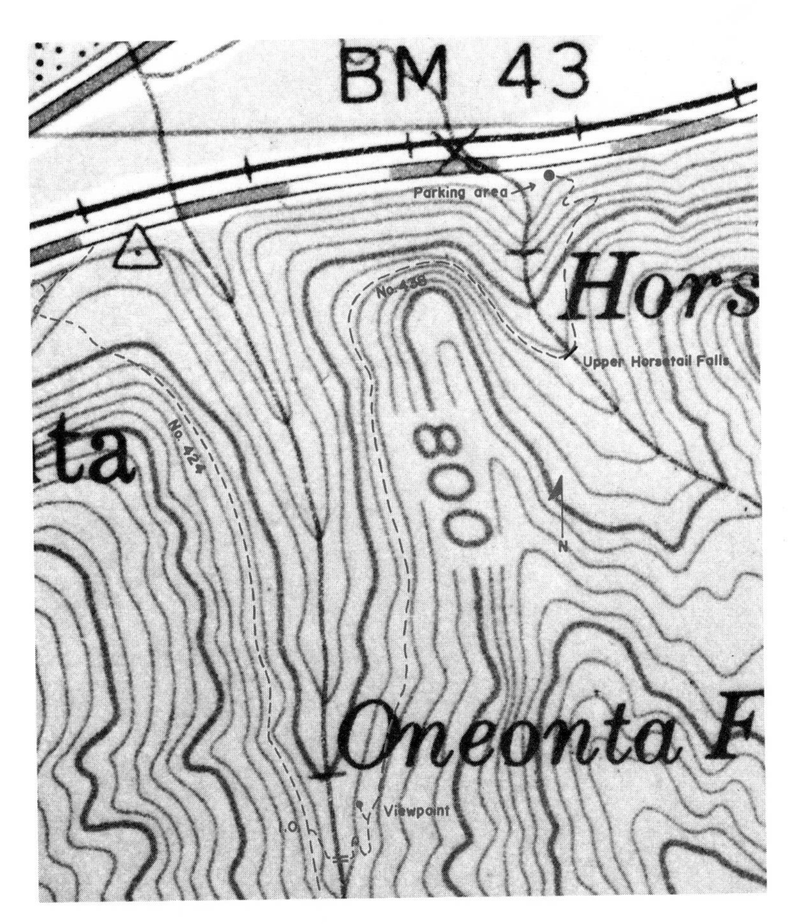

17 MUNRA POINT
COLUMBIA RIVER GORGE

One day trip
Distance: 1 mile one way
Elevation gain: 1,760 feet
High point: 1,850 feet
Allow 1½ to 2 hours one way
Usually open from March through December
Topographic map:
U.S.G.S. Bonneville Dam, Oreg.-Wash.
N4530-W12145/15
1957

Munra Point

Munra Point is an 1,800-foot high, extremely narrow rock ridge just to the west of Bonneville Dam. From the summit, the view of the dam and the Columbia River is most impressive. Mt. Adams is the dominant feature to the northeast.

This peak should not be attempted by the inexperienced hiker. In several places the trail is extremely steep with considerable exposure. Your party should be equipped with either ice axes or hiking canes and should carry at least one 100-foot length of rope for use as a hand line in descending. In wet weather, the trail is quite dangerous as the steepest parts consist of 30-degree dirt slopes which afford few footholds.

From the west, drive east on U.S. Highway 80N. Turn off at the Bonneville Dam exit and proceed north under the highway bridges. Turn left at the sign saying Portland and rejoin the freeway westbound. Continue for 1.3 miles to the next pair of highway bridges — one for each direction of travel. (Those coming from the east should drive westbound 1.3 miles from the Bonneville Dam exit). Turn left at the east end of the bridge on a short, grassy side road and park at this point. Walk under the eastbound highway bridge and turn left, so that you are paralleling the highway. The trail is marked by two blazes on a tree located a few feet behind a tall snag. Although this trail is neither marked nor maintained, it is not difficult to follow and is blazed all the way to the top.

At first the route leads up a gentle grade through dense forest. Then suddenly it climbs very steeply and continues at steep angles to the summit. After the first few hundred yards the trail follows the crest of the northwest ridge, occasionally skirting outcroppings of rock. You will not lose the trail if you follow the ridge crest. Just below the summit, the trail emerges from the woods by a large, grassy bluff. Climb a few feet straight ahead and then turn sharply to the right and contour around the western side of the ridge until reaching a gully near a thicket of oak trees. Proceed straight up to the left hand notch on the skyline. From there a trail contours to the right over to a less exposed saddle. This point provides good views of the Gorge. The best sight is from the northeast ridge which is reached by a traverse and a very narrow ridge walk.

Munra Point and Bonneville Dam

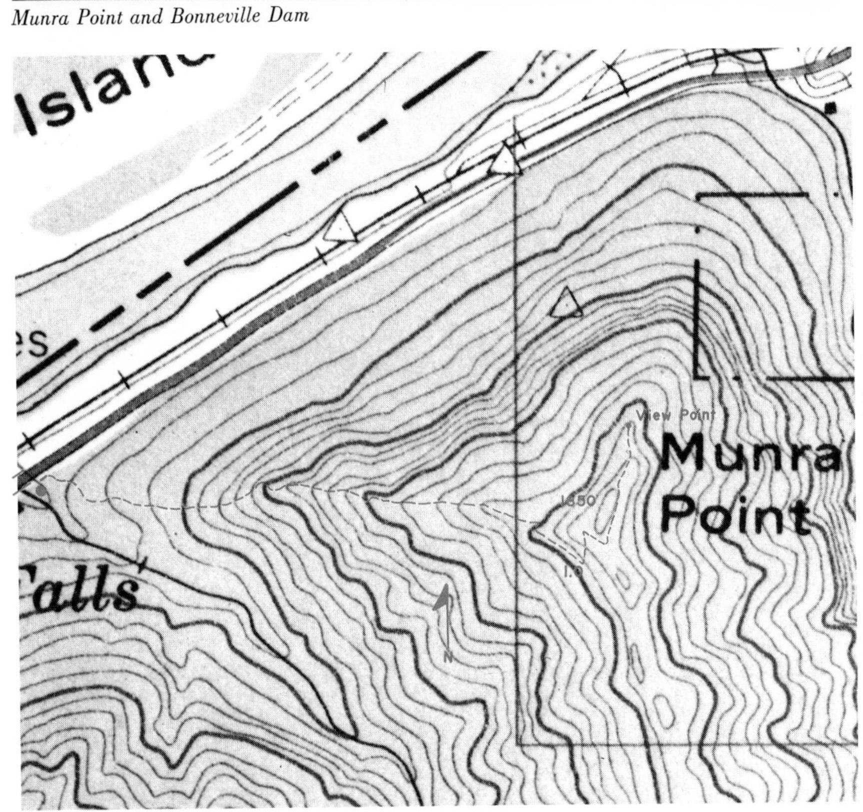

18 TANNER BUTTE COLUMBIA RIVER GORGE

One day trip or backpack
Distance: 8 miles one way
Elevation gain: 3,220 feet, loss 150 feet
High point: 4,500 feet
Allow 5 to 6 hours one way
Usually open mid-June through November
Topographic map:
U.S.G.S. Bonneville Dam, Oreg.-Wash.
N4530-W12145/15
1957

Tanner Butte is located deep in the southernmost reaches of the Columbia River Gorge between the headwaters of Tanner and Eagle Creeks. It is visited by relatively few people since, until recently, the trail has not been maintained and has been difficult to follow. If you plan a one day trip, an early start is advised as it may take as many as 10 or 11 hours to complete the round trip, depending upon your physical condition.

At one time a Forest Service fire lookout cabin stood on Tanner Butte. Only the charred ruins remain to remind the visitor of the part it once played in the prevention of forest fires, a job now largely taken over by aircraft spotters. From the summit the view in all directions encompasses wooded mountain peaks and deeply-carved stream valleys, while the face of Mt. Hood dominates the skyline a few miles to the southeast.

Drive on U.S. Highway 80N and turn off at the Bonneville Dam exit, proceeding south for about 100 yards to the Tanner Creek Road. Turn left and drive up this road. Keep to the right at the water tank and pass through a wooden gate. The trail, No. 401, begins 3.0 miles from the start of Tanner Creek Road where a yellow marker points left to Towers 6, 7, and 8. The trail sign is easy to see on the southeast side of the junction. It points to Tanner Butte 8 miles, Tanner Spur Road 5 miles, and Wauna Point Trail 1½ miles.

For the first 1,500 feet the trail climbs very steeply until joining another trail which runs the full length of the ridge. Turn right at that junction and continue through rather brushy woods until you come out on the northern end of the Tanner Spur Road at 4.7 miles. Follow the road south as it contours to the west of several small buttes. At 6.0 miles climb a few feet up a low bank to a good viewpoint overlooking Eagle Creek Canyon adjacent to a rock spire separated from the main ridge. This is a good place to stop if you do not wish to continue to the summit of Tanner Butte.

From the viewpoint hike south on the spur road which eventually drops down about 150 feet into a saddle beneath the northwestern ridge of the butte. Leave the road here and follow this ridge through bear grass and small trees to the summit. This last stretch has no trail, but the final 500-foot climb is not difficult.

If you wish to camp overnight, proceed down the south ridge from the summit or contour around the butte on the road to another saddle just below the south ridge. From here drop directly down the eastern slope to a small lake at the 3,600 foot level. This area is quite flat and is protected from the prevailing southwest winds. The lake is the only source of water near the butte.

Further travel to the south of the butte into the Bull Run Reserve is prohibited by law.

Mount Hood from Tanner Butte Trail

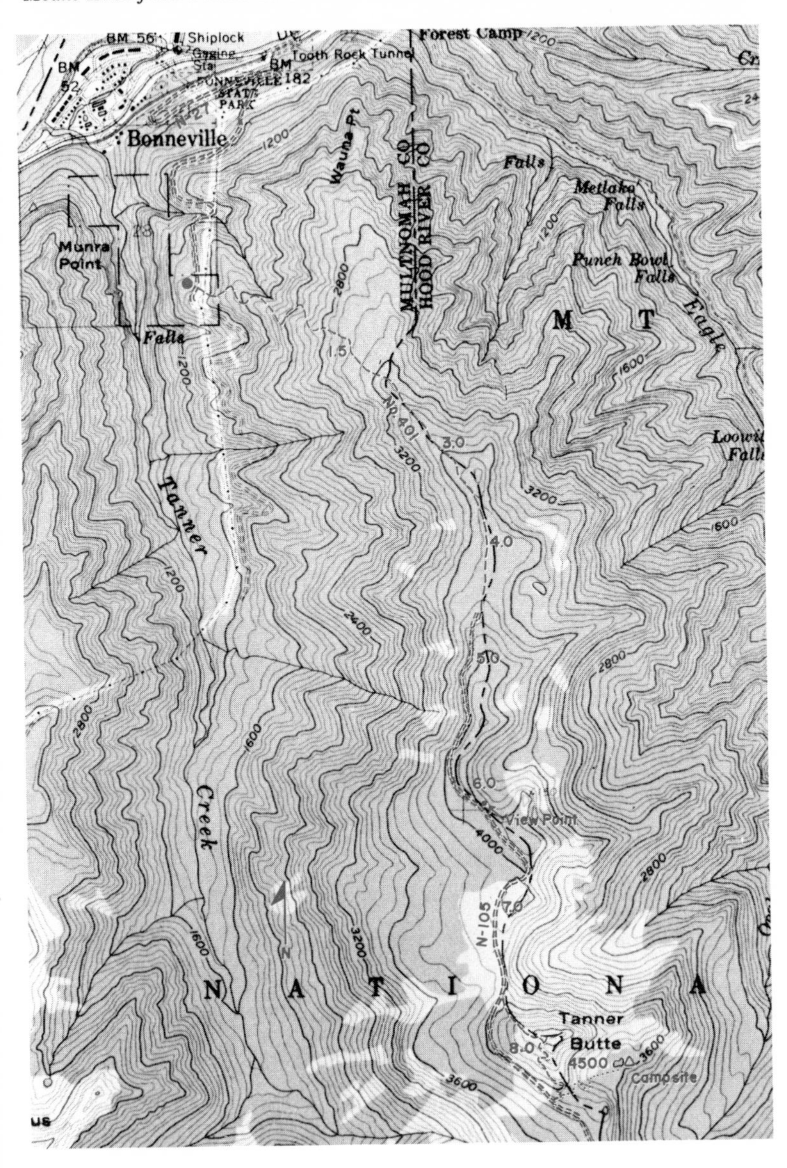

19 EAGLE CREEK COLUMBIA RIVER GORGE

Backpack (to Wahtum Lake)
Distance: 13 miles one way
Elevation gain: 3,840 feet
High point: 3,950 feet
Allow 8 to 10 hours one way
Usually open June through November
Topographic map:
U.S.G.S. Bonneville Dam, Oreg.-Wash.
N4530-W12145/15
1957

The Eagle Creek Trail offers an extraordinary variety of waterfalls, high cliffs, broad vistas, narrow gorges, campgrounds, and even a tunnel. It can be either a short afternoon stroll or a strenuous backpack for 13 miles to Wahtum Lake. Regardless of how ambitious you are, Eagle Creek is a must if you contemplate a trail trip in the Columbia Gorge.

Drive on U.S. Highway 80N to the Eagle Creek Fish Hatchery, one mile east of Bonneville Dam. Proceed south for one-half mile, past the picnic grounds, to the end of the dirt road at the small dam and intake for the fish hatchery where you will find ample parking.

The trail, No. 440, starts on the east side of the fence bordering the dam. It rises very gently through dense timber, steep grassy slopes, and an occasional cliff where ledges have been blasted out of the overhanging rock. At several points, steel cables provide hand holds to increase the safety in crossing some spots. At 1.5 miles, a very short side trail drops to the right a few feet to a view point near Metlako Falls. At two miles, another side trail to the right descends to river level at one of the most scenic attractions in Eagle Creek Gorge — Punch Bowl Falls. The upper trail also provides a spectacular view of these falls. Here Eagle Creek leaps out of a notch in the basalt and drops into a large round basin which is undercut almost all the way around. Pictures of the Punch Bowl have appeared in many national magazines and calendars.

Beyond the Punch Bowl, the trail passes through dense woods until reaching High Bridge, a steel structure spanning a very narrow gorge about 80 feet above the water. Above the next falls is Four Mile Camp, on the west side of Eagle Creek. This is a fairly well-developed campsite but has no shelter.

After leaving Four Mile Camp, the trail again crosses Eagle Creek to its east bank and shortly thereafter reaches another campsite on the left. Here there is a good shelter in addition to a large clearing among the trees where tents can be pitched.

At six miles, the trail travels into a side canyon and crosses behind the east fork of Eagle Creek at Tunnel Falls. Since there was no other way for the trail to pass this obstacle, a 30-foot tunnel was cut behind the falls. Just beyond Tunnel Falls, around a sharp bend, is another very high, twisting cataract.

At 7.5 miles the trail passes another camp on the right. This camp, which has an excellent shelter, is the highest camp on Eagle Creek. At eight miles the trail forks, switching back to the left. It is identified by a carving on a tree pointing to Wahtum Lake. The trail to the south (right fork) leads into the upper Eagle Basin. The switchback climbs to Inspiration Point at 2,400 feet offering a wide ranging view high above the southern end of Eagle Creek Canyon. The summit pyramid of Tanner Butte is visible on the western skyline.

At Inspiration Point the trail turns sharply to the right and climbs gradually through heavy timber and rhododendrons to a campsite next to a small stream which comes down from Indian Mountain. From here, the trail turns north passing yet another campsite near a stream, and then contours around a ridge joining the East Fork of Eagle Creek at the outlet of Wahtum Lake. If you walk around the southern shore of the lake, you will reach a campground at the junction of the trail and the Wahtum Lake Road.

Punch Bowl Falls, Eagle Creek

Lower Eagle Creek Trail

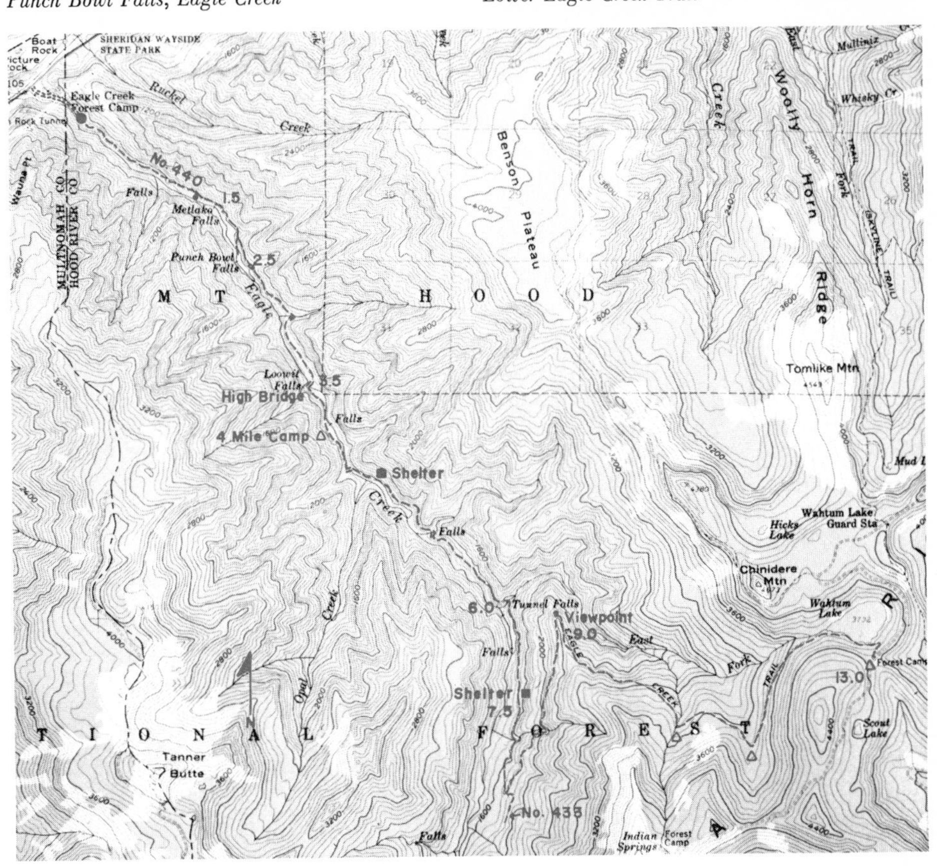

20 RUCKEL RIDGE COLUMBIA RIVER GORGE

One day trip
Distance: 3 miles one way
Elevation gain: 2,500 feet
High point: 2,900 feet
Allow 3 to 4 hours one way
Usually open May through November
Topographic map:
U.S.G.S. Bonneville Dam, Oreg.-Wash.
N4530-W12145/15
1957

Delicate wildflowers and a strenuous workout are two of the many reasons why a hike along Ruckel Ridge is one of the more enjoyable trips in the Columbia River Gorge. Also, the one trailless section through a scree field exercises the hiker's route-finding abilities. A few short rock scrambles, some exposure, and constant climbing make this a trip for the more experienced hiker. No water is available along the trail so containers should be filled before starting. An ice axe or hiking cane would be useful on some of the steeper slopes.

Take U.S. Highway 80N and turn off at Eagle Creek Forest Camp, about one mile east of Bonneville Dam. Proceed past the fish hatchery and turn left at a sign which points to the access road serving overnight camping facilities one-fourth mile beyond. Continue along this road to its termination at the eastern end of the campground.

The trail begins a few feet to the south of the large incinerator and climbs in switchbacks for about one-fourth mile until two large rocks are reached on either side of the trail. Turn left onto the path which joins the trail at this point. The main trail continues beyond this junction for about 100 yards and ends at Buck Point, where you can get a good view of the mouth of Eagle Creek and Bonneville Dam.

Continue to climb steeply in switchbacks until you reach a power transmission tower. Then, hike along the ridge top passing under the power lines and re-enter the woods. Follow the trail a short distance as it goes downhill and out of the woods onto a slope of boulders and almost disappears. Note at what place you left the woods to facilitate the return trip. Continue in a southerly direction for about 100 yards, regaining much of the elevation just lost. At this point on the south side of a rock slide of smaller stones a path leads diagonally up to the left. Follow this path to the top of the slide where the rocks become much larger. Scramble over these in a northerly direction keeping relatively close to the trees on the downslope side. The immediate goal is the west end of the open ridge, which runs in a northwesterly direction for about 200 feet from the face of the cliff looming overhead. When the end of the open ridge is reached, turn to the right and follow it up to the base of the cliff face.

The trail becomes obvious at this point and traverses to the left under the north side of the cliff for a short distance. It then turns right and climbs very steeply up the wooded slope. Although there are many small tree trunks to aid you, this section is very frustrating in wet weather and the hike is most enjoyable when there has been no recent precipitation. After you reach the ridgecrest the going becomes straightforward as the ridge is quite narrow. Whenever it becomes necessary, the trail always leaves the top of the ridge on the west side. Near the 2,000-foot level, there is some exposure along the crest of a very narrow rock ridge. However, it is short and should not present too great a problem.

Although you can turn back at any point, a logical stopping place is a large rock spire at the 2,800-foot level. It overlooks the saddle where Ruckel Ridge becomes less narrow, turns slightly to the left, and gradually climbs to the Benson Plateau.

Sunburst on Ruckel Ridge

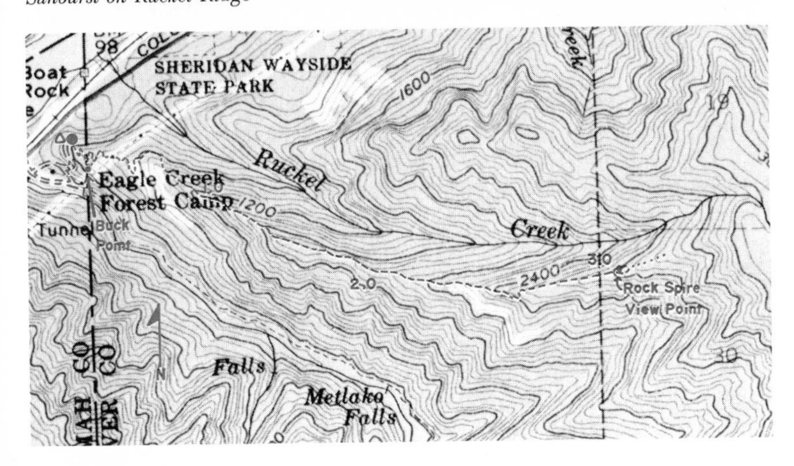

21 BENSON PLATEAU COLUMBIA RIVER GORGE

Backpack
Distance: 13 miles one way
Elevation gain: 4,940 feet, loss, 930 feet, (excluding Mt. Chinidere)
High point: 4,673 feet
Allow 8 to 10 hours one way
Usually open June through October
Topographic map:
U.S.G.S. Bonneville Dam, Oreg.-Wash.
N4530-W12145/15
1957

The Benson Trail, as it is popularly known, is the first segment of the Oregon Skyline Trail, which traverses the backbone of the Cascade Mountains for the entire length of the state. Although the trail is long, most of the climbing is in the first 6.5 miles, the remainder being primarily a ridge walk.

Approaching from the east, turn off U.S. Highway 80N at the Herman Creek exit east of Cascade Locks and proceed under the freeway to the junction with the Herman Creek Road. Turn right and drive for 0.3 mile to the Columbia Gorge Work Station. You may park your car near the buildings.

When approaching from the west, turn off U.S. Highway 80N at the Cascade Locks junction. Proceed through Cascade Locks on the main street and turn left at a sign pointing to the industrial park and airport. Continue on this road for two miles, crossing the freeway bridge, to the junction of the Herman Creek Road. Turn left, and proceed for a short distance to the Columbia Gorge Work Station.

The trail, No. 2000, begins at the west end of the work station parking lot. The trail ascends gradually about one-third mile to a power line access road, which should be followed to the west (right) a short distance until it begins to descend. At this point turn left and pick up the trail going south. This junction is not marked. After one-fourth mile, there is another unmarked trail junction; take the right hand fork and follow it to the foot bridge crossing Herman Creek.

For the next five miles the trail rises steadily to the edge of the plateau. During the climb, you will pass a heliport at about the 2,500-foot level, and Teakettle Spring a little above the heliport. The spring may be dry in late summer so carry water at that time of year.

At the end of the climb (about 6.5 miles) is the Ruckel Creek Trail junction. Be sure to turn left here and proceed south through the woods, following the Skyline Trail which, after about 1.5 miles, leaves the woods and follows the eastern edge of the plateau. All along the plateau are numerous signs pointing to sometimes obscure way trails. At several points these signs point west to the Benson Trail. This is an older, parallel route on the west side of the plateau and should not be confused with the Skyline Trail.

At 9.5 miles is Camp Smokey. Water is available 300 yards down the hillside to the west. This is a good campsite with an adequate supply of firewood and room for several tents.

At 12 miles a way trail to the left leads up about 400 feet to the summit of Mt. Chinidere where you can see the entire expanse of the Benson Plateau, with Mt. Saint Helens in the background. You will see Wahtum Lake just to the southeast.

To reach Wahtum Lake, follow the main trail to the road which circles the eastern half of the lake, or take a way trail to the right just beyond the junction of the Mt. Chinidere Trail, which joins the Eagle Creek Trail where the East Fork of Eagle Creek leaves Wahtum Lake. There is a campground at the eastern end of the lake where the Eagle Creek Trail joins the Wahtum Lake Road.

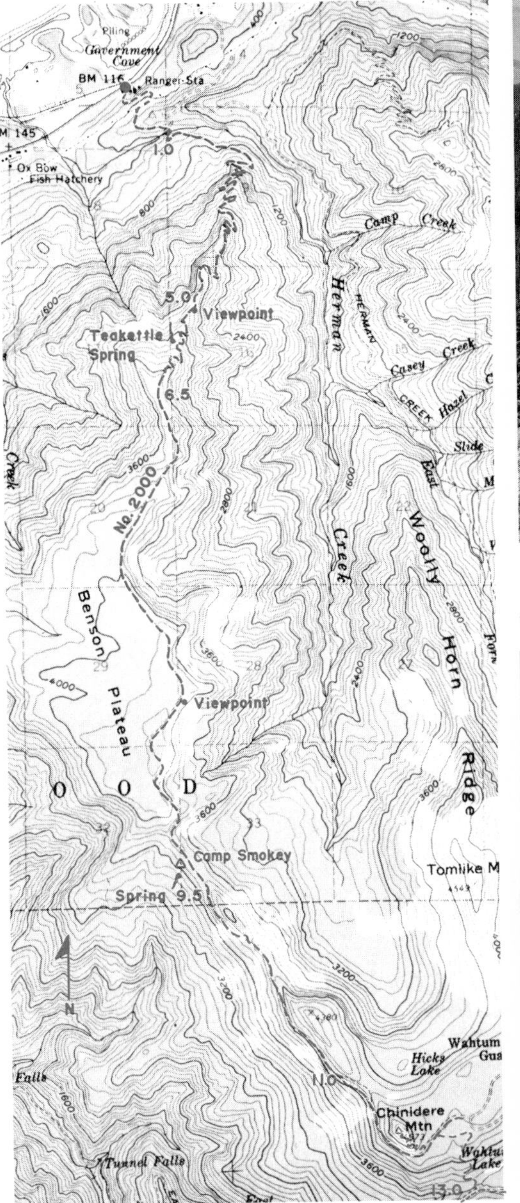

Benson Plateau from Mt. Chinidere

Columbia River from Benson Trail

22 NICK EATON RIDGE COLUMBIA RIVER GORGE

One day trip
Distance: 5½ miles one way
Elevation gain: 3,964 feet
High point: 4,080 feet
Allow 3½ to 5 hours one way
Usually open June through November
Topographic map:
U.S.G.S. Bonneville Dam, Oreg.-Wash.
N4530-W12145/15
1957

Nick Eaton Ridge is a steep hike with almost a 4,000-foot gain in elevation. Herman Creek Canyon and the Benson Plateau lie directly west of the ridge and can frequently be seen from the many good viewpoints along the trail. Oak and evergreen forests alternate with open slopes to provide a varied scene. Water is not available on the ridge.

Approaching from the east, turn off U.S. Highway 80N at the Herman Creek exit east of Cascade Locks and proceed under the freeway to the junction of the Herman Creek Road. Turn right, and drive for 0.3 mile to the Columbia Gorge Work Station (formerly a ranger station). Cars may be parked near the buildings in a lot provided for public use.

Approaching from the west, turn off U.S. Highway 80N at the Cascade Locks junction. Proceed through Cascade Locks on the main street and turn left at a sign pointing to the industrial park and airport. Continue on this road for two miles, crossing the freeway bridge, to the junction of the Herman Creek Road. Turn left, and proceed for a short distance to the Columbia Gorge Work Station.

The trail, No. 2000, begins at the west end of the work station parking lot. It climbs a few hundred feet to the powerline access road which should be followed to the west a short distance until it begins to descend. At this point turn left and pick up the trail going south. This junction is not marked. A few hundred yards above the road, the trail forks. Turn left here and climb for about one-fourth mile to a road junction. Continue on the road which goes to the east, along the south side of the ridge. After traveling about one-half mile you will pass a sign on your right pointing to water 100 yards down the slope at Bear Spring. A short distance beyond you will come to a road on the left leading to an open picnic area. Do not take this side road. A few hundred yards beyond the picnic area, a sign on the left side of the road identifies the Nick Eaton Way Trail, No. 447.

It climbs in switchbacks for three-fourths mile through a woods of deciduous and evergreen trees. The trail then travels along several large open slopes bordered by oaks. Re-enter the deep woods and, after a level stretch three miles from the highway, you will come to a junction. The trail to the left is the Ridge Cutoff Way and connects with Gorton Creek Way, a short distance to the north. A sign identifies the trail on the right as Nick Eaton Way.

Keep to the right, traversing across an open rocky slope and enter the woods. Descend a short distance, climb, and then continue on the level for one-half mile to a second junction. A sign here reads Wahtum Lake Road 5¼ miles and Green Point Mountain 4½ miles. Continue on the main trail to the left, following a sometimes obscure path that has been marked with tape in many places. At one point a false trail leads to the right about 100 yards and terminates in a steep clearing. Now the trail begins to climb more steeply, periodically meeting the ridge top but generally keeping below the crest. It goes all the way to Green Point Mountain. However, the usual stopping place is a group of large rocks on the south end of the ridge just before it begins to drop slightly. Many points on the Columbia River and the Gorge are visible from these rocks.

Nick Eaton Ridge from the air

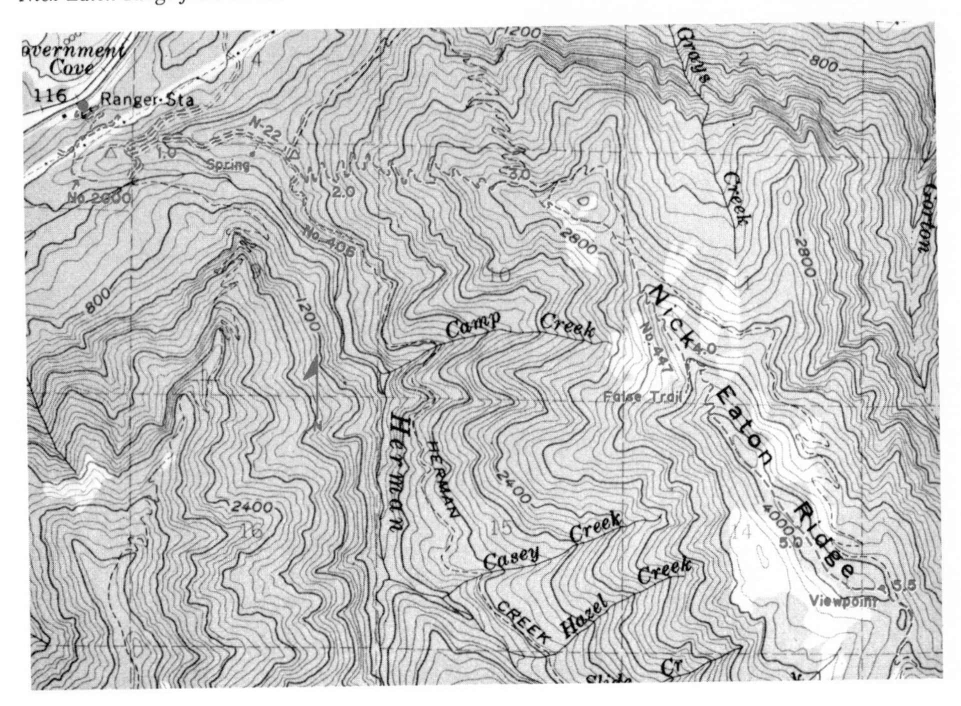

23 NORTH LAKE COLUMBIA RIVER GORGE

One day trip or backpack
Distance: 6 miles one way
Elevation gain: 3,930 feet
High point: 4,070 feet
Allow 5 to 6 hours one way
Usually open July through November
Topographic map:
U.S.G.S. Bonneville Dam, Oreg.-Wash.
N4530-W12145/15
1957

Mount Defiance from North Lake Trail

The Wyeth Trail is little used and as a consequence is not well maintained. The lower half is very steep and, according to Forest Service records, the grade at some points reaches 60 percent. North Lake is rather small and shallow, resting beneath a talus slope a short distance north of Green Point Mountain. There are no developed camping sites near the lake; however, the floor of the woods is quite clean and few rocks will have to be removed to accommodate tents.

Drive on U.S. Highway 80N and turn off at the Wyeth exit 12 miles west of Hood River. Turn left at the junction and park at the trail head about 100 feet to the east of the rock shop. A sign marks the start of the Wyeth Trail, No. 411.

Proceed south up a shallow grade which gets steeper after crossing under the powerlines and climbs in switchbacks to a rockslide at 1.5 miles. Here there is an excellent view of the Columbia River and Mt. Saint Helens. The trail continues to climb steeply up the west side of a ridge to a burned-over area near which there is a rocky outcrop. Shortly thereafter you will cross a stream which is the only source of water on the lower part of the route. Above the stream there is another small rock bluff at an elevation of 3,000 feet. This is a good place to stop if you are tired and do not want to go the full distance to North Lake.

Above the bluff the trail becomes very brushy and somewhat hard to follow. From the crest of the ridge to the lake there are a great many downed logs across the trail which have been sawed through but not removed. There are many views of the west side of Mt. Defiance from the ridge.

South of the ridge crest the trail gradually drops down to a flat area and crosses several small streams, then climbs again until reaching a point just below the lake where a very old sign points south to the Mt. Defiance Trail, one mile, and north to Wyeth, 6 miles. Turn right at the sign and proceed about 75 yards to the earth fill dam at the outlet of the lake.

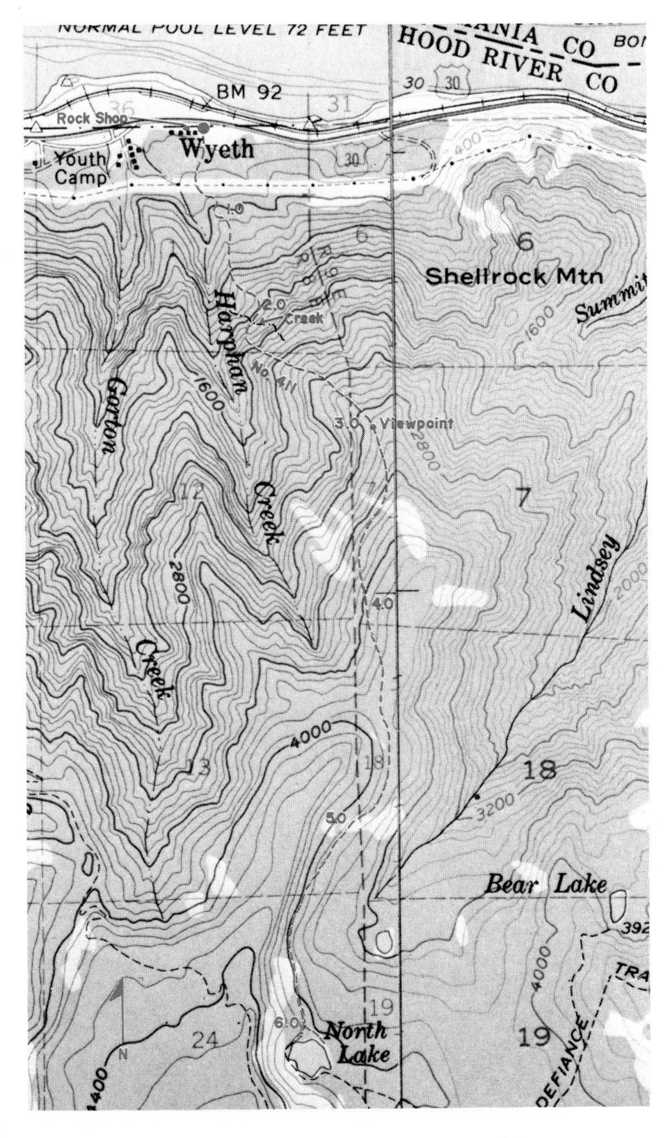
NORMAL POOL LEVEL 72 FEET
HOOD RIVER CO
BM 92
Rock Shop
Wyeth
Youth Camp
Shellrock Mtn
Summit
Harphan Creek
Creek
No. 411
Viewpoint
Gorton Creek
Lindsey
Bear Lake
North Lake
DEFIANCE
1.0
2.0
3.0
4.0
5.0
6.0
1600
2800
4000
3200
2000

24 MT. DEFIANCE COLUMBIA RIVER GORGE

One day trip or backpack
Distance: 5 miles one way
Elevation gain: 4,816 feet
High point: 4,960 feet
Allow from 4 to 6 hours one way
Usually open from June through October
Topographic map:
U.S.G.S. Hood River, Oreg.-Wash.
N4530-W12130/15
1957

Mt. Defiance, at 4,960 feet, is the highest point overlooking the Columbia Gorge. Since the trail is very steep and has a considerable elevation gain it is used frequently in the late spring by mountain climbers as a conditioning hike.

If approaching from the west, drive east on U.S. Highway 80N to the former Lindsey Creek State Park, about 150 yards west of the 52-mile highway post. A fence is adjacent to the highway, but sufficient room has been left to safely park a number of cars.

From the east, proceed west on U.S. Highway 80N and turn off at the Wyeth exit, returning to the freeway eastbound. Continue east for 2.5 miles to Lindsey Creek.

The unmarked trail, No. 413, begins just inside the east end of the fence bordering the highway. It proceeds uphill sharply behind a sign marking the location of an underground cable.

At one-fourth mile, the trail meets the powerline access road. Turn left and follow the road for 30 yards, past the remains of an old wooden ladder, to a gully leading straight uphill. Climb up this gully about 20 feet where the trail again becomes obvious. About one-half mile from the highway, a side trail (which may not be marked) descends to the left about 100 yards to a small spring. You should fill all available water containers here as this is the last source of water on the main trail.

Shortly after leaving the spring, the trail crosses an overgrown logging road and continues up on the right side of the ridge crest. A rock cairn identifies the point where the trail re-enters the woods on the opposite side of the road.

At two miles, the trail flattens out for a short distance, then turns left through an area of young trees. A sharp turn to the right follows very soon thereafter and is marked by a fallen log which has been blazed. It is easy to lose the trail here so be sure to watch closely for the downed log.

One mile below the summit, the trail climbs to a rocky bench and turns left, proceeding generally eastward for about one-fourth mile through a lava flow. It turns right again and in another one-fourth mile joins the road that leads up to the summit.

If you wish to spend the night, a good campsite is available at Warren Lake, 1.5 miles to the northeast. To get to the lake, follow the summit road down the mountain for one-half mile where it forks. Take the left fork for an additional one-half mile, following the orange blaze marks in the trees to the Warren Lake Trail sign. Turn left and follow this trail to Warren Lake. As indicated on the map, this trail returns to the Mt. Defiance trail, but it is very hard to follow west of the lake. However, you can reach the Mt. Defiance trail easily by contouring for one-half mile across the lava flow directly below the summit.

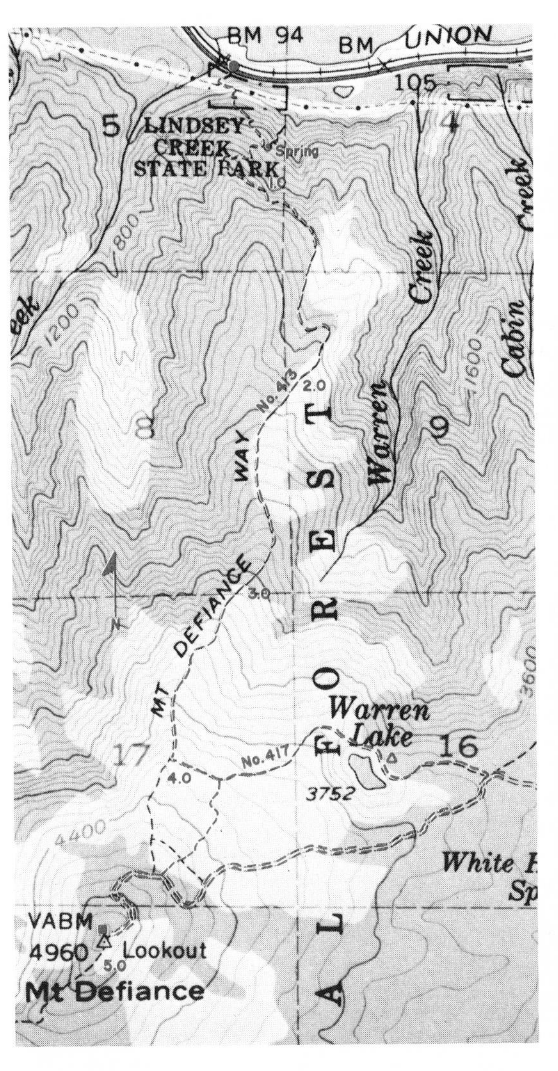

Warren Lake, Mt. Defiance

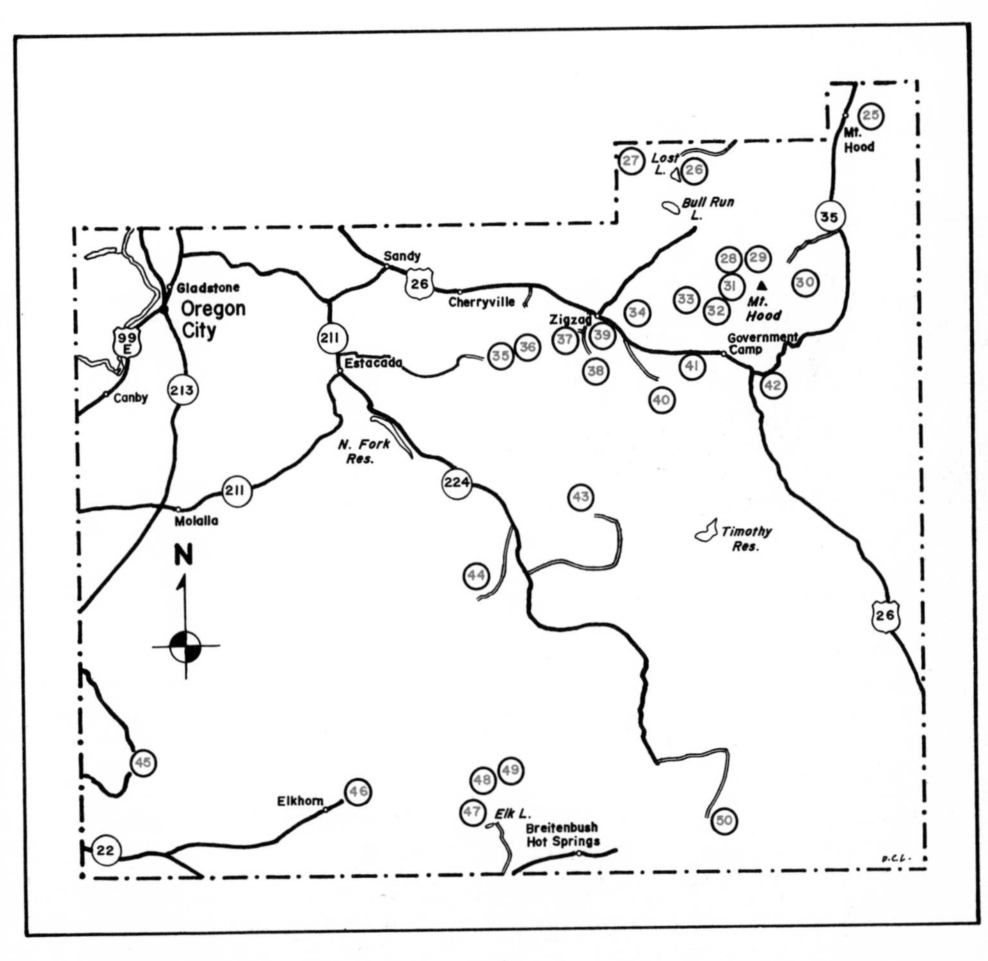

Mt. Hood
Lost L.
Bull Run L.
Sandy
Gladstone
Oregon City
Cherryville
Zigzag
Mt. Hood
Government Camp
Estacada
Canby
N. Fork Res.
Molalla
Timothy Res.
N
Elkhorn
Elk L.
Breitenbush Hot Springs

NORTHERN OREGON

Mt. Hood, at 11,245 feet, is the highest peak in Oregon and is the dominant feature on the skyline from two-thirds of the trails in this section. Famous throughout the world for its asymmetrical beauty, it is believed to be the second most frequently climbed mountain in the world, the first being Japan's Fuji, which imparts a religious significance to the believers who ascend to its summit.

Geologically, Mt. Hood is composed of numerous lava flows and a great quantity of volcanic ash. Due to the deep scoring of its flanks by many large glaciers, which have long since receded to their present size, the mountain is known to have been in existence sometime prior to the last great glacial advance. Barrett Spur, standing somewhat apart on the northwest side of the mountain is a remnant of an older volcano which once stood on the site of the present peak. The summit of the mountain forms about one-half of a large crater, the southern portion of which is believed to have collapsed when a lake near the summit broke through and swept down the mountain forming the unusually smooth south side. However, this is only a theory and has so far not been proven.

Timberline Lodge, at the 6,000-foot level on the southeast side of the mountain, is perhaps the best known alpine hotel in existence. It was built during the Depression by W.P.A. labor. Its huge timbers, ornate wrought iron work, wood carvings, and massive stone masonry remain a monument to the skilled craftsmen and artisans who labored for many years to construct a truly unique building.

Circling the mountain at about 6,000 feet above sea level is the 36-mile Timberline Trail which is covered in part by five of the trails in this section. This is very beautiful alpine country, with stone and wooden shelters placed at strategic locations.

The decision whether to do a one-day hike or a backpack trip on the trails in Northern Oregon will depend upon the intensity of the wilderness experience you wish to absorb. The trails are not excessively long and most are within easy reach of the Portland and Salem metropolitan areas. Most of the trails lead to high points with broad views of the surrounding mountains. Fine campgrounds can be found almost anywhere.

Seven of the trails are in the rugged terrain between Mt. Hood and Mt. Jefferson near the headwaters of the Clackamas River, where there are few roads and little logging. The loop trail at Silver Creek Falls should be a must for everyone. It is only a short distance east of Salem and is not a strenuous trip. In the late fall, multitudes of deciduous trees deposit a layer of leaves so thick that in places they come up to your ankles. Another must trip for the more hardy hiker is the steep trail up to the lower part of Yocum Ridge, which separates Sandy and Reid Glaciers, on the west side of Mt. Hood. In the summer, glacial ice and a profusion of wild flowers form a beautiful contrast to the fluted spires of the mountain's west face. The upper part of Yocum Ridge was the last major route on the mountain to be climbed, having resisted the efforts of mountaineers for decades.

Most of the forested mountains of Northern Oregon are covered with rhododendron bushes, which in the spring are ablaze with delicate pink blossoms. Beargrass, with its long stalks and bulbous white blooms will delight a photographer, particularly when whole fields of these plants are in flower.

25 BALD BUTTE NORTHERN OREGON

One day trip
Distance: 1.5 miles one way
Elevation gain: 2,039 feet
High point: 3,779 feet
Allow 1½ to 2 hours one way
Usually open April through November
Topographic map:
U.S.G.S. Hood River, Oreg.
N4530-W12130/15
1957

Bald Butte Lookout Tower

Bald Butte is a high, grassy-topped mountain just to the east of the little town of Mt. Hood in the Upper Hood River Valley. The Butte is quite exposed to the prevailing westerly winds which are accelerated by the presence of nearby Mt. Hood. (Winds have been estimated near the lookout tower in excess of 80 miles per hour. Persons climbing the butte in cold, windy conditions are advised to carry extra-warm clothing as a precautionary measure.) The view of Mt. Hood from the top is extraordinarily impressive as the foreshortening effect of looking directly across at the steep northeast face makes it appear almost vertical. The now-closed Cloud Cap Inn can be distinguished among the trees at the 6,000-foot level on the northeastern shoulder of the mountain.

Proceed south on Oregon Highway 35 from Hood River (or north from U.S. Highway 26) to the town of Mt. Hood in the Upper Valley. From the post office on the west side of the highway, continue south for 0.3 mile and turn left on a side road opposite a utility pole bearing the numbers 205-22. Drive on this road for 0.7 mile, turning left at the junction and proceeding across an irrigation canal to a large clearing. Park here.

Walk up the logging road which contours along the north side of the clearing and then continue east up the south side of a canyon for 0.9 mile. Just before a mud slide turn left and drop down to a creek bottom (usually dry). From here climb diagonally up the cleared area to the right, making use of the many animal trails. The formal trail is all but impossible to find. You will climb through the woods, cross a logging road, and emerge eventually on the northwest corner of the grassy summit dome. Go almost straight up to the lookout tower staying to the left of a lone tree in the middle of the slope. If the wind is blowing from the west, refuge can be found in the trees to the southeast of the tower, down a short slope.

Bald Butte from the west

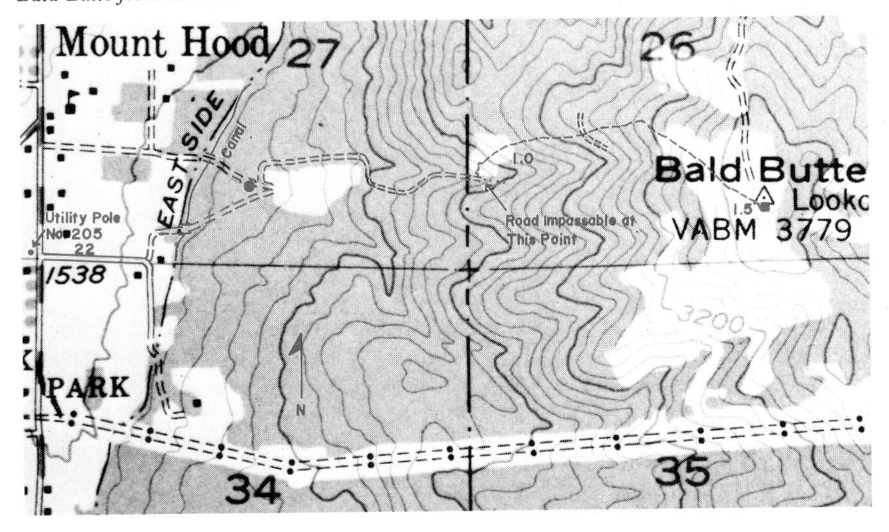

26 LOST LAKE BUTTE NORTHERN OREGON

One day trip
Distance: 2 miles one way
Elevation gain: 1,288 feet
High point: 4,468 feet
Allow 1½ to 2 hours one way
Usually open June through October
Topographic map:
U.S.G.S. Bull Run Lake, Oreg.
N4522.5-W12145/7.5
1962

The trail ascending Lost Lake Butte offers an easy two-mile hike to the summit of a cinder cone on the northeast side of Lost Lake near the slopes of Mt. Hood. The lake is a very popular summer resort area with well-developed campgrounds on its north shore. The serenity of the surrounding peaks and valleys is left largely undisturbed since no power boats are allowed on the lake.

Lost Lake may be reached by following Oregon Highway No. 35 north from Hood River or south from the Government Camp area to the plywood mill at the settlement of Dee, between the Upper and Lower Hood River Valleys. From here, the road to the lake is well marked. However, at several places there are signs pointing in different directions to Lost Lake. Follow the signs with the lowest mileage. These will be on Forest Service road No. S-100.

If the Lolo Pass road from U.S. Highway 26 is used, follow it north of the pass to a junction one mile beyond the point where it crosses the West Fork of the Hood River. Turn left on road S-100 and proceed to the lake.

The trail to Lost Lake Butte, No. 616, begins at the junction of road S-100 and the campground service road at the lake shore. A sign on the east side of the junction marks the trail head.

Climb the bank and proceed east for one-fourth mile to where the Jones Creek road crosses the trail. The trail continues east on the opposite side of the road and has signs showing both directions. It is wide and well maintained and ascends in a series of gentle switchbacks to the rocky crest at the site of a former lookout tower.

In favorable weather conditions, many of the peaks of the Columbia Gorge can be seen to the north and west; among them are Larch Mountain, Tanner Butte, Indian Mountain, Mt. Chinidere, and Mt. Defiance. You will be treated also to an extraordinary view of the northwest face of Mt. Hood, as well as Lost Lake which lies at the foot of the butte.

It is suggested that adequate water be carried as none is available on the trail.

Lost Lake from Lost Lake Butte

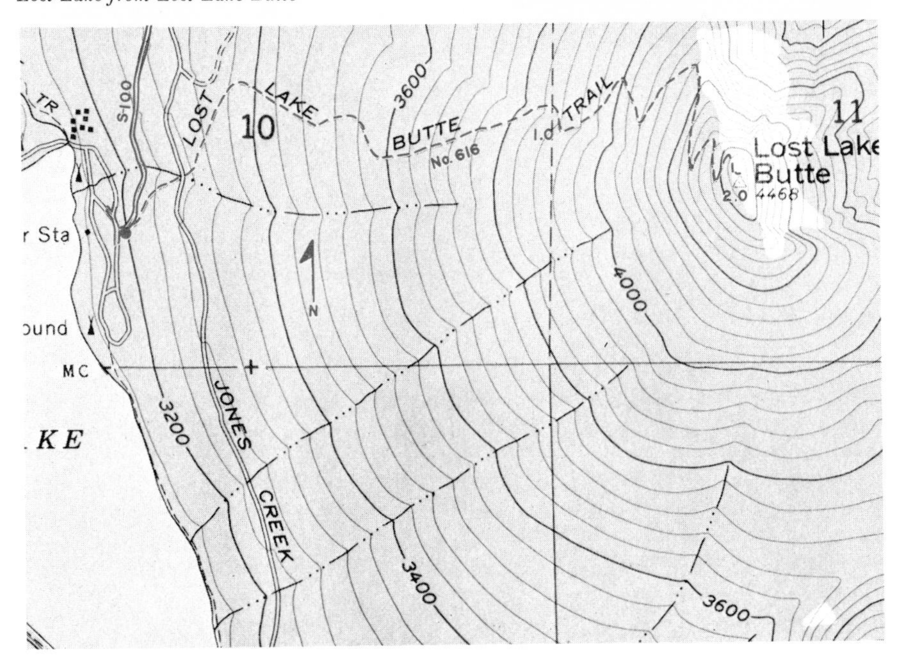

27 BUCK PEAK NORTHERN OREGON

One day trip
Distance: 7½ miles one way
Elevation gain: 1,860 feet, loss 580 feet
High point: 4,751 feet
Allow 4 to 5 hours one way
Usually open mid-June through October
Topographic map:
U.S.G.S. Bull Run Lake, Oreg.
N4522.5-W12145/7.5
1962

Mt. Adams from the Skyline Trail

From Buck Peak you can look southeast directly down on popular Lost Lake and across to the rugged northwest face of Mt. Hood. Even more spectacular is the view to the west, which includes the high country south of the Columbia Gorge.

Drive east of Portland on U.S. Highway 26 and turn north on the Lolo Pass Road across from the Zigzag Ranger Station. Continue for 11 miles to the summit of Lolo Pass where there is parking space. A sign on the north side of the road identifies this new section of the Skyline Trail, No. 2000. Be sure to carry water, as this trail is dry most of the year.

Hike along the gravel road west of the sign for about 50 yards until you meet the path that goes under the power lines. After crossing the powerline access road, the trail climbs gradually along the wooded eastern slopes of Hiyu Mountain. The trail has been cut out of rock at about the one-half mile point and from here the massive summit of Mt. Adams is visible to the north and the extremely steep west face of Mt. Hood rises close by on the east. Re-enter the woods and travel on the level before crossing a large rocky slope one mile from the pass. The trail continues through the woods for the next three miles, generally contouring along the northeast slopes of Sentinel Peak.

After four miles, the trail travels along an overgrown fire break. At the Preachers Peak saddle it comes to the junction of Trail No. 617, which descends to Lost Lake. Here you continue straight ahead. The trail re-enters the woods and one-half mile later switchbacks several times to the saddle between Preachers Peak and the Devils Pulpit. A large rock outcropping one-half mile beyond the saddle offers a good resting place with a view of Bull Run Lake and Mt. Hood. Past this point the trail is level for one mile and then turns to the left and descends on the north side of the ridge to another saddle. From the north side of the ridge, Buck Peak is visible as the high point to the northwest. Climb gently for another one-half mile to the junction of the Buck Peak Trail, No. 615. Turn right and follow this trail for one-third mile to the summit of the peak, site of a former fire lookout station.

Mt. Hood from Buck Peak

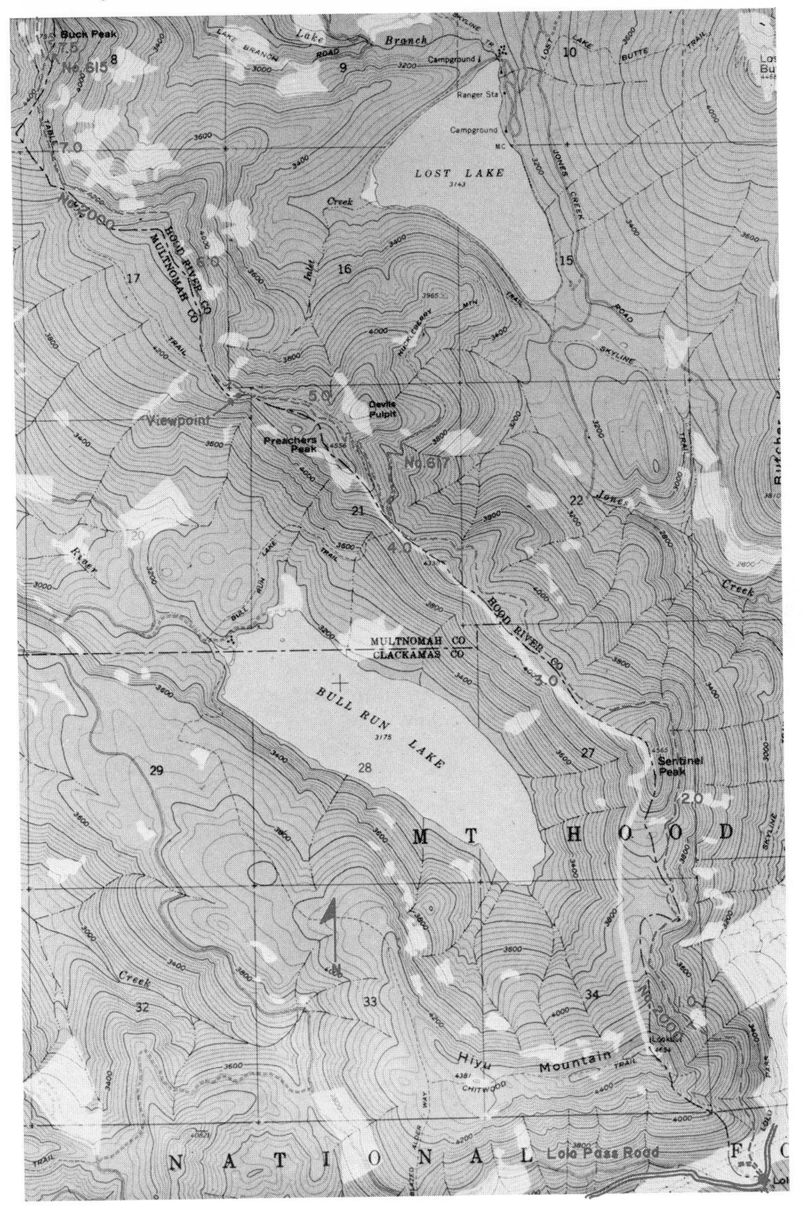

28 CAIRN BASIN NORTHERN OREGON

One day trip or backpack
Distance: 5 miles one way
Elevation gain: 2,310 feet, loss 400 feet
High point: 5,720 feet
Allow 3 to 4 hours one way
Usually open July through October
Topographic maps:
U.S.G.S. Bull Run Lake, Oreg.
N4522.5-W12145/7.5
1962
U.S.G.S. Cathedral Ridge, Oreg.
N4522.5-W12137.5/7.5
1962

Mt. Hood from South Fork of Ladd Creek

The country surrounding Cairn Basin is an exceptionally beautiful part of the Mt. Hood Wild Area. Alpine tarns vie for attention with the many meadows, streams, and waterfalls. Close-up views of the northwestern face of Mt. Hood and Sandy Glacier may be had as soon as you reach the crest of Bald Mountain Ridge. There is a very good rock shelter at Cairn Basin and if the shelter is occupied, another such structure is located nearby on the top of McNeil Ridge. The latter hut is frequently used by climbers attempting an ascent of Mt. Hood via Cathedral Ridge.

Take U.S. Highway 26 to the Lolo Pass Road opposite the Zigzag Ranger Station. Proceed to the summit of Lolo Pass and turn right on a gravel logging road, No. S-238. At 3.1 miles beyond this junction turn sharply left on road No. S-238J and proceed for 1.0 mile to the trail head located on the east side of the road.

The trail, which angles sharply up to the right, is identified only by a small red marker on a stump. After about 100 yards, it joins the Skyline Trail, No 2000. Turn left here and follow the Skyline Trail for one mile to the Bald Mountain Shelter at the junction of the Timberline Trail, No. 600. Here, an unmarked way trail climbs to the southeast for about one-third mile to the top of Bald Mountain, 4,591 feet, the former site of a Forest Service fire lookout cabin.

From the Bald Mountain Shelter, follow the Timberline Trail, No. 600, to the east as it contours around the north side of Bald Mountain. One-half mile beyond the shelter is the junction of the McGee Creek Trail, No. 627. A short distance later the trail leaves the heavy timber and follows the top of Bald Mountain ridge directly above the canyon of the Muddy Fork. At the east end of the ridge, the trail drops down into the timber below McNeil Ridge. At the point where the trail reaches heavy timber, a sign points left to a camping area on the South Fork of McGee Creek. This campsite is popular with packers as there is ample pasture for horses and abundant water.

The trail contours up to Cathedral Ridge, passing the beautiful green cascade of McGee Creek, crosses rocky slopes and passes near several tarns which may evaporate into lush meadows in the early fall. From the sign marking Cathedral Ridge

Trail, No. 625, the route drops down and crosses the South Fork of Ladd Creek, climbs a low ridge and descends into Cairn Basin. The stone shelter is to the right about 200 feet, and there are many excellent campsites in open woods. A small stream passes near the shelter.

The McNeil Ridge shelter cabin may be reached by returning to where the trail crosses McGee Creek. From here, proceed straight uphill gaining about 600 feet in elevation, and contour to the right to the ridge crest. The shelter can be seen standing on the westernmost point on the ridge. Water usually is available just below the northeast end of this ridge.

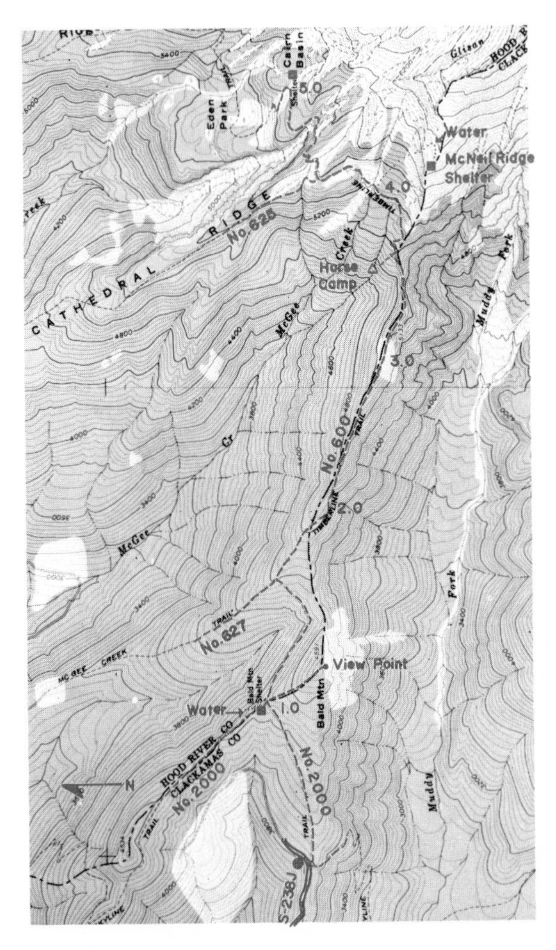

29 ELK COVE NORTHERN OREGON

One day trip or backpack
Distance: 4 miles one way
Elevation gain: 780 feet, loss 900 feet
High point: 6,020 feet
Allow 3 hours one way
Usually open August through October
Topographic map:
U.S.G.S. Cathedral Ridge, Oreg.
N4522.5-W12137.5/7.5
1962

The north side of Mt. Hood, with its multitude of rock ridges, small canyons, and nearby ice fields is an excellent place to enjoy a truly alpine experience without the necessity of a lengthy backpack. From Cloud Cap to Elk Cove and return is a comfortable day's journey on the Timberline Trail without a great deal of altitude gain. The Cove is a wonderful place to camp, too, with an abundance of water and magnificent scenery. However, the stone shelter, which stood for many years, was destroyed by an avalanche and is no longer usable except as a windbreak.

Approaching from either Government Camp or Hood River, drive along Oregon Highway 35 to the Cooper Spur junction. Proceed to the little community of Cooper Spur and turn off on Cloud Cap Road, No. S-12, and drive 11 miles to Cloud Cap Saddle Campground, directly below the old inn, where a sign points to Elk Cove — 4 miles.

Proceed to the east on the Timberline Trail, No. 600. At one-fourth mile you will cross Eliot Creek, usually on a small, improvised wooden foot bridge. From there, the trail climbs steeply at first and then more gradually, leading in and out of small side canyons to Stranahan Ridge. Then it descends gradually to Compass Creek where late in the summer an ice cave over the creek may be explored.

From Compass Creek the trail goes down into Coe Creek Canyon and crosses the creek at a point just above the falls. *Caution:* The Timberline Trail has recently been relocated, crossing Coe Creek at a lower altitude which is considerably safer than the former high-trail crossing. However, the rock slab on the east side of the creek is very slippery. Use the anchored wire hand line in descending to the stream bed. (This crossing is very hazardous for horses.)

After crossing Coe Creek, the trail climbs gradually until it reaches the edge of Elk Cove. The Cove proper is a meadow a few hundred yards wide. Unfortunately, some of the natural beauty of the area has been affected by heavy avalanches which have splintered many of the trees during the last 20 years. Above and to the southwest is Barrett Spur. Geologists state that this large rib of rock was once a part of an older mountain which stood long before the present Mt. Hood was formed.

Adventurous hikers can climb to Barrett Spur, elevation 7,853 feet, from Elk Cove and obtain an excellent view of Ladd and Coe Glaciers as well as Cathedral Ridge, a route to the summit of Mt. Hood that is not often climbed.

North Face of Mt. Hood

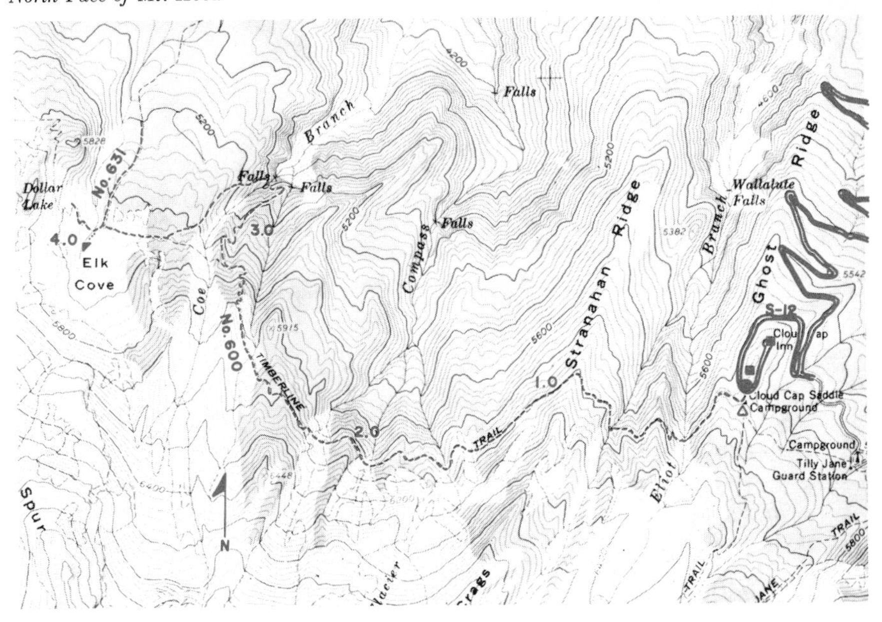

30 GNARL RIDGE
NORTHERN OREGON

One day trip or backpack
Distance: 4½ miles one way
Elevation gain: 2,156 feet
High point: 6,633 feet
Allow 3 to 4 hours one way
Usually open from mid-July through October
Topographic maps:
U.S.G.S. Timberline Lodge, Oreg.
N4515-W12137/7.5
1962
U.S.G.S. Badger Lake, Oreg.
N4515-W12130/7.5
1962

Mt. Hood from Elk Meadows

This area of Mt. Hood is truly a hiker's paradise with rushing streams, waterfalls, and European-type alpine vistas of broken glaciers and deep canyons as well as a beautiful campsite at Elk Meadows. To fully appreciate this trip, you are urged to wait for good weather conditions.

Drive to Hood River Meadows Campground on Oregon Highway 35, the Mt. Hood Loop, via Hood River or from U.S. Highway 26. (Highway 35 joins U.S. Highway 26 three miles east of Government Camp.) The campground is on the old highway which can be reached from the Mt. Hood Meadows cut off at Bennett Pass on the south, or from a junction a few miles to the north of the pass where a sign points to Hood River Meadows. There is ample parking space available at the Meadows. To avoid unnecessary walking it is wise to park cars as close to the highway as possible.

The trail, No. 666, starts on a dirt road leading north just to the right of the entrance to the campground.

Follow this road for one-fourth mile until it meets the main trail. The trail crosses Clark Creek on a large log and then goes over Kate Creek on a small log. It crosses Warren Creek on a foot bridge and a short distance later drops down to the sandy bed of Newton Creek. This fording can be made on a log, just beyond which the trail turns right and climbs several switchbacks to the base of a ridge below Elk Mountain. Follow the trail north to Elk Meadows where, 2.5 miles in, there is an open shelter cabin that looks out to the east face of Mt. Hood. This beautiful meadows is an excellent place to camp if you wish to spend some time in the area.

From the shelter cabin, walk diagonally northwest across the lower portion of the meadow to the edge of the woods. The trail is marked by a red painted blaze on a tree which can be seen from some distance away. You are now on Trail No. 652 which follows the lower portion of Gnarl Ridge and climbs through open woods for one-half mile and then leads up the ridge crest for another one-half mile until it reaches the Timberline Trail, No. 600. Here a sign points left to Timberline Lodge 8 miles and right to the Cloud Cap road at 5 miles.

Turn right and follow the Timberline Trail for one mile to the viewpoint just below Lamberson Butte. Just short of the viewpoint is the ruins of a stone shelter which was destroyed by an avalanche a number of years ago.

From the viewpoint turn east and climb straight up to Lamberson Butte for a magnificent view of the east face of the mountain and Newton-Clark Glacier and the surrounding country to the east.

GNARL RIDGE

Gnarl Ridge

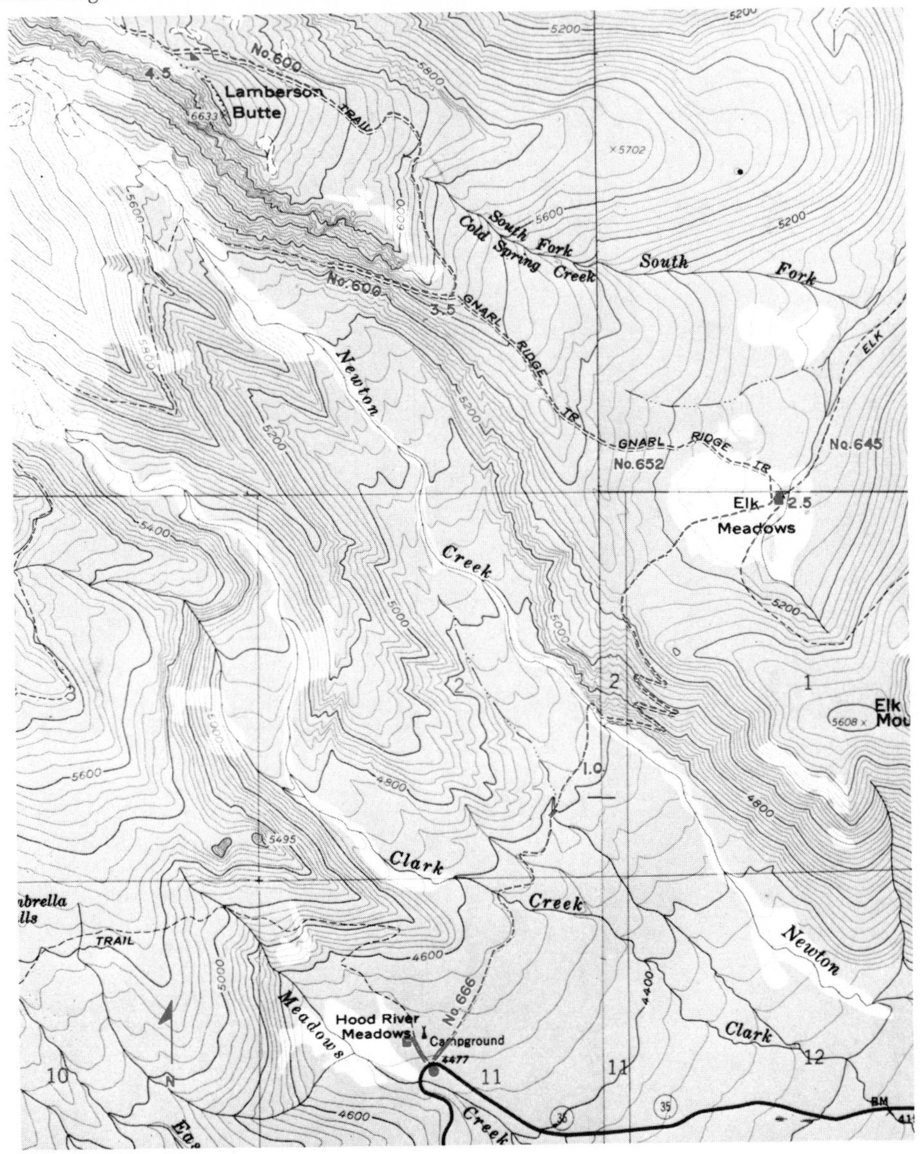
No.600
4.5
Lamberson Butte
6633
TRAIL
5200
5800
6000
×5702
South Fork
Cold Spring Creek
South Fork
5600
No.600
3.5
GNARL RIDGE TR
Newton
ELK
GNARL RIDGE TR
No.652
No.645
Elk Meadows
2.5
5400
Creek
5000
2
1
Elk
5608
1.0
4800
5495
Clark
Creek
TRAIL
4600
Newton
Meadows
No.666
Hood River Meadows
Campground
4477
4400
Clark
10
11
12
35
Creek
BM

31 YOCUM RIDGE NORTHERN OREGON

One day trip or backpack
Distance: 5 miles one way
Elevation gain: 3,585 feet
High point: 6,285 feet
Allow 4 to 5 hours one way
Usually open from late July through October
Topographic maps:
U.S.G.S. Bull Run Lake, Oreg.
N4522.5-W12145/7.5
1962
U.S.G.S. Cathedral Ridge, Oreg.
N4522.5-W12137.5/7.5
1962

Although most Portlanders are familiar with the western face of Mt. Hood, few have viewed the mountain from the vantage point of Yocum Ridge, the most westerly of Mt. Hood's many buttresses. Here, just above the timberline, one can see the Little and Big Sandy Glaciers and Reid Glacier, from which huge ice blocks constantly plunge off a high cliff and fall several hundred feet into the canyon of the Sandy River.

Above Ramona Falls the route consists only of blazes on the trees for the last mile. Due to its difficulty, that portion of the trail should not be attempted by inexperienced hikers without competent leadership.

Proceed to the town of Zigzag on U.S. Highway 26 and turn north on the Lolo Pass Road opposite the Zigzag Ranger Station. Drive north on this road for 4.3 miles and turn right at a sign marking Road S-25. Keep on S-25, driving past McNeil Campground, for a total of four miles, to the turnaround at the head of the Sandy River Trail, No. 770.

The trail immediately crosses the Sandy River on a new concrete and steel foot bridge, then turns right at the Portage Trail junction and proceeds east along the north side of the Sandy River until reaching the Timberline Trail junction. Keep to the left and continue on to the Upper Sandy Guard Station. The trail then climbs to a low plateau and continues on to Ramona Falls at two miles.

At Ramona Falls Forest Camp there is a small shelter cabin enclosed on three sides, an out building, and several nice campsites. Ramona Falls, a 100-foot lacey cascade, tumbles down over a fractured surface of black rock.

The Yocum Ridge Trail is marked by a sign just west of the foot bridge at the base of the falls. One and one-quarter miles after the switchback, the trail appears to end. Turn steeply up hill and carefully follow the sometimes obscure foot path and blazes on the trees. A short distance after leaving the main trail paths lead both to the left and to the right. On both sides, there are large notched stumps. Proceed past the stump on the *right* where the trail again becomes clear. After a steep climb the trail tops out on the ridge crest near a small pond and meadow. Turn right and continue up the crest of the ridge past two grassy meadows until you reach a rock pile.

This section is very difficult to follow as the blazes are far apart and the foot path is all but invisible. Go around the right side of the rock pile and climb up the ridge crest about 500 yards to a small north-south spur where the entire west face of the mountain can be seen. This is a good place to stop, or you may wish to climb above timberline to the right for better views of Reid Glacier and the Upper Sandy River Canyon.

Ample water is available near slopes of heather about 100 feet down on the northeastern side of the ridge.

Yocum Ridge

32 PARADISE PARK NORTHERN OREGON

One day trip or backpack
Distance: 4.8 miles one way
Elevation gain: 1,140 feet, loss 900 feet
High point: 6,040 feet
Allow 3 to 3½ hours one way
Usually open mid-July to mid-October
Topographic map:
U.S.G.S. Timberline Lodge, Oreg.
N4515-W12137.5/7.5
1962

This trail, which contours just below timberline, is a scenic combination of alpine meadows, woods, and canyons. To the north you see frequent and impressive closeup views of Mt. Hood; looking south, you can enjoy expansive scenes of the northern Oregon Cascades, highlighted by Mt. Jefferson.

Proceed to Timberline Lodge via the Timberline Road which joins U.S. Highway 26 one-half mile east of Government Camp opposite the Summit Ranger Station. Cars may be parked at Timberline Lodge, either in the upper or lower parking lots.

To get on the Timberline Trail, No. 2000, walk to the back of the lodge past the reflection pond and follow a connecting path north for about 100 yards to a large sign marking the beginning of the trail. This portion of the Timberline Trail is also the Skyline Trail. Paradise Park is 4.6 miles west of this point.

Three-quarters of a mile west of the lodge on the south side of the trail is the site of the old Timberline Cabin, for many years the only shelter available to skiers and climbers on this side of the mountain. Today, only the foundation remains. A short distance after this, the trail crosses Little Zigzag Canyon.

Just west of Little Zigzag Canyon a sign marks Trail No. 779 to Hidden Lake, 2.5 miles. This trail continues for another 2.5 miles past the lake and terminates on the old Mt. Hood Loop Highway near Twin Bridges Campground.

At two miles, the Skyline Trail reaches the edge of Zigzag Canyon. The panorama from this vantage point is one of the most spectacular found anywhere on the mountain. The top of the canyon is dominated by Mississippi Head, a one-quarter mile wide band of 200-foot high vertical rock.

From the rim the trail descends 740 feet to the floor of the canyon and crosses the Zigzag River. Then it rises gradually 980 feet through woods and meadows to the opposite edge. During August and September huckleberries are plentiful on this side of the canyon.

At 4.5 miles is the junction of Trail No. 778 which connects with the old Mt. Hood Loop Highway seven miles to the south. A short distance from here the trail descends into a small valley formed by Lost Creek, on the other side of which is a well-constructed stone shelter. A few very good campsites can be found close by.

The meadows constituting Paradise Park are located on a bluff just above the shelter.

Paradise Park

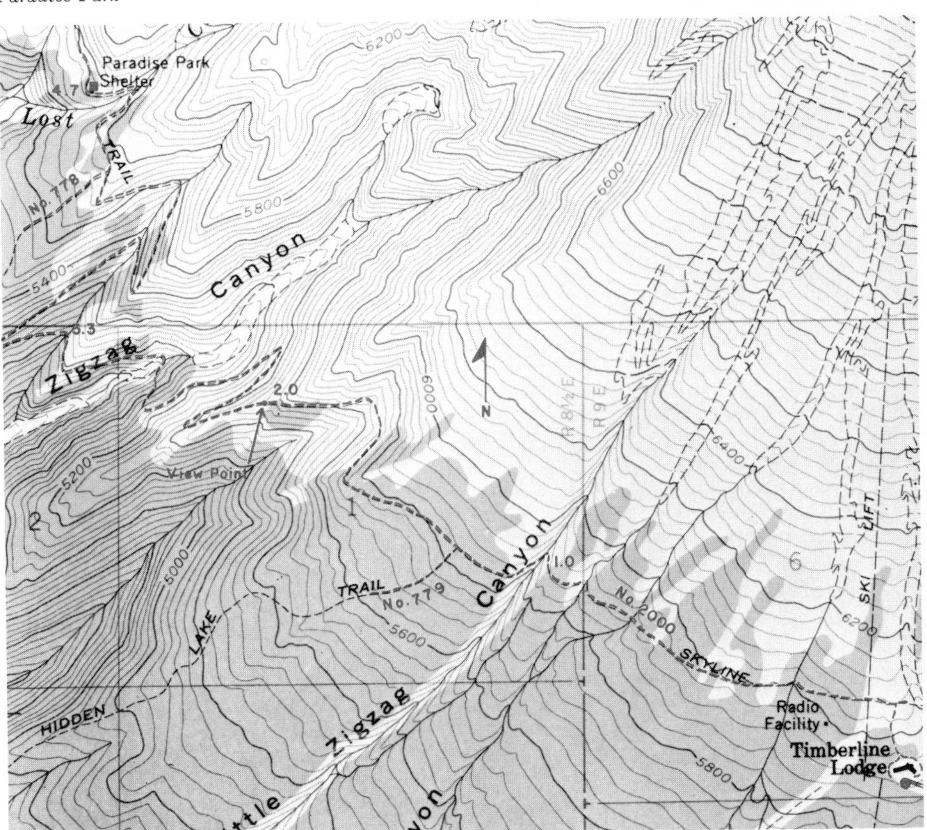

33 BURNT LAKE NORTHERN OREGON

One day trip or backpack
Distance: 5.5 miles one way
Elevation gain: 2,321 feet
High point: 4,971 feet
Allow 3 to 4 hours one way
Usually open June through November
Topographic map:
U.S.G.S. Government Camp, Oreg.
N4515-W12145/7.5
1962

Burnt Lake

If you like to float on your back in a warm lake and gaze up at a rugged snow capped peak this is a trip you will want to make. And, a short hike to the top of East Zigzag Mountain above the lake offers a close up view of Mt. Hood and several other major peaks. For the most comfortable swimming, be sure to do this hike in the late summer after a hot spell.

Drive east of Portland on U.S. Highway 26 and turn north on the Lolo Pass Road opposite the Zigzag Ranger Station. Drive for 4.2 miles, turn right on Road No. S-25, and follow the signs pointing to McNeil and Lost Creek campgrounds. One-half mile farther turn right, cross a bridge, and continue past McNeil Campground. At the junction of the road to Lost Creek Forest Camp, remain on Road No. S-25. At the next junction turn right onto Road No. S-239 and follow the sign reading Burnt Lake Trail 2 miles. About one-half mile further, turn right onto Road No. S-239G, cross a bridge and wind around to the south side of a ridge. Continue for 0.9 mile to where the road terminates at the end of a clear cut. There is parking for several cars.

A small sign on a tree points to the Burnt Lake Trail, No. 772. Hike along the cat road which follows the south edge of the clearcut. After one-fourth mile, the road turns to the right and enters the woods. Pass a small dilapidated shed and continue along the road until it veers to the left. At this point the trail proper leads to the right and is marked by a blaze and an unofficial sign. After 2.5 miles of level travel the trail crosses a creek and then climbs very steeply for three-fourths mile. You will then cross a brush-covered flat area followed by a short climb to the lake. Hike along the west side of the lake to the south end where there is a good camping spot. Fresh water can be obtained from a small creek a short distance further along the main trail.

To reach East Zigzag Mountain, which is only a 30 minute hike from the lake and well worth the effort, continue south along the main trail through a flat, marshy area then climb via switchbacks through brush and small trees. Turn right at the junction on the crest. The last one-fourth mile climbs along the open ridge top. From the summit you can look down on Burnt Lake and across to the southwest face of Mt. Hood.

Burnt Lake and Mt. Hood

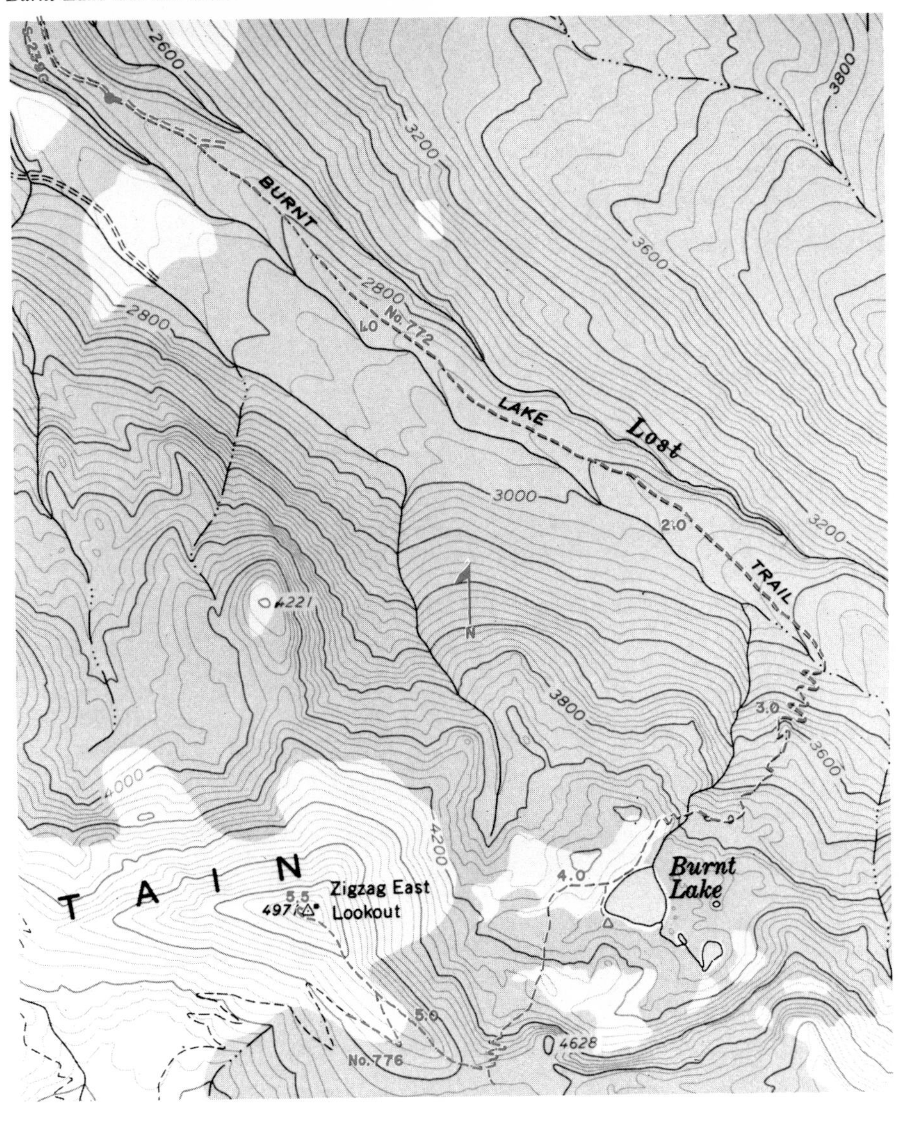

34 WEST ZIGZAG MOUNTAIN NORTHERN OREGON

One day trip
Distance: 5 miles one way
Elevation gain: 3,400 feet, loss 480 feet
High point: 4,525 feet
Allow 3 to 4 hours one way
Usually open June through mid-November
Topographic map:
U.S.G.S. Rhododendron, Oreg.
N4515-W12152.5/7.5
1962

Zigzag Mountain is a long, high ridge that joins Mt. Hood on the east and overlooks the Sandy River to the north and the town of Rhododendron and the Zigzag River Valley on the south. Until a few years ago a fire lookout cabin stood on the West Peak and could be seen from Rhododendron, nearly 3,000 feet below.

There is a very heavy deer population on the lower slopes of West Zigzag Mountain, and if you are reasonably quiet, you almost certainly will see these animals.

Carry water on this trail, since the only available water is a small spring just off the trail on the north side of the mountain, about 200 yards east of the site of the old lookout cabin.

Take U.S. Highway 26 to Zigzag. Turn north on the Lolo Pass Road opposite the Zigzag Ranger Station, and drive 0.4 mile from the highway, crossing the Zigzag River bridge. Turn right on an unmarked road with power lines on the north side. A utility pole opposite the junction bears the symbols B1, 15, and L9. Proceed on this road for 0.7 mile. The start of the West Zigzag Mountain Trail, No. 348, is marked with a sign a few feet off the road on the left. It reads West Zigzag Mountain Lookout 5 miles, Paradise Park Trail 15 miles, and Timberline Trail 16 miles.

The trail climbs quite steeply for several miles with numerous switchbacks. During the course of the climb it is interesting to observe the changes in plant life as altitude is gained. It varies from dense deciduous growth and large mature trees on the valley floor to open beargrass slopes and stunted trees on the summit. At four miles the trail tops out on the rocky summit ridge and then contours across it for another mile to the site of the former lookout cabin. From here Mt. Hood seems very close and you can also see Mt. Saint Helens, Mt. Rainier and Mt. Adams to the north, and Mt. Jefferson and Olallie Butte to the south.

There are no adequate campsites on the West Peak. The ridge is quite exposed and usually windy, but there are enough trees to afford some shelter.

West Zigzag Mountain and Zigzag River

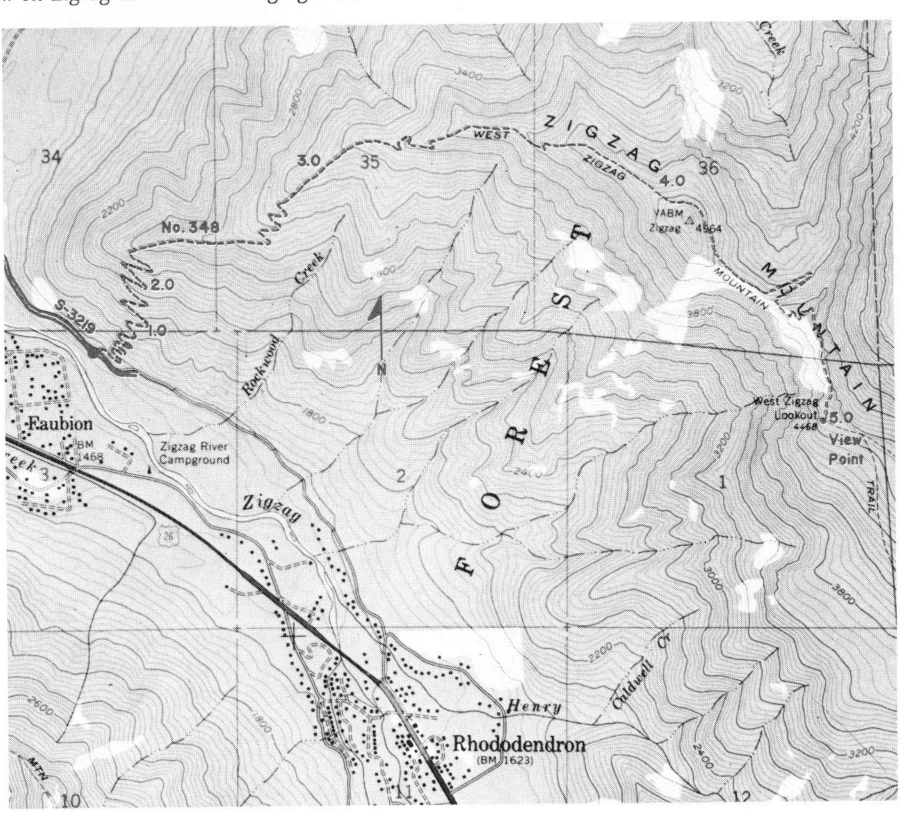

35 EAGLE CREEK NORTHERN OREGON

One day trip
Distance: 3.5 miles one way
Elevation gain: 560 feet
High point: 2,160 feet
Allow 1½ to 2 hours one way
Usually open March through December
Topographic map:
U.S.G.S. Cherryville, Oreg.
N4515-W12200/15
1955

A warm, summer day is the perfect time to take this cool, shady hike along a new trail which follows the banks of Eagle Creek between Wildcat and Old Baldy Mountains. It is level for the first four miles, and the stream offers good fishing in many places.

Drive southeast of Portland on Oregon Highway 224 to the community of Eagle Creek, where State Highways 211 and 224 merge. Nine-tenths of a mile south of Eagle Creek, on the highway to Estacada, turn left on Firwood Road at a sign pointing to Eagle Fern Park. At the first junction at the end of a long, straight stretch, keep right on Clackamas County Road 40. A sign here points to Bissell, George, Eagle Fern Park, and the fish hatchery. About two miles later cross a bridge and again keep to the right staying on Clackamas County Road 40 past Eagle Fern Park. Several miles later you will pass a road on your right that leads to the fish hatchery. Drive about three miles past the hatchery junction to an unmarked road on the right just before several right angle turns. Turn onto this gravel road and after a few hundred feet pass a white metal gate which is closed only during periods of severe fire danger. One and six-tenths miles further keep right at a junction and drive two more miles until coming to the road's end at the bottom of a steep hill, where adequate parking is available. If the hill is muddy, you can park at the top of the grade and walk down the road for about one mile to the beginning of the trail. There is a barbed wire gate part way down the hill.

Just before the parking area is the beginning of the old Eagle Creek Trail which now has been abandoned. Follow a cat track on the east side of the turnaround which soon leads to the trail head and a sign reading, Eagle Creek Trail, No. 501.

The trail follows the north bank of Eagle Creek through spectacular old growth rain forest at an almost level gradient. Cattle Camp or The Farm as it is sometimes known, 3.5 miles from the beginning of the trail, is a large, open, grass-covered area that makes an ideal stopping place. Beyond here the canyon narrows and the trail climbs gently above the creek to where it soon terminates at the end of the new construction.

Cattle Camp at Eagle Creek

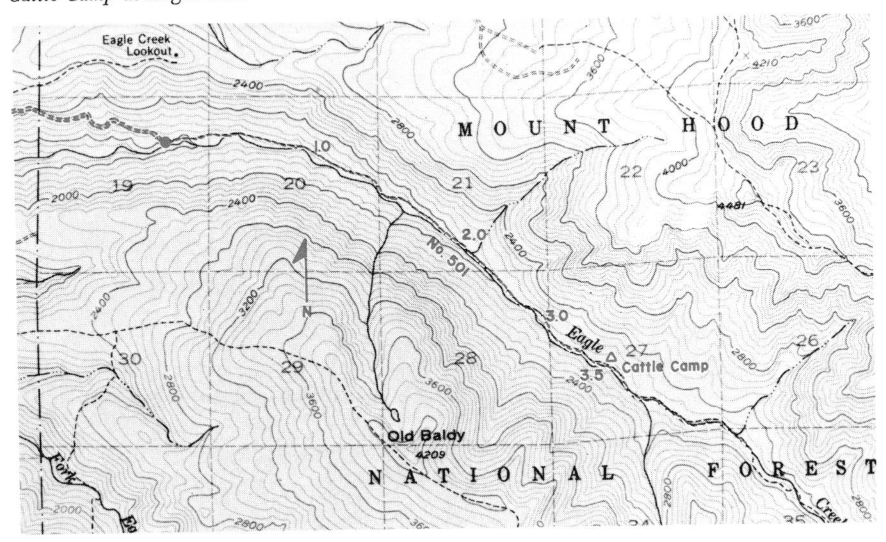

36 WILDCAT MOUNTAIN NORTHERN OREGON

One day trip
Distance: 5 miles one way
Elevation gain: 1,641 feet, loss 100 feet
High point: 4,481 feet
Allow 2½ to 3½ hours one way
Usually open June through November
Topographic map:
U.S.G.S. Cherryville, Oreg.
N4515-W12200/15
1955

The Wildcat Mountain Trail starts fairly high on a long, north-south ridge about 20 miles from Mt. Hood. From the crest you have a broad vista, extending far north of Vancouver, Wash., west to the summit of the Coast Range, and as far south as Salem. The view to the east is also very expansive with several of the Northwest's major snow-capped peaks dotting the horizon. Many years ago a lookout stood on the high point of the ridge, and the grassy slopes along the length of the mountain used to support flocks of sheep.

Drive east of Portland on U.S. Highway 26, between Sandy and Brightwood to a point just east of the 36-mile post and turn south on the Wildcat Creek Road. This road is 0.3 mile east of the Chapel of the Hills and just around the bend from a Chevron service station. Drive 3.5 miles up this rough, single-lane road to the trail head. A sign on the left-hand side of the road marks the Wildcat Trail, No. 782. Parking is limited and you may have to back down a short distance to find a suitable place.

The trail climbs for about one-third mile through overgrown slash, turns sharply to the right and enters dense woods. It travels through the forest, gradually descending and then climbing. When you come to the first open ridge, keep to the east (left) and follow the clear area south for a short distance. The rather faint trail re-enters stunted woods, traveling parallel to the ridge and veers slightly to the left as it enters more dense forest. Shortly hereafter you will come to the Alder Creek Way trail sign pointing right to the Loop Highway, 7.3 miles and the Cherryville Road, 5 miles. The trail to which this sign refers is completely overgrown and impassable. Trail 782 then travels along the bottom of a rocky slope below a rim of cliffs.

South of the cliffs it climbs steeply in switchbacks, makes a sharp left turn and levels off. Note this turn as it is easily missed on the return trip. Continue a short distance up to the open ridge where you will see the summit of Wildcat Mountain, the high point to the south. The trail becomes a bit obscure here so look to the rear occasionally to establish suitable landmarks for your hike back along the ridge. The trail continues along the ridge top, re-entering the woods, then comes out onto a longer, more open expanse of tall beargrass. A few feet ahead is a flag on a large cairn which marks the junction with the now abandoned 3-6 trail. Follow along a double track through the beargrass for about one-half mile. The trail then becomes more distinct, traverses the east side of the ridge, drops down to the junction of the Douglas Camp Trail, No. 781, and then climbs gradually to the summit. Mt. Hood is the predominate feature from the site of the former lookout cabin.

Wildcat Mountain and Mt. Hood

37 PLAZA TRAIL NORTHERN OREGON

One day trip
Distance: 4 miles one way
Elevation gain: 2,764 feet
High point: 4,045 feet
Allow 3 to 4 hours one way
Usually open June through November
Topographic map:
U.S.G.S. Rhododendron, Oreg.
N4515-W12152.5/7.5
1962

The Plaza Trail offers a steady climb of almost 3,000 feet through heavy timber and culminates in a rocky outcrop near the summit of Huckleberry Mountain. From here you will be rewarded with excellent views of Mt. Hood, and the Sandy, Salmon, and Boulder Creek Valleys.

Drive on U.S. Highway 26 to the settlement of Wemme, three miles west of Rhododendron. Turn south at Welches School and proceed for 1.1 miles past the Mt. Hood Golf Course to a fork in the road. Take the right hand road and continue for 0.2 of a mile on the paved road which turns right and crosses the Salmon River. On the west side of the bridge, turn right at the sign pointing to the Plaza Trail and follow a private road to the trail head at the end of the road. Parking is limited here, so it may be necessary to park by the bridge.

The start of the trail, No. 783, is well marked. After a few feet it crosses a small creek on a wooden footbridge. Turn to the left and go in a southwesterly direction for about 75 feet through a swampy area. To avoid losing the trail, be sure to follow the small arrows and signs for the first few hundred yards. The trail then becomes obvious again as it climbs up the bank on the south side of the creek. After crossing several rocky stream beds it follows an old logging road for a few yards and then turns sharply uphill to the right. This junction of the trail and the logging road is not marked, so take care to avoid walking past it.

For the next 2.5 miles, the trail switchbacks up the crest of a narrow ridge through dense timber that obstructs the views of the golf course and the surrounding countryside. On the summit of the ridge, about three miles in, a sign points right to the Arrah Wanna Trail No. 784, which returns to the valley floor on the north side of the Salmon River opposite Camp Arrah Wanna.

From this junction, proceed south following the ridge of Huckleberry Mountain until emerging onto a rocky knob just short of the highest point on the ridge. This exposed area affords an excellent stopping point since the views are no better farther on as most of the summit ridge is covered with trees.

On the Plaza Trail

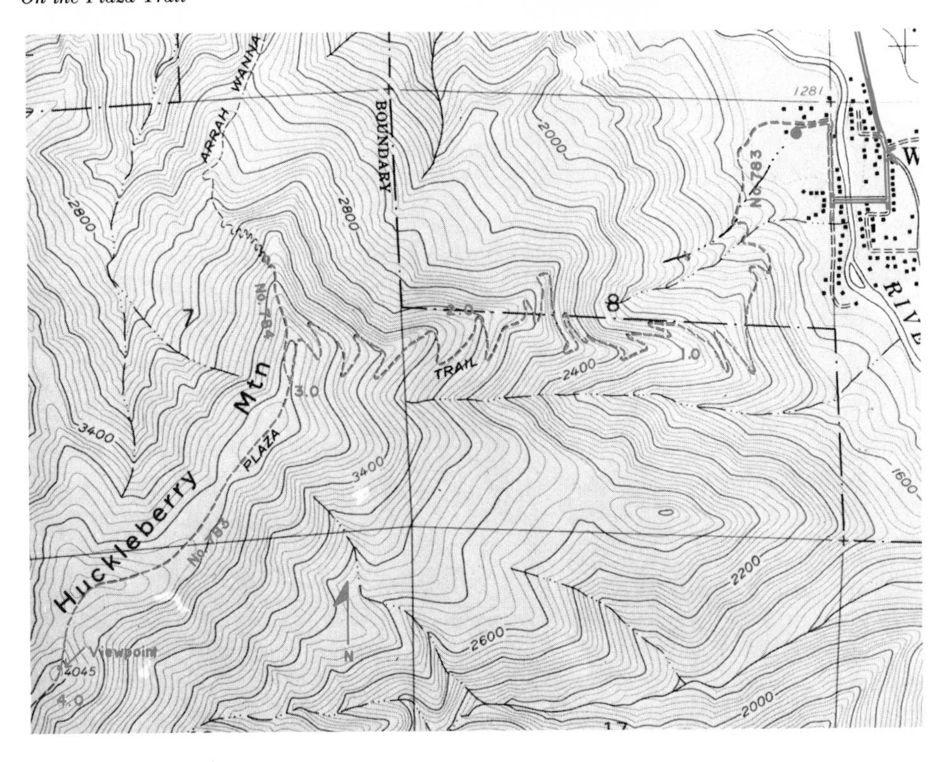

38 SALMON RIVER NORTHERN OREGON

One day trip
Distance: 4 miles one way
Elevation gain: 890 feet, loss 400 feet
High point: 2,490 feet
Allow 2 to 2½ hours one way
Usually open March through December
Topographic map:
U.S.G.S. Rhododendron, Oreg.
N4515-W12152.5/7.5
1962

Final and Frustration Falls — Salmon River Trail

The first 1.7 miles of this trail contours just above the Salmon River offering a pleasant and easy hike for the entire family. Bighorn Campground is well-developed with fire grates and tables and is a fine place for a picnic lunch before returning. For those wanting a more strenuous hike, farther up the trail there are spectacular views of the Salmon River Canyon and Final and Frustration Falls. Be sure to carry water as there are few creeks in the first four miles, and they may be dry in the middle and late summer.

Drive on U.S. Highway 26 about 44 miles east of Portland, and turn south on the Salmon River Road about one-fourth mile west of Zigzag. Proceed five miles, passing the Green Canyon Guard Station, to the north end of the Salmon River Bridge. Ample parking space is available off the road. The trail, No. 742, is marked by a large sign near the northeast corner of the bridge.

In the beginning the trail climbs a short pitch, drops down to the river's edge, and then climbs again leveling off about 100 feet above it. Periodically, it travels a short distance into the woods away from the river. At one and three-quarter miles you will come to Bighorn Forest Camp.

The junction with Hambone Trail, No. 792, on the other side of the river is one-eighth mile beyond. Continue one-fourth mile further to Rolling Riffle Campground, another well-developed site. From here the trail travels up and away from the river. At one point two signs with arrows indicate a sharp left turn. For an exceptional view of this narrow and rocky portion of the Salmon River Canyon, continue straight ahead on the path which goes partway across an open slope.

To reach a view of Final and Frustration Falls, continue through the woods on the main trail for about one-fourth mile past the arrows and turn right onto a side trail leading down through the trees to a steep, grassy slope. Make a right turn where the terrain becomes steep, descend a short distance, then turn left and contour around to the ridge crest. Continue hiking down the grassy slope, keeping to the left until the falls become visible. Near the bottom of the slope is a level area that makes a good lunch stop.

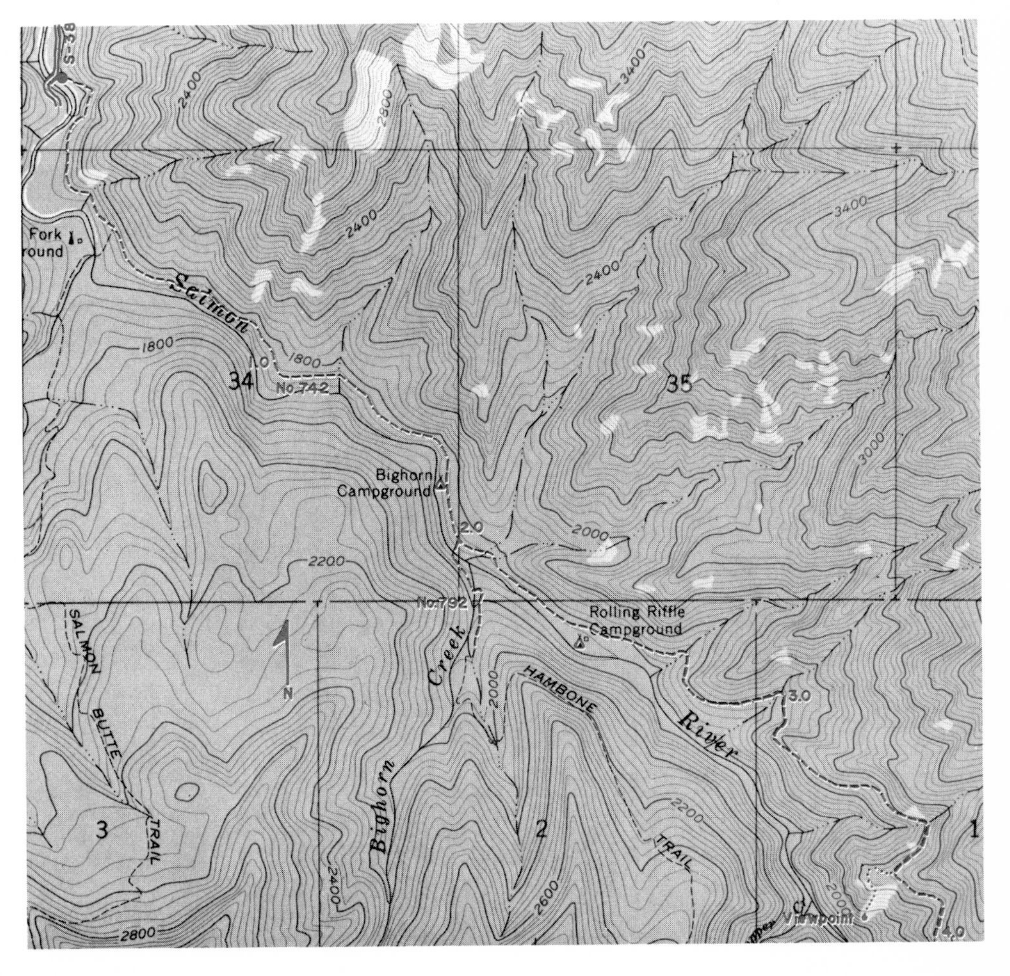
Fork
round
Salmon
1800
34
No.742
Bighorn
Campground
2.0
2200
No.792
Rolling Riffle
Campground
35
2400
3400
3000
2000
2800
SALMON
BUTTE
TRAIL
N
Creek
HAMBONE
River
3.0
3
Bighorn
2
2200
TRAIL
1
2400
2600
2800
Viewpoint
4.0

39 HUNCHBACK RIDGE NORTHERN OREGON

One day trip
Distance: 4.5 miles one way
Elevation gain: 2,818 feet, loss 210 feet
High point: 4,033 feet
Allow 3 to 4 hours one way
Usually open June through November
Topographic map:
U.S.G.S. Rhododendron, Oreg.
N4515-W12152.5/7.5
1962

This delightful and easily-accessible hike features rocky cliffs and views down the Salmon River Canyon to the community of Welches. The trail is not hazardous for experienced hikers, but animals, very young children, and those bothered by mild exposure should not take this trip.

Take U.S. Highway 26 to the Zigzag Ranger Station, 44 miles east of Portland. Parking is available in front of the main building. Hike south along the gravel road, past the utility buildings, and turn left and follow a dirt road a few hundred feet to the trail. The trail sign reads Hunchback Trail, No. 793 — Sherar Burn Road No. S-32, 10 miles, Devils Peak Lookout 9 miles, and Cool Creek Trail, No. 794, 9 miles.

The trail switchbacks past a spring and climbs gradually to a level saddle. It again climbs in switchbacks for about one mile, then crosses to the west side of the ridge, dropping down along an open slope to a small saddle and then climbing steeply to a precipitous viewpoint. The trail then crosses to the east side of the ridge and continues ascending just below the crest. A small rocky area is reached after one particularly steep, but short pitch. Continue across this slope and re-enter the woods. The ridge becomes wider and more level here, and the trail follows along its crest.

At about 2.7 miles, the trail begins to descend along the east side of the ridge and is interspersed with a few level stretches and short climbs. At 4.3 miles the trail leaves the eastern slope and climbs steeply along the ridge crest for one-fourth mile. To go to the viewpoint, continue straight ahead where the trail leaves the ridgetop and makes a sharp downslope switchback to the left. Follow the ridge for about 150 feet to a rocky outcrop. Mt. Hood is close by to the east, and Devils Peak, which may be reached by continuing another five miles along the Hunchback Trail, is visible as the high point to the southeast.

Hunchback Ridge

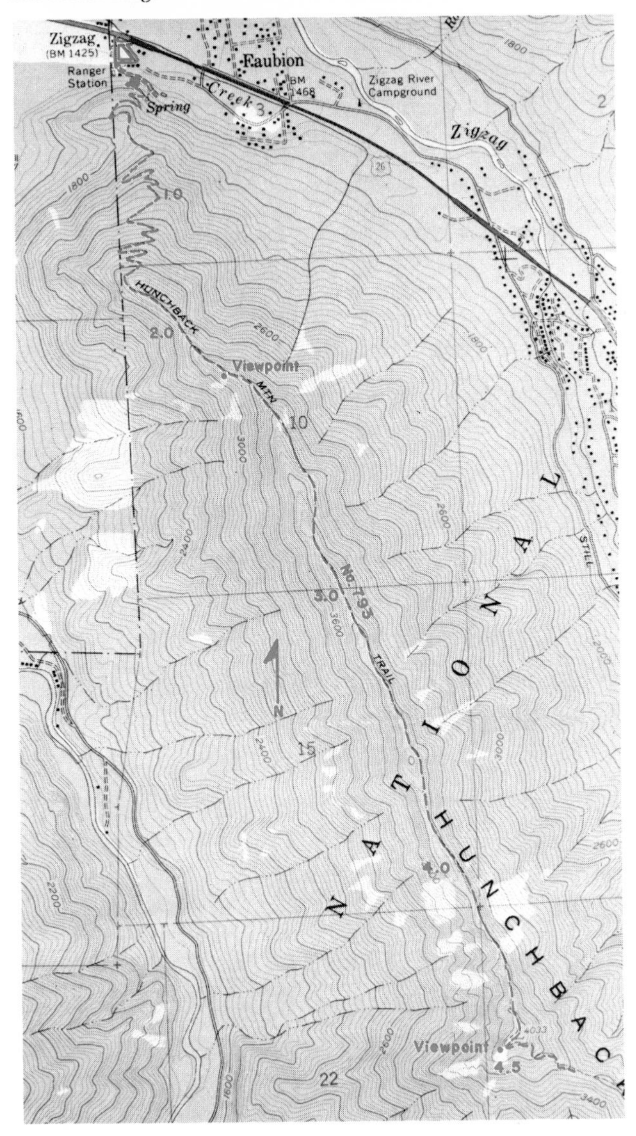

40 DEVILS PEAK NORTHERN OREGON

One day trip
Distance: 4 miles one way
Elevation gain: 3,205 feet
High point: 5,045 feet
Allow 3 to 4 hours one way
Usually open late June through November
Topographic maps:
U.S.G.S. Rhododendron, Oreg.
N4515-W12152.5/7.5
1962
U.S.G.S. Government Camp, Oreg.
N4515-W12145/7.5
1962

Devils Peak is the highest point on the ridge separating Still Creek and the Salmon River and commands an exquisite view of Mt. Hood, Mt. Saint Helens, Mt. Adams and Mt. Rainier to the north, and Mt. Jefferson and Three Fingered Jack to the south. Even though the trail to the peak is only four miles long, it is rather steep as the total elevation gain is more than 3,000 feet.

There are two ways to approach the start of the trail: from the east, proceed west on U.S. Highway 26 through Government Camp until reaching the outskirts of the town of Rhododendron. Turn left on Vine Maple Road No. 20 which crosses Still Creek and after one mile junctions with the Still Creek Road No. S-39. Turn left at that junction and follow Still Creek Road for 1.8 miles. The Devils Peak Trail is marked by a sign on the right, but is hard to see because it is a few yards in from the road.

Approaching from the west, drive along U.S. Highway 26 to a point just west of the Zigzag River Bridge, 1.5 miles east of the Zigzag Ranger Station. Turn right on the Old Loop Highway, No. 10, and drive 0.2 mile to the junction of the Still Creek Road No. S-39 and follow it for 2.9 miles to the trail head.

The sign at the beginning of the Cool Creek Trail (No. 4204) reads Devils Peak Lookout, 4 miles, Hunchback Trail No. 793, 4 miles and Sherar Burn Road No. S-32, 5 miles.

At first the gradient is quite steep with many switchbacks. At about three-fourths mile a ridge is reached and the character of the woods changes from second growth to very mature trees. The forest floor is covered with blowdowns, and decaying stumps giving it a somber, yet beautiful appearance.

During the dry season the only source of water is a small rivulet about two miles up from the road. It is advisable to carry a good supply of water at that time of the year.

Throughout the entire trip you are surrounded by rhododendron bushes which, when in bloom, display their pastel pink flowers against the dark background of the widely-spaced trees.

Near the top of Devils Peak, the trail leaves the dense timber and follows along the west side of a rocky ridge. Just short of the lookout is the junction of the Hunchback Ridge Trail, No. 793. The Sherar Burn Road is to the left 1.5 miles, and to the right the trail leads down Hunchback Ridge to the Zigzag Ranger Station, ten miles northwest.

The lookout is straight up a small spur trail about 100 yards. The views from the summit are quite expansive, and on a clear day, Portland and the Coast Range can be seen.

S-39
24
19
19
COOL
2200
2000
2800
Cool
1.0
CREEK
NO. 4204
3000
Water
3200
2.0
TRAIL
25
30
30
TRAIL
3800
Creek
3600
4000
3.0
CREEK
26
4400
COOL
N
TRAIL
36
31
31
4400
4770
No. 793
Spr
Heliport
Devils Peak
Devils Peak
Lookout
4.0
HUNCHBACK
4200

Devils Peak Lookout

41 MIRROR LAKE AND TOM DICK MOUNTAIN NORTHERN OREGON

One day trip
Distance: 3 miles one way
Elevation gain: 1,646 feet
High point: 5,066 feet
Allow 45 minutes to the lake and 2½ hours to the summit
Usually open late June through November
Topographic map:
U.S.G.S. Government Camp, Oreg.
N4515-W12145/7.5
1962

Mirror Lake, 1,000 feet below the summit of Tom Dick Mountain, is probably the most frequented off-highway area in the Mt. Hood National Forest. Many years ago it was used by Portlanders late in the fall as a natural ice skating rink before the snow became too thick, although in recent years early freezes to the required depth have been rare. The lake is only one mile from the highway, but the trail continues on another 1.5 miles almost to the summit of Tom Dick Mountain, and affords an excellent ridge walk with good views of Mt. Hood as well as the lesser peaks of the region.

The trail, No. 662, starts two miles west of Government Camp on the south side of U.S. Highway 26. A footbridge over Camp Creek connects the trail with the highway and is clearly visible to the motorist. An extension of the highway shoulder assures ample parking space.

A short distance from the beginning the trail crosses the exit creek from Mirror Lake. You should not use any water below the lake as it may be contaminated by the out buildings and from other sources. After crossing the creek, the trail turns right and follows an old logging road for a short distance. Rhododendrons are abundant here and grow all the way to the top of Tom Dick Ridge.

As you near the lake, keep to the right if you intend to follow the trail to the top of the ridge. If not, take the first trail to the left for 100 yards to the northern side of the lake.

At one mile you will reach a sign which indicates Mirror Lake is to the left and Tom Dick Ridge one mile to the right. The route to the ridge traverses an open hillside covered with huckleberries which, in season, are very succulent due to the northern exposure. At two miles, the trail reaches the crest of the ridge at 4,550 feet elevation. A very large rock cairn marks the point where the trail turns left and follows the ridge crest for about one-half mile before it fades away. Follow small rock cairns to the left until the first crest is reached at 4,965 feet. From there walk east one-third of a mile along the crest of the ridge to the site of a former lookout at the highest point, 5,066 feet. A tall, thin rock cairn marks the summit.

Mirror Lake and Mt. Hood

Cairn on Tom Dick Mountain

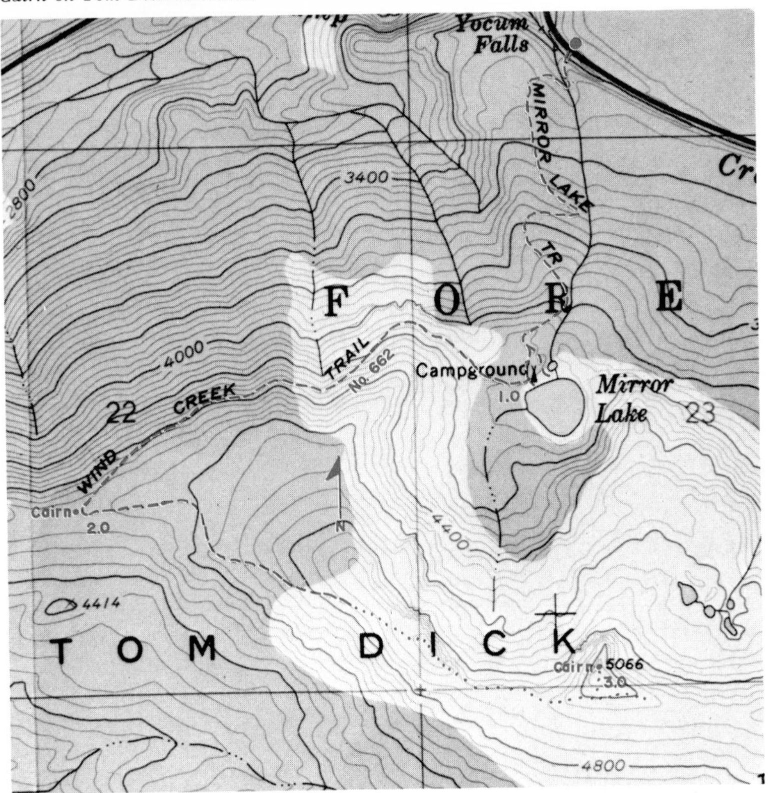

42 TWIN LAKES NORTHERN OREGON

One day trip or backpack
Distance 3¾ miles one way
Elevation gain: 423 feet, loss 200 feet
High point: 4,500 feet
Allow two hours one way
Usually open from July through mid-November
Topographic maps:
U.S.G.S. Timberline Lodge, Oreg.
N4515-W12137.5/7.5
1962
U.S.G.S. Mt. Wilson, Oreg.
N4500-W12130/15
1956

These two lakes, about three-fourths mile from each other, offer an easy day's hike with fine views of Mt. Hood, Barlow Ridge, and the Barlow Creek Valley. The upper lake is very shallow, averaging only about two to three feet in depth during the summer months. Animal tracks may sometimes be seen on the lake bottom, as deer, bear, and an occasional coyote cross from one side to the other.

Take U.S. Highway 26 east of Government Camp to its junction with Oregon Highway 35 to Hood River. Follow Highway 35 for 0.4 mile and turn right on the Old Loop Highway and proceed east for 2.5 miles to Barlow Pass. The trail begins about 50 yards west of the pass on the south side of the road. There is enough space for a few cars to park adjacent to a large wooden map of the Twin Lakes area.

A sign at the start of the Skyline Trail, No. 2000, reads Upper Twin Lake 3 miles and Lower Twin Lake 3¾ miles. (Actually the sign says Trail No. 2069, the old designation of the Skyline Trail.)

The first mile is through thinning timber which gradually gives way to an open ridge. The trail then proceeds along the east side of a small butte, elevation 4,925 feet, and skirts Bird Butte through dense areas of first growth timber. All along this section you will see many burned stumps and snags indicating a sizable fire sometime in the past.

Beyond Bird Butte the trail drops gently to Upper Twin Lake, which is very shallow with no fishing. However, there are several excellent campsites on the north side of the lake and the tip of Mt. Hood is visible from the shoreline.

To get to Lower Twin Lake, follow the trail south along the east side of the upper lake beyond which it drops several hundred feet to a small depression north of Frog Lake Buttes. Near the lake turn left on a side trail that goes down to the shore. The main trail goes on down 1.5 miles to Highway 26.

The lower lake is larger and deeper than the upper and has some fishing possibilities. Excellent campsites also can be found here.

Except for the lakes, there is no water, and you are advised to boil or chemically treat the lake water as a precautionary measure.

Mt. Hood from Upper Twin Lake

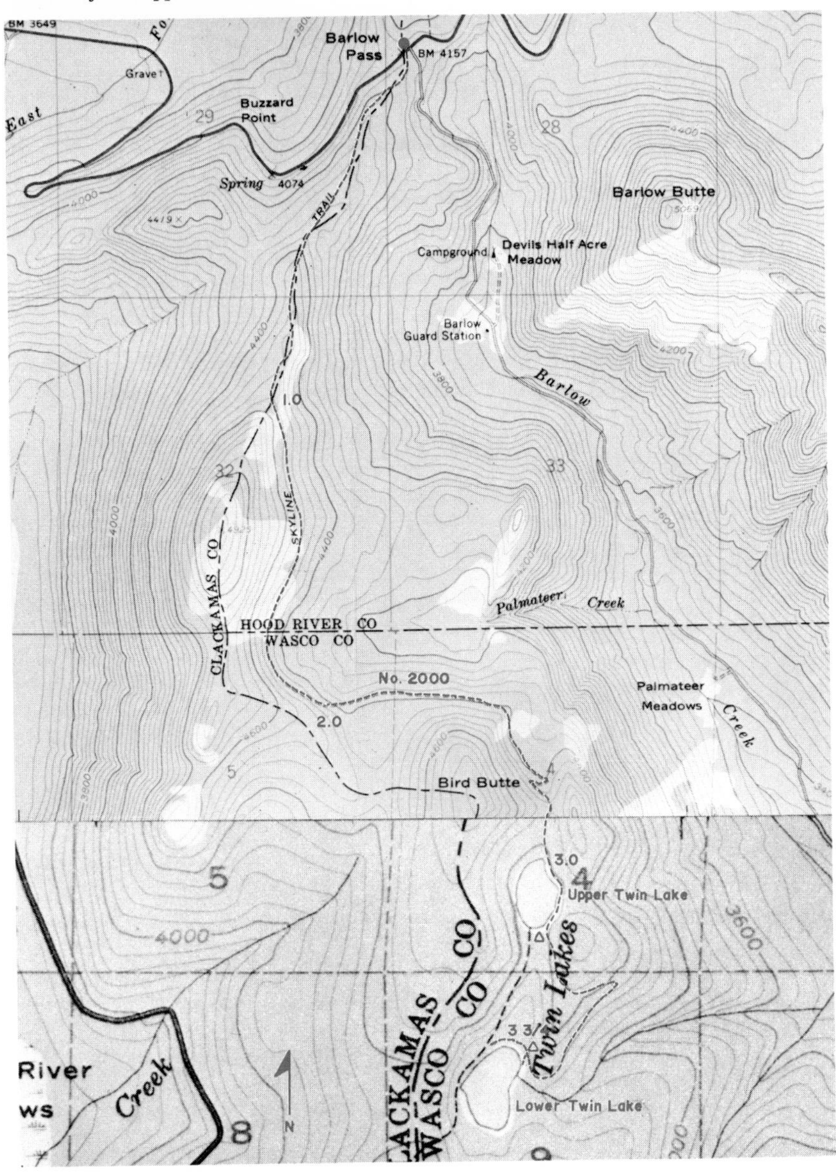

43 SERENE LAKE NORTHERN OREGON

One day trip or backpack
Distance: 3 miles one way
Elevation gain: 440 feet, loss 800 feet
High point: 4,666 feet
Allow 1½ hours one way
Usually open July through October
Topographic maps:
U.S.G.S. Fish Creek Mtn., Oreg.
N4500-W12200/15
1956
U.S.G.S. High Rock, Oreg.
N4500-W12145/15
1956

Serene Lake, like other lakes in this region, is noted for its fine fishing. The very scenic trail is only three miles long, with minimal elevation gain. If you enjoy expansive views of the Northern Oregon Cascade Mountains, a walk out along the Signal Buttes or a short trip to High Rock is recommended.

Drive 26 miles east of Estacada on the Clackamas River Road (Oregon 224) to the bridge at Ripplebrook Forest Camp. On the south side of the bridge, turn left onto Road S-57, and follow it for seven miles to the junction of Road S-58, on the east side of Shellrock Creek. Turn left and follow this road for seven miles to the junction of Road S-457. (Be careful here not to turn onto Road S-596 leading to Hidaway Lake.) Turn left onto Road S-457 and proceed two miles to the saddle directly west of High Rock. At the saddle, there is a four-way junction. Turn left onto Road S-456 and drive west four miles, passing Signal Buttes, to the junction of Road S-456A. Turn left and drive one-fourth mile to the Frazier Turnaround and Campground where you will find parking space for several cars.

The Serene Lake trail, No. 512, which is well-marked, begins on the west side of the road at the campground. For the first mile, it descends through open forest. Just beyond the one-mile marker, a side trail to the left, No. 513, leads one-fourth mile to a very good campsite at Middle Rock Lake. Lower Rock Lake can be reached by an unmarked trail to the right, somewhat below the junction of trail No. 513.

Just before reaching the two-mile marker, the trail passes several small tarns and ascends the side of a ridge in a series of switchbacks. It then levels out and gradually descends to the northern tip of Serene Lake. A small campsite is just to the left of the outlet stream, and others exist in the woods on the lake's west shore.

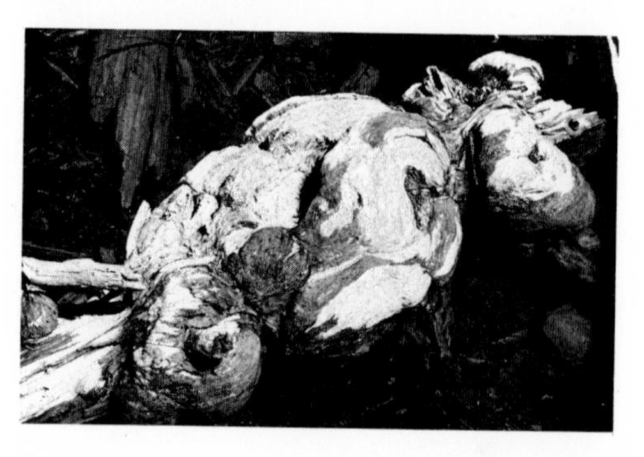

Campsite at Serene Lake

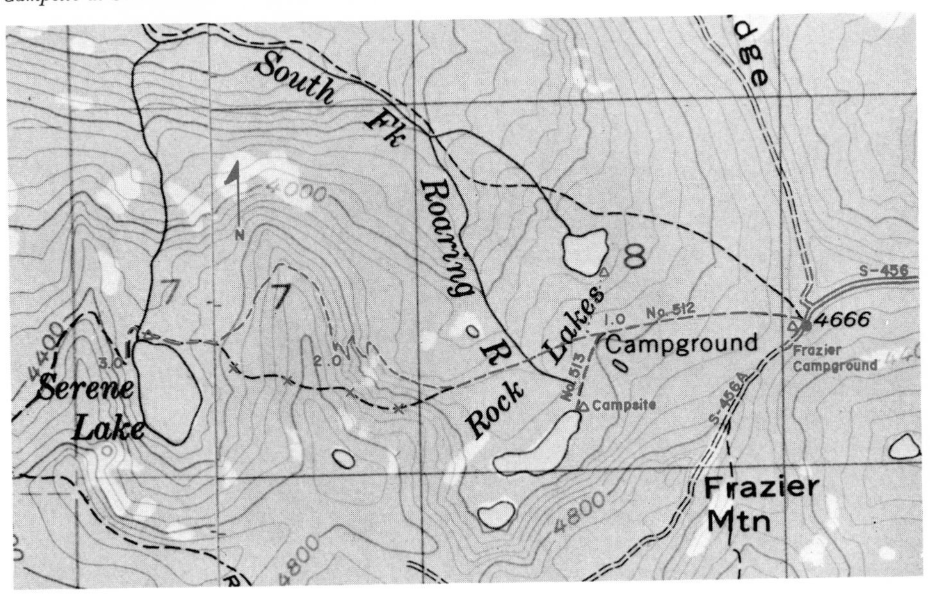

44 FISH CREEK MOUNTAIN NORTHERN OREGON

One day trip
Distance: 3 miles one way
Elevation gain: 1,450 feet
High point: 5,098 feet
Allow 1½ hours one way
Usually open June through November
Topographic map:
U.S.G.S. Fish Creek Mtn., Oreg.
N4500-W12200/15
1956

This trip offers you the combination of a scenic drive along the upper Clackamas River and a pleasant hike with good views from the 5,000 foot summit of Fish Creek Mountain.

From Estacada, drive 23 miles east on Oregon Highway 224 past the Three Lynx power station. Turn right at the Sandstone Junction just before the bridge at Cripple Creek Campground. Proceed south for four miles along the Sandstone Road (No. S-53) and turn right at a sign pointing to Fish Creek Lookout Trail, five miles. Continue along Road S-53 until the next junction is reached, and turn left at another sign pointing to the trail. This was the trail's original beginning, but subsequent logging operations in the area forced relocation higher up on the ridge. Continue on S-53 to the next junction and turn right onto Road S-53C at a sign reading Fish Creek Lookout Trail, one mile. Drive along this road for one-half mile to the next junction and turn right onto Road S-504B and proceed north a short distance to the trailhead where the ridge meets the road.

The trail, No. 541, climbs steadily north along the western side of the ridge. The woods are relatively open and dotted with interesting rock outcroppings. At 2.3 miles, the trail levels off for several hundred yards. Here, a sign marks the junction of the way trail to High Lake, a small pond less than a mile from the ridge, which is well worth taking the time to see. It is, also, the only source of water on this portion of the Fish Creek Divide.

From the High Lake Junction, the trail climbs slightly, then drops down to a small saddle, climbs again, contours around a rocky area, and leads out onto the summit and the charred remains of the old fire lookout. In good weather the view from the summit encompasses a vast array of snow-capped peaks and rich timberlands.

Beaver pond — Fish Creek Mountain

Remains of lookout tower — Fish Creek Mountain

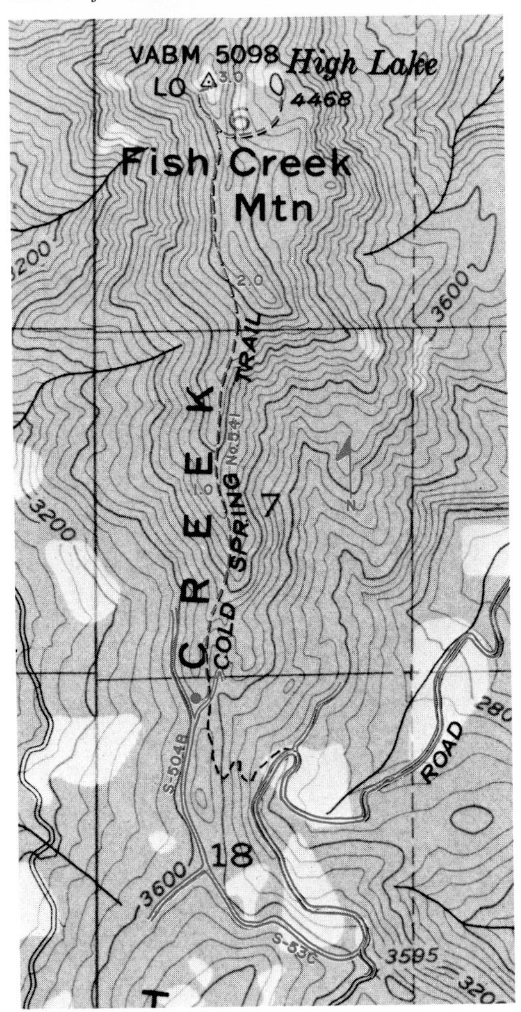

45 SILVER CREEK FALLS NORTHERN OREGON

One day trip
Distance: 7 miles round trip
Elevation gain: 560 feet
High point: 1,520 feet
Allow 3 to 4 hours round trip
Usually open all year
Topographic map:
U.S.G.S. Lyons, Oreg.
N4445-W12230/15
1951

Unnamed falls — Silver Creek Falls

Silver Falls State Park, comprising more than 8,000 acres, is a place of outstanding beauty. It lies at the confluence of the North and South Forks of Silver Creek, 26 miles east of Salem on Oregon Highway 214. The main attraction is the 14 waterfalls, five of which are 100 or more feet in height. Geologically, the region consists of a basaltic overflow above irregular sandstone. The caverns which exist behind many of the falls are believed to have been formed by the undercutting action of water on the tuff, which is assisted during the winter months by alternating cycles of freezing and thawing. This is a very good place for a family outing as four loop trips are possible varying in length from two to seven miles with very little elevation gain.

Drive east on Highway 214 from either the Santiam Pass Highway, No. 22, or the town of Silverton, proceeding to the South Falls picnic area where cars may be parked near the park buildings.

The trail starts on the north side of a fence at the edge of South Falls and is marked by a sign giving the names of the various falls in the park. It drops down in switchbacks, passing behind South Falls, 177 feet high, continuing downstream on the west bank a short distance until a side trail leads to the right, crossing the stream on a bridge and returning to the picnic grounds. Proceed downstream to Lower South Falls, 93 feet. The trail descends in a series of stone and wooden stairs, going behind the falls and following the South Fork of Silver Creek on the east bank.

Just before the confluence of the North and South Forks of Silver Creek, the trail climbs a low ridge. Here a return trail one mile in length proceeds south along the bluff to the parking area. Follow the sign pointing to Winter Falls. After leaving this junction, the trail follows a roadbed for some distance on the south side of the North Fork of Silver Creek. It descends to a log footbridge and climbs on the other side until it reaches Lower North Falls, 30 feet. Near here, a short side trail to the left goes one-tenth mile to the base of Double Falls, 178 feet. Continue on for two-tenths mile to Drake Falls, the smallest of the group at 27 feet. A short distance later Middle North Falls at 106 feet can be seen. A side trail passes behind this lacy cataract to the opposite side of the canyon and dead ends. Another two-tenths mile brings you to the junction of the Winter Creek Trail which crosses the stream, returning one-half mile to Highway 214 at Winter Falls. Continue on past Twin Falls, 31 feet, and a side trail leading to the North Falls Youth Camp. At four miles, the trail goes into a huge cavern behind North Falls, 136 feet, and switches back up to the North Falls parking area. Across the road from the parking lot a sign points east three-tenths of a mile to Upper North Falls, 65 feet high.

The return trip to the South Falls parking lot is made by following a trail next to the highway which leads west for one mile to the Winter Falls overlook, and another 1.5 miles to the parking lot.

Middle North Falls — Silver Creek Falls

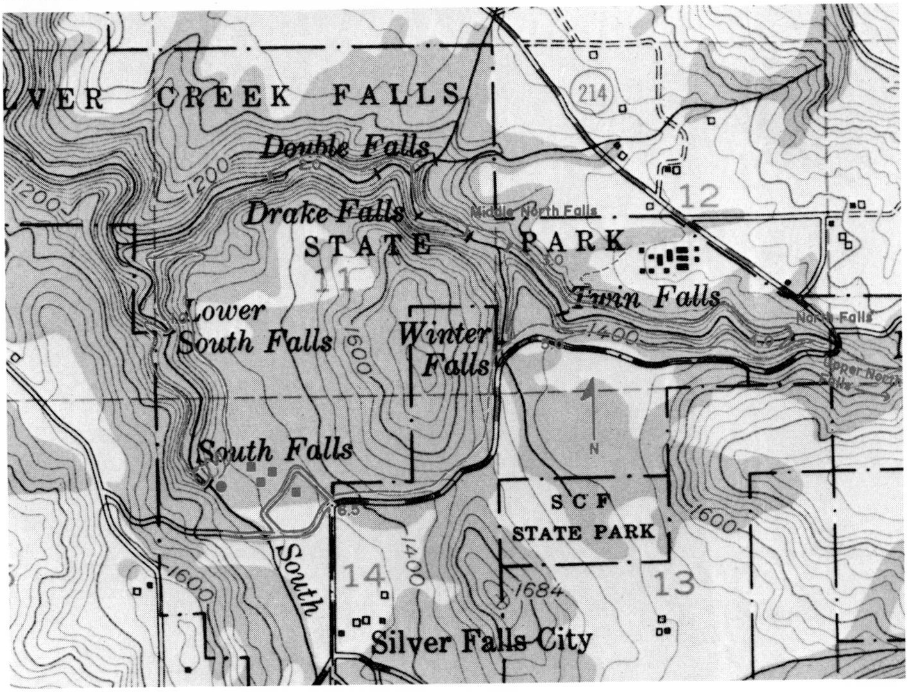

46 HENLINE MOUNTAIN NORTHERN OREGON

One day trip
Distance: 3 miles one way
Elevation gain: 2,515 feet
High point: 4,115 feet
Allow 2 to 3 hours one way
Usually open June through November
Topographic map:
U.S.G.S. Mill City, Oreg.
N4445-W12215/15
1955

Henline Mountain is a very steep and craggy peak located at the east end of the Elkhorn Valley, which was formed by the Little North Santiam River. The trail leads to the south summit, which commands a panoramic view of the Elkhorn Valley and surrounding mountains. You will not find any water on the trail.

Drive east on the North Santiam Highway, Oregon 22, to a point 23 miles east of Salem where a sign points left to the Little North Fork Road and Elkhorn Valley. Turn left (north) and follow the Little North Fork Road for 18.5 miles to the Henline Mountain Trail, 0.9 miles east of a sign pointing right to the Pearl Creek Guard Station, Shady Cove, and Opal Lake. The trail sign can be seen on the north side of the road on a rocky slope. Contrary to the map, the trail head is no longer located at the Pearl Creek Guard Station.

Those approaching from the east on Highway 22, should turn north at the Gates Hill Road just east of the 33 mile highway post and drive six miles to Elkhorn Valley. Turn right at the junction of the Little North Fork Road and proceed to the trail head.

Henline Mountain Trail, No. 3352, climbs most of the way to the summit in a series of switchbacks with gentle grades. For its entire length the surface of the trail is very rocky, so you should not wear tennis shoes.

Five hundred feet below the summit the trail leaves the southern face of the mountain and skirts the base of a high cliff to the right. There it continues around to the northeast side where it traverses a large rock slide before coming out again above the cliffs on the southern slope.

Here you will find several large pinnacles, the highest of which is the south summit of Henline Mountain. Remnants of the old lookout cabin are still visible, and almost the entire Elkhorn Valley can be seen from the summit.

Trail near the lookout

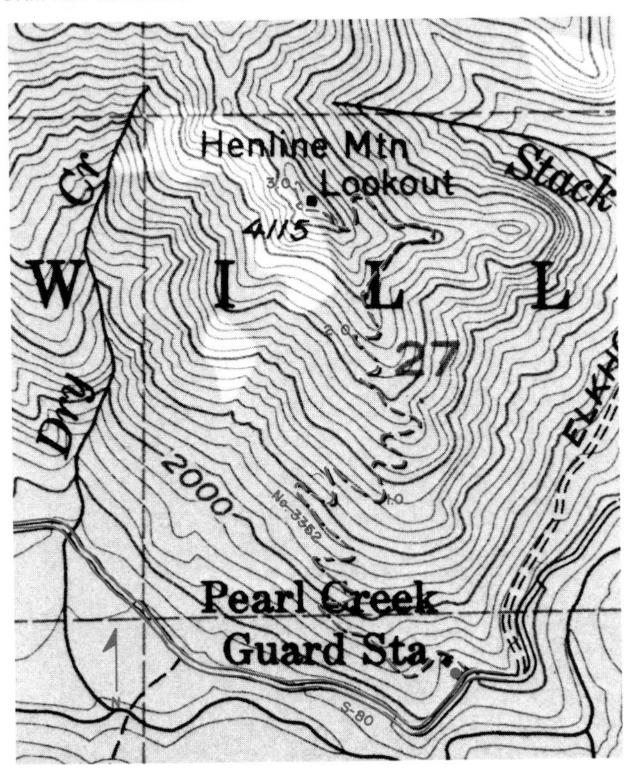

47 BATTLE AX NORTHERN OREGON

One day trip
Distance: 2 miles one way
Elevation gain: 1,244 feet
High point: 5,558 feet
Allow 1 hour one way
Usually open late June through October
Topographic map:
U.S.G.S. Battle Ax, Oreg.
N4445-W12200/15
1956

Few trails offer such expansive views in exchange for so little hiking. The slopes of Battle Ax lack dense vegetation so you can enjoy the scenery all the way up. This is definitely a hike to do on a clear day. Water is usually available from several small creeks along the road about a mile east of the trail head.

Drive east of Salem on Oregon Highway 22 to the community of Detroit and turn northeast onto the Breitenbush Road, S-46, on the south side of the Breitenbush River Bridge. Proceed for 4.2 miles and turn left on Road S-80 at the Elk Lake sign. Continue for 0.8 mile, then turn left keeping on Road S-80 and following the sign to Elk Lake. A few miles further keep to the right when the road switchbacks and follow it up to a saddle at the Gold Butte Lookout Road.

Turn left here and continue on the level, crossing the bridge over Elk Lake Creek at the north end of Elk Lake, and drive past the north shore of the lake as far as possible. The road becomes increasingly rocky and rutted and you will probably have to stop short of the trail head at the Beachie Saddle which is about 1.5 miles west of the west end of Elk Lake. The only parking spaces just below the saddle consist of a few turnouts.

If necessary, hike the remaining distance to the trail head at the Beachie Saddle. A sign at the north side of the saddle locates the Battle Ax Trail, No. 3340.

The trail climbs in a straight line for the first one-third mile and then switchbacks for the remaining distance. Many interesting large rock formations can be seen along various portions of the trail. From the summit every major peak in the Cascade Range is visible, from Mt. Rainier in the north to the Three Sisters in the south. The Beachie Saddle can be seen directly below and you can look down on Elk Lake by walking along the ridge to the southeast of the lookout.

Elk Lake and Mt. Jefferson from Battle Ax Mountain

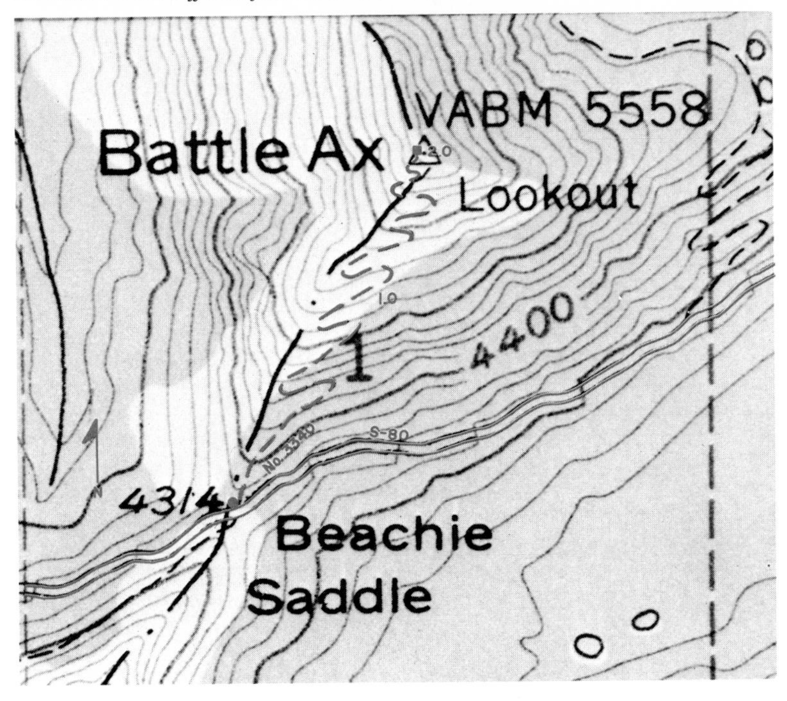

48 BAGBY SPRINGS-TWIN LAKES NORTHERN OREGON

One day trip or backpack
Distance: 5.5 miles one way
Elevation gain: 775 feet (not including Silver King Mt.), loss 775 feet
High point: 4,755 feet (not including Silver King Mt.)
Allow 3 hours one way
Usually open late June through October
Topographic map:
U.S.G.S. Battle Ax, Oreg.
N4445-W12200/15
1956

This scenic and varied trail winds through deep woods, crosses boulder fields, traverses open slopes, and travels along bare ridge crests. Except for the first mile and the last one-half mile, the trail is fairly level.

Drive east of Salem on Oregon Highway 22 to Detroit and turn east onto the Breitenbush Road, S-46, on the south side of the Breitenbush River Bridge. Proceed for 4.2 miles and turn left on Road S-80 at the Elk Lake sign. Continue for 0.8 mile, then turn left keeping on Road S-80, and following the sign to Elk Lake. A few miles further keep to the right when the road switchbacks and follow it up to a saddle at the Gold Butte Lookout Road.

Turn left here and continue on the level, crossing the bridge over Elk Lake Creek at the north end of Elk Lake, and drive past the north shore of the lake to the trail head about one-third mile beyond the road which leads off on the left to the campgrounds. The only parking is that which can be found alongside the road. A sign at the trail head on the north side of the road locates the Bagby Springs Trail, No. 3370.

For the first mile the trail switchbacks up the slope to the north of Elk Lake. At the top, the trail travels through dense woods and passes several ponds. The vegetation then becomes less dense and the ponds along this portion of the trail are inhabited by vociferous frogs. You will cross a large boulder slope and re-enter the woods, then follow the eastern side of a ridge to the 3.2 mile point where the trail crosses to the western slope. Valleys and ridges of the Clackamas River drainage can be seen to the west.

One mile further north you will come to the junction of the Twin Lakes Trail, No. 573. A good side trip is to hike along the ridge the 1.5 miles to Silver King Mountain. From its ridge-like summit you can look directly down onto Twin Lakes.

To reach Twin Lakes, keep to the right on Trail No. 573 and travel along an open ridge for one mile. If you look back to the south and west, you can see the terrain that has just been covered. At the five-mile point, the trail turns sharply to the north and switchbacks steeply down to Upper Twin Lake where there are excellent campsites and a shelter as well as good fishing.

Shelter at Upper Twin Lake

Beargrass blooms on Twin Lakes Trail

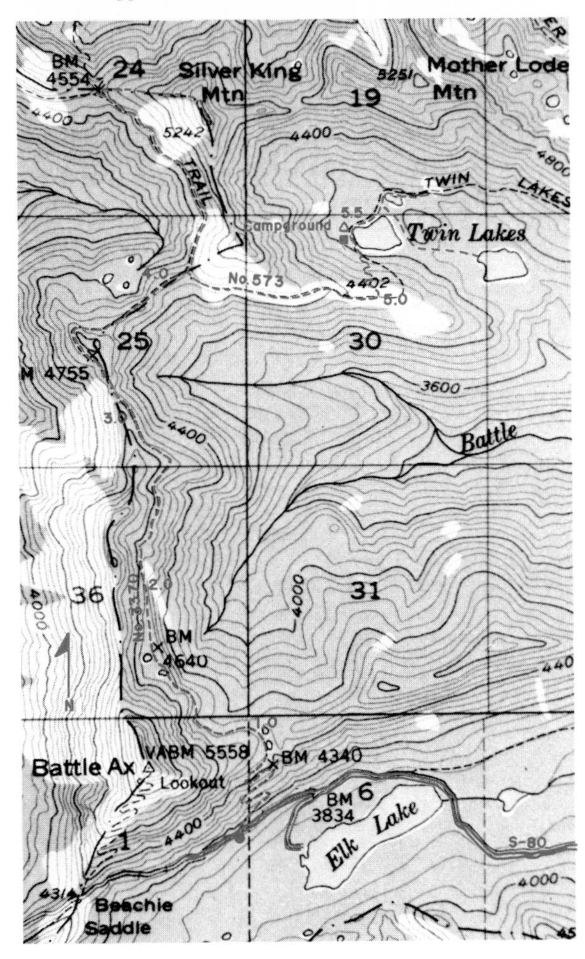

49 BULL OF THE WOODS NORTHERN OREGON

One day trip or backpack
Distance: 8 miles one way
Elevation gain: 2,723 feet, loss 1,100 feet
High point: 5,523 feet
Allow 5 to 7 hours one way
Usually open late June through October
Topographic map:
U.S.G.S. Battle Ax, Oreg.
N4445-W12200/15
1956

After hiking to Bull of the Woods Lookout, you will feel as though you have really penetrated far into the wilderness. A side trip to the Welcome Lakes offers good camping and is close to several other trails which fan out in different directions.

Drive east of Salem on State Highway 22 to the community of Detroit and turn east onto the Breitenbush Road, S-46, on the south side of the Breitenbush River Bridge. Proceed for 4.2 miles and turn left on Road S-80 at the Elk Lake sign. Continue for 0.8 mile, then turn left keeping on Road S-80 and following the sign to Elk Lake. A few miles further keep to the right when the road switchbacks and follow it up to a saddle at the Gold Butte Lookout Road. Turn left here and continue on the level, crossing the bridge over Elk Lake Creek at the north end of Elk Lake. You will have to park your car here or on the other side of the bridge as there is no parking space at the trail head.

Walk along the road to the west for a few hundred yards to a sign on your right that reads, Elk Creek Trail, No. 3371. The nearly level trail travels along a wooded slope of first-growth timber for two miles then begins descending. At four miles, you will come to Battle Creek Shelter, located at the confluence of Elk Lake Creek and Battle Creek. The three-sided shelter is well-preserved and has a concrete fire pit and a steel grate.

From the shelter, follow the trail heading west, which is marked by a sign pointing to Twin Lakes and Bull of the Woods. A few hundred feet beyond the shelter cross Battle Creek (no bridge) and pick up the trail about 60 feet upstream. Continue through the woods for about one-quarter mile to the junction of the Welcome Lakes Ridge Trail, No. 557. Turn right here and begin climbing. A short distance from the junction, you will pass a collapsed cabin on your right. Continue up the very steep ridge. Just after the trail becomes less steep, it crosses an open slope covered with beargrass which, when in bloom, is a magnificent sight. Keep to the left, passing a brass survey marker in the middle of the field and re-enter the woods on the left side, continuing to ascend to the ridge crest.

At 6.3 miles, the Welcome Lakes Trail, No. 554, drops down about 300 feet to the first and smallest of the Welcome Lakes. If you are planning to camp, the campground at the east end of this lake is perhaps the best spot in the entire group. Bull of the Woods can be reached either by proceeding northwest along the top of the ridge or by descending to the Welcome Lakes. If you choose the latter route, hike northwest on Trail 556 past the West Welcome Lake junction and return to the ridge by turning left at the junction of the Shriners Peak Trail, No. 555. Follow the signs to Bull of the Woods Lookout, rejoining Trail 554 on the ridge.

Shortly after the trail begins to climb at the west end of the ridge, pass the Mother Lode Trail, No. 558, on the left and continue on to the west ridge of the summit pyramid where the trail switchbacks to the right and climbs a short distance up to the lookout cabin. Here you will enjoy panoramic views of the many peaks, canyons, and lakes in this very rugged southern part of the Mt. Hood National Forest.

A good loop trip can be made by returning to the Mother Lode Trail and following the signs to Twin Lakes on this sometimes steeply descending, sometimes marshy trail for about six miles back to the Battle Creek Shelter. Be sure to stay left at the junction of the Twin Lakes Trail, No. 573, about two miles before reaching the shelter.

West Welcome Lake

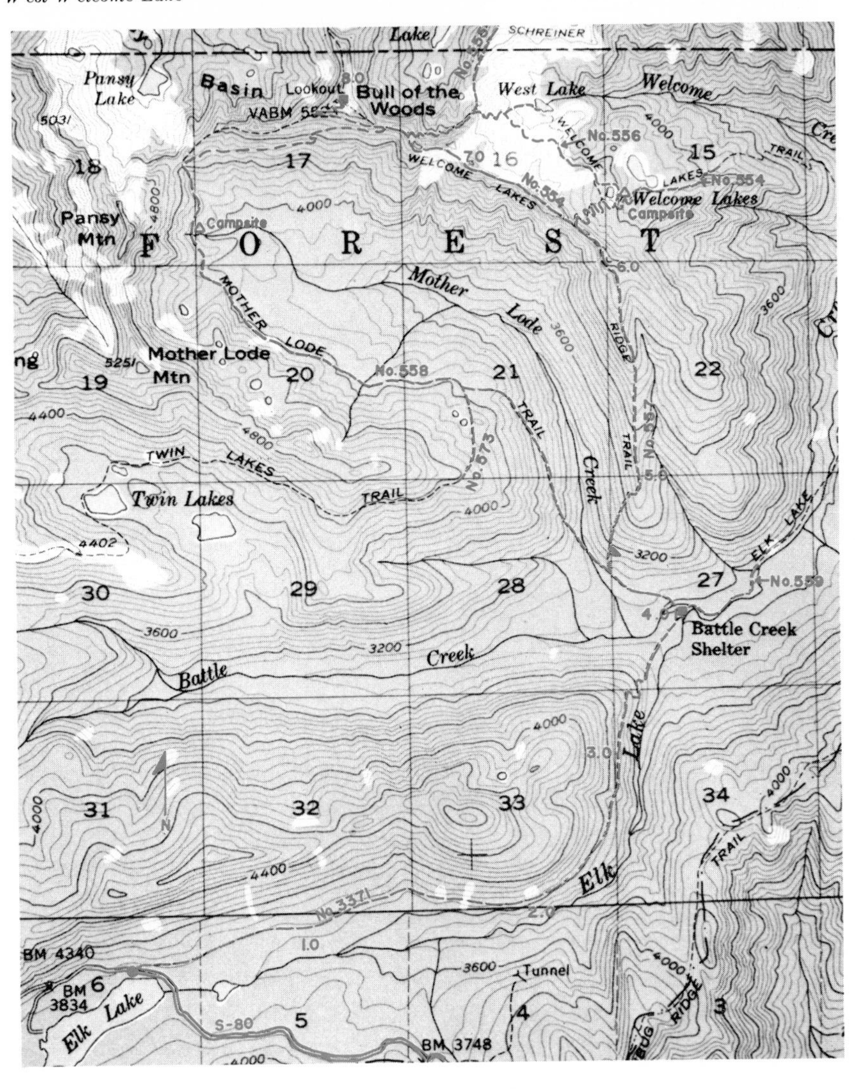

50 OLALLIE BUTTE NORTHERN OREGON

One day trip
Distance: 4 miles one way
Elevation gain: 2,525 feet
High point: 7,215 feet
Allow 3 to 4 hours one way
Topographic map:
U.S.G.S. Breitenbush Hot Springs, Oreg.
N4445-W12145/15
1961

This is one of the highest points in the Oregon Cascades that can be reached by trail, and the view from the top is a full panorama. Here you will see the only remaining example in Oregon of the cupola-type lookout cabin which years ago stood on the summits of many of the major mountains in the Northwest.

Drive east of Portland on the Clackamas River Road, Oregon Highway 224, and turn left on Road S-806, 48 miles east of the town of Estacada. Stay on Road S-806 for about nine miles, following the signs to Olallie Lake, until its junction with Skyline Road, No. S-42. Turn right and proceed south on S-42 for three miles to the trail head on the left side of the road directly underneath the most southerly of the three power lines. A sign marks the Olallie Butte Trail, No. 720.

Travel east almost on the level in semi-open woods for one-half mile. The trail then turns south and climbs steadily for the remaining distance, winding through trees that become more dense as you gain elevation, except near the summit where the prevailing southwest wind has stunted the vegetation. From the abandoned lookout cabin you can see the golden fields of Eastern Oregon, the Three Sisters, Broken Top, Mt. Hood, and the north side of Mt. Jefferson. For additional views of the surrounding country, hike across the flat summit to the steep southeast slope with its interesting jagged rock formations. Olallie Lake and many lesser lakes lie at the foot of the butte and can be seen from this vantage point.

Mt. Jefferson from the Olallie Butte Lookout

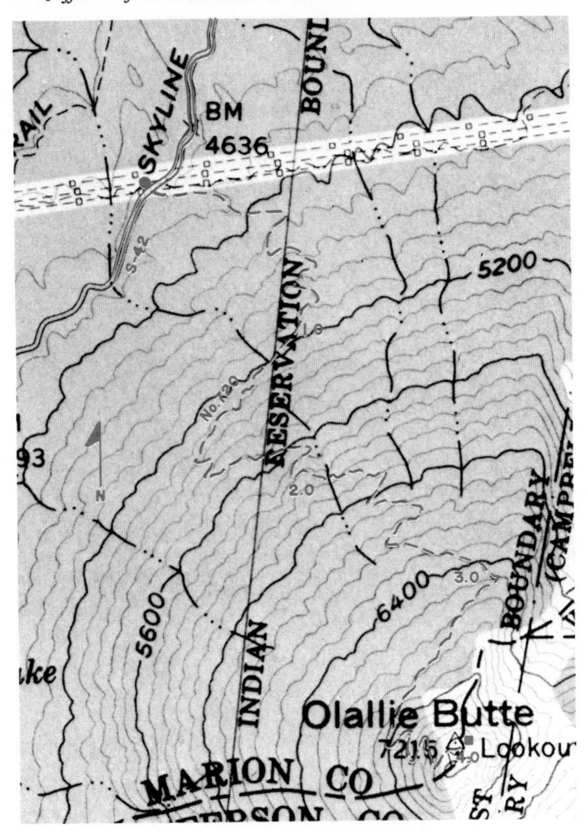

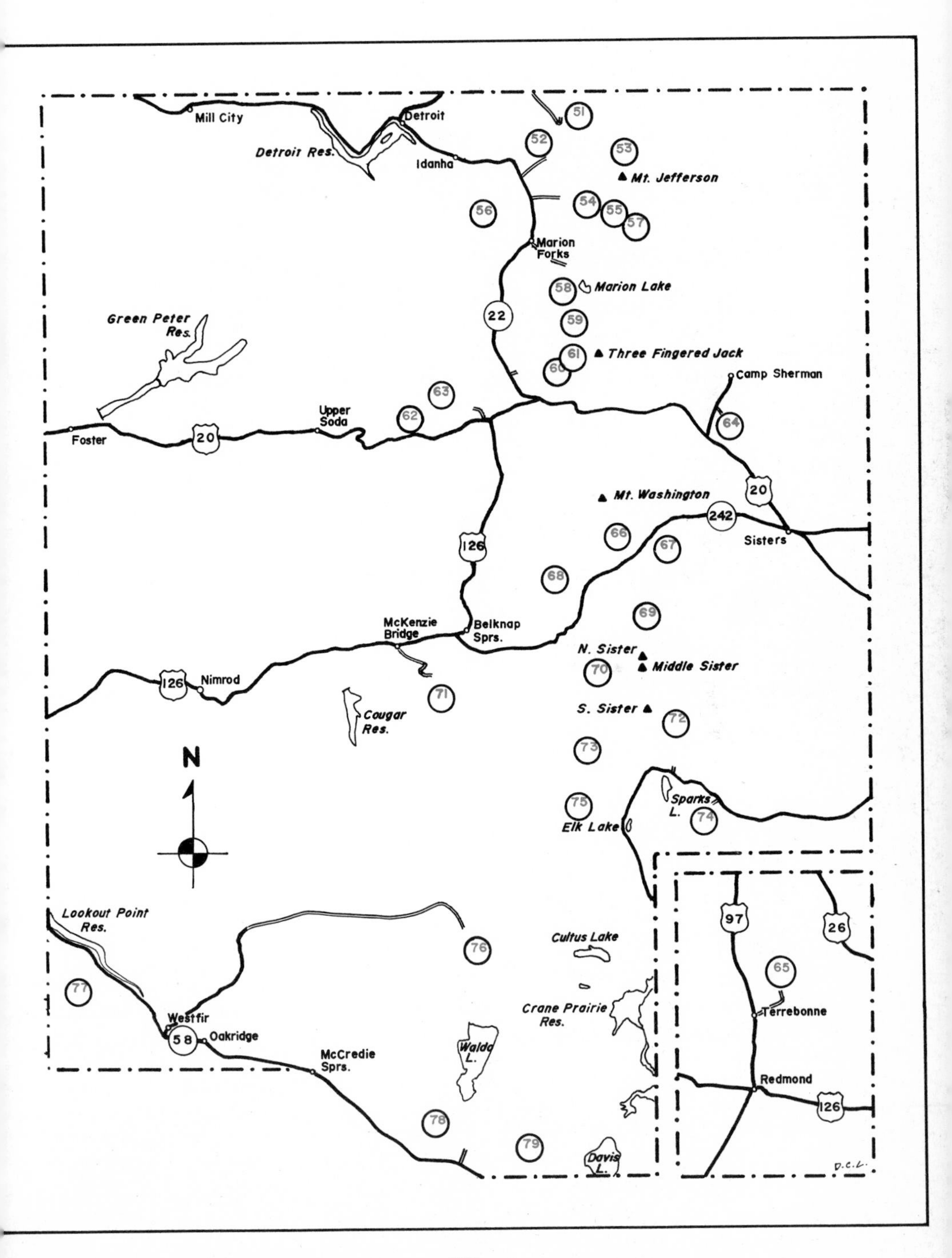
Mill City
Detroit
Detroit Res.
Idanha
51
52
53
Mt. Jefferson
54
55
57
56
Marion Forks
58
Marion Lake
22
59
Green Peter Res.
61
Three Fingered Jack
60
Camp Sherman
63
Upper Soda
62
Foster
20
64
20
Mt. Washington
242
66
67
Sisters
126
68
69
McKenzie Bridge
Belknap Sprs.
N. Sister
Middle Sister
70
126
Nimrod
71
Cougar Res.
S. Sister
72
N
73
Sparks L.
75
74
Elk Lake
97
26
Lookout Point Res.
76
Cultus Lake
65
77
Crane Prairie Res.
Terrebonne
Westfir
58
Oakridge
Waldo L.
McCredie Sprs.
Redmond
126
78
79
Davis L.
D.C.L.

CENTRAL OREGON

Oregon has had a fiery past and many varied examples of volcanic activity can be seen in the central part of the state. Probably the most obvious remnants are the major peaks that form the backbone of the Cascades — Mt. Jefferson, Three Fingered Jack, Mt. Washington, the Three Sisters (North, Middle, and South), Broken Top, and Bachelor Butte.

There are only a few foothills east of the Cascades, whereas on the west side rugged country continues for 50 miles to the Willamette Valley. This wide, lower area, termed the Western Cascades, was formed before the narrower High Cascades to the east. Another interesting contrast between the east and west sides is the rain shadow effect that the Cascades create. As air from the coast rises over the mountains, the moisture in it is condensed and falls either as rain or snow. After passing the crest of the Cascades, the air mass descends to a lower elevation where it becomes more dense and the clouds tend to evaporate. Consequently, the western slopes are covered with dense vegetation and the eastern ones are comparatively arid.

The outer layers of material around the summits of Mt. Washington and Three Fingered Jack have eroded away, leaving only volcanic plugs, the solidified inner core. Theoretically, as the process of erosion continues, Mt. Jefferson and the Three Sisters will eventually resemble their two older neighbors. Less impressive than the major peaks, but more numerous, are the many cinder cones scattered throughout the region. Some of these are easily identified by their symmetrical shape and others, because of erosion, are irregular in appearance. Four of the most prominent cinder cones — Black Butte, the youngest in this area, Black Crater, Bachelor Butte, and Maiden Peak — have trails to their summits, and are described in this section. In addition to the peaks and cinder cones, recent lava flows (those where vegetation is very sparse or non-existent) are on the edge of many of the trails.

Not all of Central Oregon consists of jagged mountains, rock strewn cinder cones, and barren lava flows. Although you will less often encounter stands of timber as dense as those found in the northern part of the Cascades, the vegetation often is lush, particularly around Mt. Jefferson and south of Bachelor Butte. The trails along the slopes of Mt. Jefferson and the North Sister travel through many alpine meadows. Oranges, purples, and pinks from the Indian paint brush, lupine, and heather blend with other blooms to present expanses of remarkably beautiful color combinations. The most concentrated display can be seen on Iron Mountain, a short, easily-accessible hike that is a popular trip during the spring and early summer.

The whole region is dotted with all kinds of lakes, both large and small. Many are warm and deep enough for enjoyable swimming.

A contrast to the mountainous terrain of the Western and High Cascades is the desert setting of Smith Rocks. The aptly-named Crooked River winds around three sides of this formation. Rising apart from the western slope is the 350-foot high tower of Monkey Face, one of the more interesting and difficult rock climbs in Oregon since the spire overhangs on all sides.

A great many trails in this section climb to the summits of smaller peaks, and the ones to the lakes are generally longer than in other regions. Since most of these trails are in mountainous areas, they are closed during the late fall, winter, and spring.

51 BEAR POINT CENTRAL OREGON

One day trip
Distance: 4 miles one way
Elevation gain: 2,941 feet
High point: 6,043 feet
Allow 3 hours one way
Usually open July through October
Topographic maps:
U.S.G.S. Breitenbush Hot Springs, Oreg.
N4445-W12145/15
1961
U.S.G.S. Mt. Jefferson, Oreg.
N4430-W12145/15
1961

This short hike winds up the open southwest slopes of Bear Point for the last 1.5 miles, where Mt. Jefferson can be seen rising prominently to the east. The lookout cabin on the summit is one of the few remaining in Oregon.

Take the North Santiam Highway, Oregon 22, to the community of Detroit. Turn south onto the Breitenbush Road, S-46, and continue east for 11 miles past Breitenbush Hot Springs to the South Breitenbush Road, S-918. Turn right and drive south for 4.4 miles to the South Breitenbush Trail, No. 3375, where the road makes a sharp hairpin turn to the left.

The sign at the trailhead reads South Breitenbush Trail — Bear Point Lookout 4 miles, Skyline Trail and Russell Lake 6 miles. Climb gently through deep woods crossing several small streams and open areas. At 1.5 miles you will come to an old cabin on the left. Beyond the creek to the east of the cabin, the trail turns to the left. Continue for one-half mile, climbing gently through increasingly brushy vegetation to the junction of Trail No. 3342 to Bear Point Lookout.

Turn to the left here and continue on the level through tall brush for one-quarter mile. Water is available from a stream a short distance after the junction. The trail then begins to climb in short but not steep switchbacks. Just before the final pitch to the summit it veers to the west and travels through some trees. Fire Camp Lakes can be seen below to the northwest and scores of other lakes are scattered about. Jefferson Park Glacier is the main ice field that can be seen on the mountain's slopes.

Mt. Jefferson from Bear Point Lookout

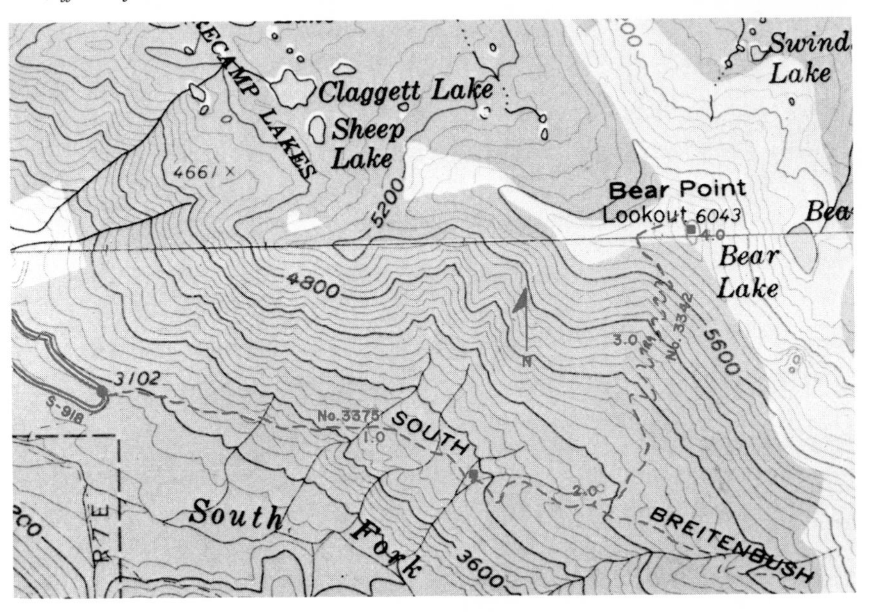

52 TRIANGULATION PEAK CENTRAL OREGON

One day trip
Distance: 6.5 miles one way
Elevation gain: 2,474 feet, loss 200 feet
High point: 5,434 feet
Allow 4 to 5 hours one way
Usually open July through October
Topographic map:
U.S.G.S. Mt. Jefferson, Oreg.
N4430-W12145/15
1961

A large meadow, interesting rock formations, and views of the northwest side of Mt. Jefferson are three of the sights to be enjoyed by the hiker on this trip. Indian Paint Brush and other vivid wildflowers are abundant along the upper portions of the trail during the spring and early summer.

Take the North Santiam Highway, Oregon 22, and turn off on the Whitewater Road, No. 1044, about mid-way between Idanha and Marion Forks. Proceed east for 3.3 miles past the junction of Road 1044B — which leads downslope to the right — to the trailhead at Cheat Creek, where there is parking at a turnout. A sign identifies the Cheat Creek Trail, No. 3431.

Follow the logging road for about 200 yards until it turns down toward the creek. The trail begins here on the left hand side of the road and climbs through thick woods crossing several branches of Cheat Creek. At the two-mile point it levels off and then enters a meadow which is named for the wild cheat grass that grows here. Posts mark the way across this five-acre field.

Re-enter the woods and climb for one-half mile on a deeply rutted trail to the ridge crest. Continue for a few hundred feet and keep left at the junction of the Jefferson Park Trail. Park Ridge and other landmarks around Mt. Jefferson's north side can be seen by turning off the trail to the right a short distance beyond the junction and walking a few feet to an opening on the ridge crest. The trail contours around the ridge, alternating between open and wooded slopes. Periodically, Wild Cheat Meadow can be seen directly below, and Mt. Jefferson, Three Fingered Jack, and Mt. Washington appear on the skyline.

At four miles come to the junction of the Devils Peak Trail, No. 3345. Keep left, on Trail 3373, and continue on the level for another 1.5 miles, crossing several boulder fields and passing under large rock formations. At the 5.5 mile point, enter deep woods and go around a bend. One-quarter mile beyond is the junction of the Triangulation Peak Trail, No. 3374, which is marked by a sign pointing to the summit, three-quarters of a mile further. Turn left here and climb gradually to the peak. The foundation is all that remains of the former lookout cabin.

Wild Cheat Meadow

Spire Rock

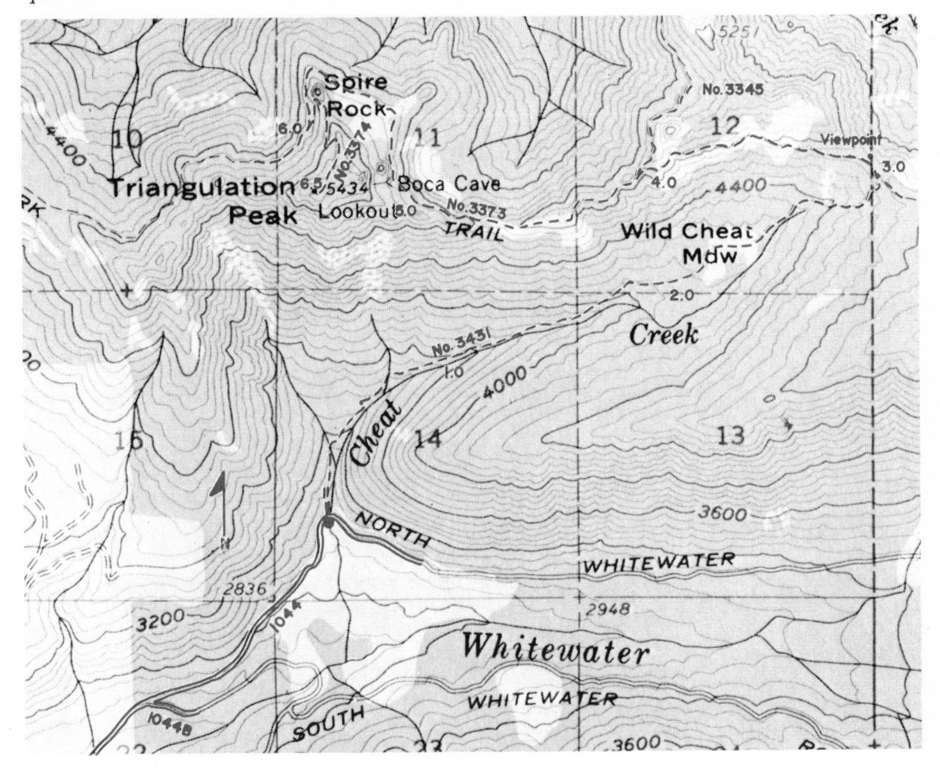

5251
Spire Rock
No.3345
10
11
12
Viewpoint
3.0
4400
No.3374
Triangulation Peak
5434
Boca Cave
Lookout
No.3373
TRAIL
4.0
4400
Wild Cheat Mdw
2.0
Creek
No. 3431
1.0
4000
Cheat
15
14
13
3600
NORTH
WHITEWATER
2836
3200
1044
2948
Whitewater
WHITEWATER
10448
SOUTH
3600

53 JEFFERSON PARK CENTRAL OREGON

One day trip or backpack
Distance: 6 miles one way
Elevation gain: 1,510 feet, loss 1,168 feet
High point: 6,890 feet
Allow 3 to 4 hours one way
Usually open mid-July through October
Topographic map:
U.S.G.S. Mt. Jefferson, Oreg.
N4430-W12145/15
1961

Jefferson Park is a very flat, lake-dotted meadow about a mile long and one-half mile wide at the 5,800-foot level on the north side of Mt. Jefferson. From here you have close-up views of the mountain's major glaciers, and the park provides an excellent base camp for climbing parties attempting the north side routes. In the late summer, it is a carpet of Indian Paint Brush and heather blossoms.

Drive on the North Santiam Highway (Oregon 22) to the town of Detroit. Turn north on the Breitenbush Road, No. RS-46, and continue past Breitenbush Hot Springs to the boundary of the Mt. Hood National Forest where the unpaved road leaves the North Fork of the Breitenbush River. At this point, turn right on the Skyline Road, No. S-42, and drive to the Breitenbush Lake Campground, bordering the lake on the west. Ample parking is available here.

The trailhead is at the southern end of the campground and is marked by a sign pointing to Jefferson Park, 6 miles. Several hundred yards beyond, the trail passes under a large suspended wood carving identifying this as the Skyline Trail, No. 2000.

At one mile a path to the right leads to the 6,095 foot summit of Pyramid Butte. Those who do not wish to make a long hike can enjoy a far-reaching view of Mt. Jefferson and the surrounding lake country from this point. From this junction, the trail then turns south climbing gradually for several miles through the thinning forest, passing several very beautiful tarns. Eventually it leaves the woods, climbs up the lava fields and continues up to the crest of Park Ridge at 6,890 feet. Here you suddenly see the entire north face of Mt. Jefferson and the broad green expanse of Jefferson Park a thousand feet below.

To proceed down into the park, turn sharply left and continue along the trail which descends in switchbacks across open volcanic slopes to Russell Lake. Excellent camping sites can be found throughout the park. However, the most scenic areas lie in the southwestern section near Park, Scout, and Bays Lakes. Rock Lake is especially interesting as it is surrounded by high rock walls. Fresh water is available near the Park Butte drainage and from the many streams coming directly off the north side of Mt. Jefferson.

Jefferson Park and Scout Lake

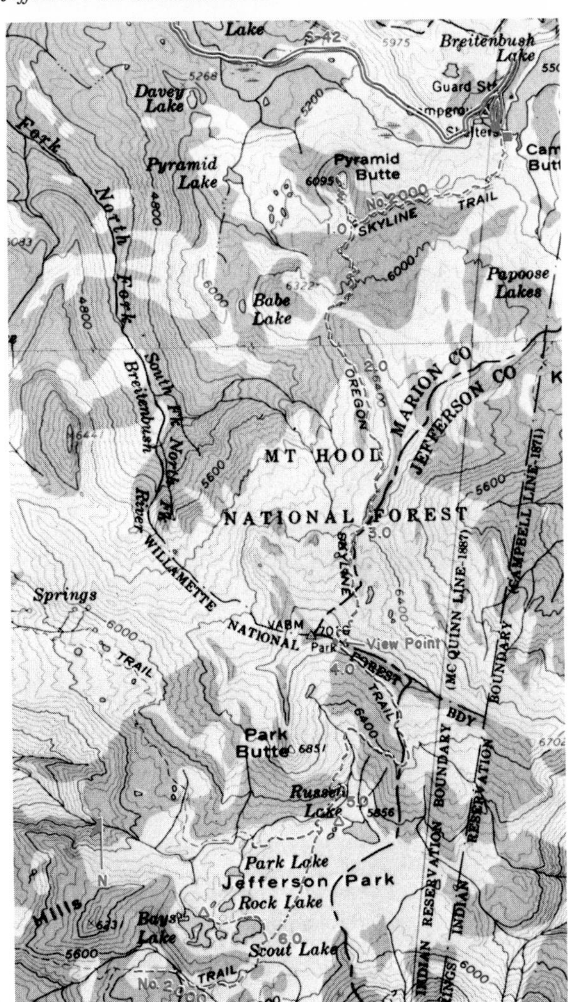

54 GRIZZLY PEAK CENTRAL OREGON

One day trip
Distance: 5 miles one way
Elevation gain: 2,699 feet
High point: 5,799 feet
Allow 4 to 5½ hours one way
Usually open July through October
Topographic map:
U.S.G.S. Mt. Jefferson, Oreg.
N4430-W12145/15
1961

Grizzly Peak is the closest you can get to Mt. Jefferson's rugged south face without actually being on its slopes. Equally close appearing is Pamelia Lake which seemingly lies almost directly beneath your feet.

Take Oregon Highway 22 (North Santiam) and turn east on the Pamelia Lake Road, No. 109, about 7.5 miles east of Idanha and 1.5 miles south of the Whitewater Campground. Drive the four miles to the trailhead located on the left hand side of the road just north of the Pamelia Creek crossing. It is identified by a sign reading, Pamelia Lake Trail, No. 3439 — Pamelia Lake 2 miles, Skyline Trail 2¼ miles, and Hunts Lake 6 miles. Ample parking is available.

For the first two miles, the trail climbs gradually and follows Pamelia Creek through lush woods. At one-half mile, Milk Creek almost meets the trail on the north side. A large, undeveloped campsite is to the south of the trail just before the exit creek from Pamelia Lake reappears from its underground channel. A short distance further you will come to the junction of the Grizzly Peak Trail, No. 3428. Turn right here and cross the rocky area over Pamelia Creek which flows underground at this point.

The trail travels to the west for about three-quarters mile, climbing gradually through deep forest. At the three-mile point it heads in a southerly direction and then switchbacks several times. One-half mile further the trail climbs in an easterly direction. The tree cover becomes less dense the higher you climb and more of the south face of Mt. Jefferson comes into view. The trail heads south for the last three-quarters mile and turns sharply to the left just before reaching the summit.

In addition to the proximity of Mt. Jefferson's slopes and Pamelia Lake, Hunts Cove and the Cathedral Rocks can be seen to the northeast and the summits of Three Fingered Jack, the Three Sisters, Broken Top, and Mt. Hood jut up along the horizon.

Mt. Jefferson from Grizzly Peak

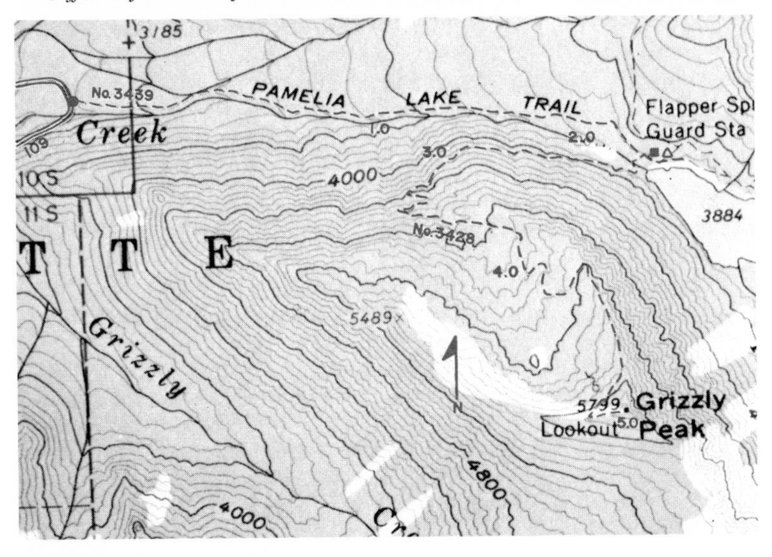

55 HUNTS COVE CENTRAL OREGON

One day trip or backpack
Distance: 6 miles one way
Elevation gain: 2,127 feet
High point: 5,236 feet
Allow 3 to 4 hours one way
Usually open July through October
Topographic map:
U.S.G.S. Mt. Jefferson, Oreg.
N4430-W12145/15
1961

Pinnacle on Hunts Cove Trail

This very scenic hike along the southwestern shoulder of Mt. Jefferson passes three lakes. The open rocky slopes above the cove are a complimentary contrast to the luxurious forest that borders the trail.

From Oregon State Highway 22 (North Santiam) turn east on the Pamelia Lake Road, No. 109, about 7.5 miles east of Idanha and 1.5 miles south of the Whitewater Campground. Drive the four miles to the trailhead located on the left hand side of the road just north of the Pamelia Creek crossing. It is identified by a sign reading, Pamelia Lake Trail, No. 3439 — Pamelia Lake 2 miles, Skyline Trail 2¼ miles, Hunts Lake 6 miles. Ample parking is available.

In the first two miles the trail climbs gradually and follows Pamelia Creek through lush woods. At one-half mile Milk Creek almost meets the trail on the north side. A large undeveloped campsite is to the south of the trail just before the exit creek from Pamelia Lake reappears from its underground channel. A short distance further you will come to the junction of the Grizzly Peak Trail, No. 3428. Continue straight ahead to the Flapper Springs Guard Station, which looks out across Pamelia Lake. This station is manned during the summer.

Tree trunks poking out of the lake indicate that it is of comparatively recent formation. Chipmunks, looking for food left by hikers and campers, scamper among the many rhododendron bushes that line the shore.

Hike along the trail one-eighth of a mile to the junction on the left of the Skyline Trail, No. 2000, and a fisherman's trail leading down to the lake on the right. Keep straight ahead and continue around to the eastern shore of the lake. At 3.5 miles, you will come to Hunts Creek. Cross the first branch and go downstream a short distance following a sign on a tree. Then cross the main stream on a large log. The trail now becomes very clear and begins climbing along a wooded slope. It switchbacks once and then crosses an open slope where Mt. Jefferson dominates the view to the northeast.

After gaining additional altitude you can look to the northwest and see Pamelia Lake and the country just covered. Shortly before the 5.5 mile point, where large rock pinnacles rise overhead, the trail comes to the junction of the Hunts Cove Trail, No. 3430. Turn left and hike one-half mile to Hanks Lake. Although there are campsites here, Hunts Lake, one-half mile further, is more scenic and makes a better stopping place. The jagged spires overlooking the lakes to the east are the Cathedral Rocks. You can scramble up the slopes to the north of Hunts Lake for a close-up view of Mt. Jefferson.

Hanks Lake — Hunts Cove

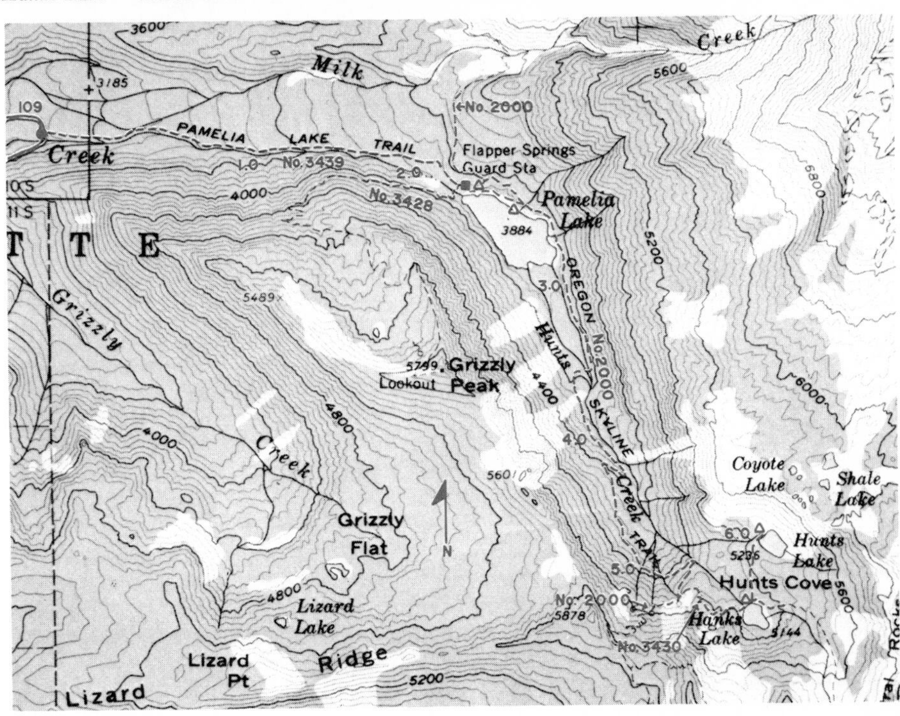

56 BACHELOR MOUNTAIN CENTRAL OREGON

One day trip
Distance: 3.5 miles one way
Elevation gain: 1,943 feet
High point: 5,593 feet
Allow 1½ to 2 hours one way
Usually open late June through October
Topographic maps:
U.S.G.S. Detroit, Oreg.
N4430-W12200/15
1956
U.S.G.S. Mt. Jefferson, Oreg.
N4430-W12145/15
1961

Mt. Jefferson from Bachelor Mountain

An easy trail to the summit of Bachelor Mountain, a few miles west of the Cascade crest, will reward you with panoramic views of most of Oregon's snow-capped peaks. During the spring and early summer, brightly colored wildflowers bloom on its open slopes.

Take the North Santiam Highway, Oregon 22, east of Detroit Reservoir and turn east onto Road 1155, about one and three-quarter miles south of Marion Forks. Cross the Bugaboo Bridge and stay on Road 1155 for 3.3 miles to the west end of a clearcut just before the road is straight for some distance. Parking space is available on the shoulder of the road, and the Bachelor Mountain Trail, No. 3420, is marked by a sign at the edge of the clearcut.

Hike north for about 150 feet along the logging road, which borders the west side of the clearcut until it forks. Keep to the right and continue along the partly overgrown road to a point near the north end of the clearcut. The beginning of the trail is not clearly marked so if you have trouble finding it, the best solution is to go into the woods a few feet and then walk parallel to the clearcut until you cross the trail which is very well-defined and runs perpendicular to the northern side of the logged area. You will see a three-mile marker on the right soon after the trail enters the trees.

The path climbs gradually through the woods for almost a mile before coming to a switchback. At one and three-quarter miles the trail contours just below a ridge crest on the semi-open southern side and passes the unmarked junction of the old Bruno Meadows Trail, No. 3424. Shortly thereafter it crosses a grassy area and a creek and climbs in switchbacks recrossing the same creek. A short distance further the trail traverses a quarter-mile long rocky slope which offers a good view of Mt. Jefferson, Three Fingered Jack, the Three Sisters, and the Husband. Re-enter the woods and one-quarter mile further come to the junction of the side trail to Bachelor Mountain.

Keep to the right and climb up through the woods for one-quarter mile. The remaining distance to the summit is across the open southeast side of the peak, which is covered with beargrass.

Bachelor Mountain and Mt. Jefferson

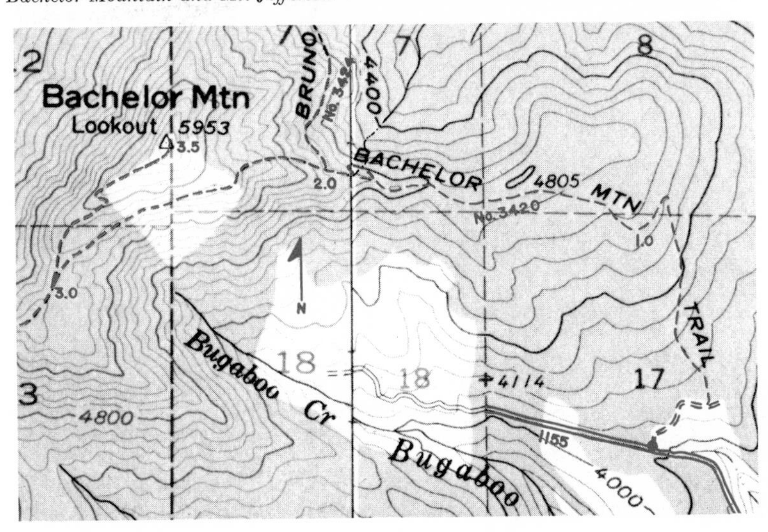

57 SUMMIT TRAIL CENTRAL OREGON

Backpack
Distance: 12 miles one way
Elevation gain: 2,200 feet, loss 1,480 feet
High point: 6,010 feet
Allow 6 to 8 hours one way
Usually open July through October
Topographic maps:
U.S.G.S. Mt. Jefferson, Oreg.
N4430-W12145/15
1961
U.S.G.S. Whitewater River, Oreg.
N4430-W12130/15
1961

Lava flows near Forked Butte

Numerous lakes, each totally different in scenic appeal, and interesting lava formations highlight the Summit Trail which traverses the eastern crest of the Cascade Range just south of Mt. Jefferson.

Drive on the Santiam Highway, U.S. 20, a few miles east of Suttle Lake and turn north on Road 1210 at a sign pointing to Todd Lake and Abbot Butte Lookout. This sign is one-fourth mile west of a sign pointing south to Cache Mountain and Camp Tamarack.

Just after you cross Lake Creek, turn right onto Road 1138 and follow the sign to Abbot Butte Lookout and Jack Lake. Five miles from the highway and just beyond the bridge over Jack Creek, follow Road 1211. A sign here also points to Abbot Butte Lookout and Jack Lake. At the Jack Lake junction, continue north on Road 1210 and drive past the Bear Valley Trail and several side roads until reaching a sign reading Loader No. 2, which is 9.8 miles from the highway. Turn left and follow the red-rocked road, No. 1210B, for 1.9 miles to its end at the Cabot Lake Trail head, where ample parking is available.

Hike west on the Cabot Lake Trail, No. 68, through almost level woods to Cabot Lake. Here, the trail turns south and climbs in switchbacks for about one-fourth mile through less-dense timber. The trail again becomes level and passes several large ponds. The southeast face of Mt. Jefferson is often visible on the skyline. At four miles you will come to the junction of the Summit Trail, No. 65. Keep to the right, and climb gradually for about one-half mile before arriving at Carl Lake. Three sides of this lake are surrounded by forested slopes, but the east end appears to be suspended in space. Campsites are available on the southeast side of the lake.

North of Carl Lake the trail climbs in short switchbacks, then travels through a semi-open area dotted with tarns. At Junction Lake, really a large pond, is the junction with the Sugar Pine Trail, No. 67. Continue to the left on the main trail and contour through a tree-dotted lava flow. The large cinder cone rising to the northeast is Forked Butte. The trail curves along the edge of a field of large rocks and comes to an open slope of volcanic ash. From here you overlook the terrain surrounding the southern slopes of Mt. Jefferson. The trail then drops down to the right and enters the woods, switchbacking down to Patsy Lake, nestled between steep, forested slopes. There are good campsites here. The Jefferson Lake Trail, No. 66, leads off to the east at the outlet of the lake.

Keep to the left on the Summit Trail which climbs directly above Patsy Lake. The trail is level for the next three-quarters mile, traveling through a rocky meadow. There is a slight drop down to Table Lake which, unlike the other lakes seen on this hike, is surrounded by flat open ground. Campsites are plentiful as are mosquitos during the summer months. Hole-in-the-Wall Park can be reached by contouring east along the Summit Trail, crossing a pass near Bear Butte, and descending about 600 feet to the small pond in the center of an open meadow.

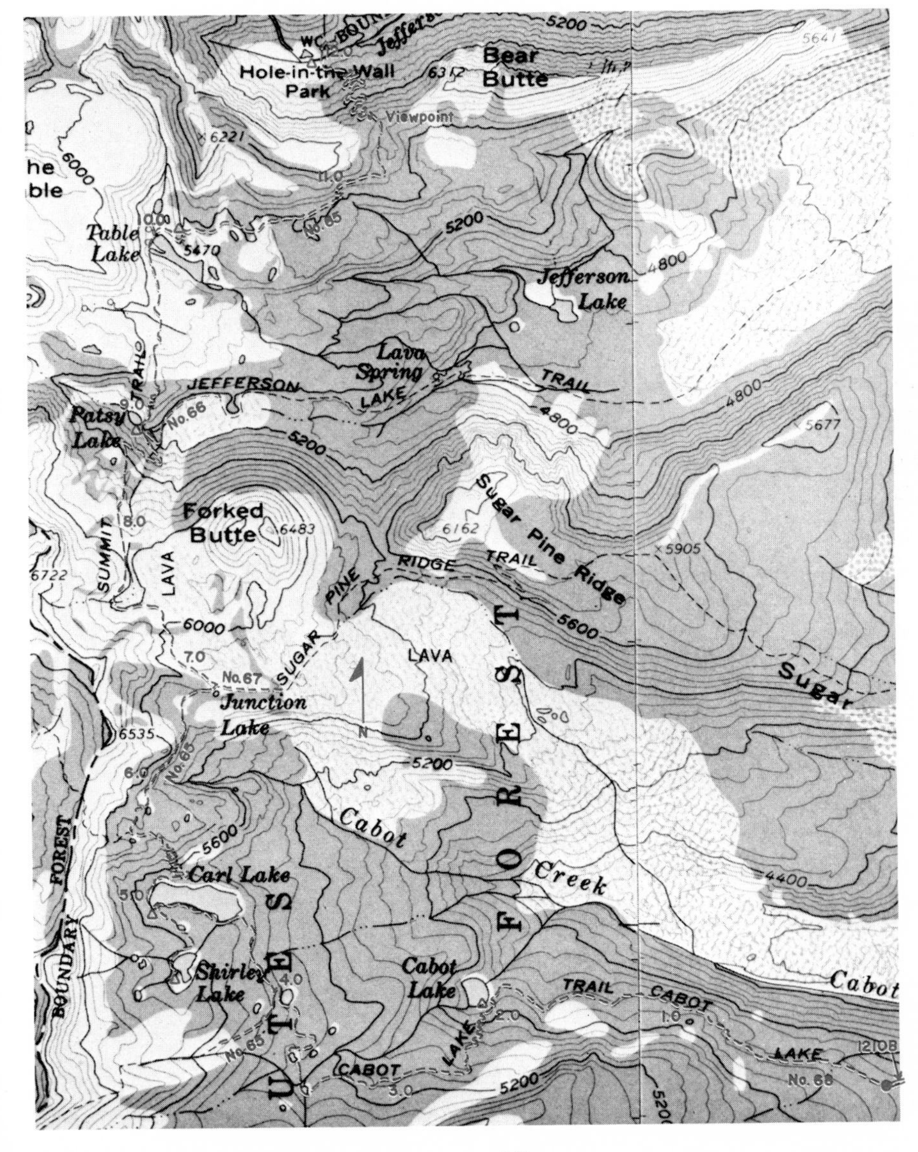

Hole-in-the-Wall Park
Bear Butte
Viewpoint
Table Lake
Jefferson Lake
Lava Spring
JEFFERSON LAKE TRAIL
No. 66
Patsy Lake
Forked Butte
SUMMIT TRAIL
LAVA
Sugar Pine Ridge
SUGAR PINE RIDGE TRAIL
No. 67
Junction Lake
No. 65
LAVA
Cabot Creek
Carl Lake
Shirley Lake
Cabot Lake
CABOT LAKE TRAIL
No. 68
FOREST BOUNDARY
U S F O R E S T
Sugar
Cabot

58 MARION MOUNTAIN CENTRAL OREGON

One day trip or backpack
Distance: 5 miles one way
Elevation gain: 1,201 feet
High Point: 5,351 feet
Allow 2½ to 3 hours one way
Usually open June through October
Topographic map:
U.S.G.S. Mt. Jefferson, Oreg.
N4430-W12145/15
1961

The entire expanse of Marion Lake, one of Oregon's most easily accessible wilderness fishing areas, is visible from the top of Marion Mountain. The jagged summits of both Mt. Jefferson and Three Fingered Jack rise to the northeast and southeast.

Drive on Oregon Highway 22 to Marion Forks, a community about midway between Detroit and the junction of the North and South Santiam highways to the southeast. Turn east on the Marion Creek Road, No. 1157, just north of the Marion Creek bridge. Proceed for 4.5 miles to the road's end where there is parking. Carry drinking water as there are few creeks along this trail.

The trail starts on the south side of the road near the turnaround and is marked by a sign reading, Marion Lake Trail, No. 3436 — Lake Ann 1½ miles, Marion Lake Forest Service Station 2 miles, and Oregon Skyline Trail 7 miles. The trail climbs gently through old timber until reaching Lake Ann. Campsites are available at the west and south end of the lake. About one-fourth mile beyond Lake Ann you will reach the junction of the Marion Lake Outlet Trail, No. 3495. If you wish, you can make a small loop trip here by continuing on No. 3436 to the guard station, one-half mile east, then taking the connecting trail southwest along the northwest shore of the lake. The more direct route, however, is to keep to the right on Trail 3495.

Three-quarters of a mile further is a second junction where the Marion Lake Outlet Trail meets the Blue Lake Trail, No. 3422. The branch of the Blue Lake Trail which heads to the east is the one you would have been on had you taken the loop. Follow the sign which says Marion Mountain 2½ miles.

Cross the bridge over the outlet creek and traverse along the rocky slope above Marion Lake. Travel through less-dense timber for one mile to the junction of the Pine Ridge Trail, No. 3443. Turn right on this trail following the sign to Marion Mountain and Camp Pioneer. At first the trail climbs and then becomes level, passing several small ponds. A short distance beyond the ponds you will come to the Marion Mountain Trail, No. 3435. Turn left here and climb the final three-fourths mile to the ridge crest. Turn to the left to get to the promentory where a fire lookout was once located.

Fine views of Mt. Jefferson, Three Fingered Jack, Marion Lake, Lake Ann, and Mt. Hood can be seen to the north and the North and Middle Sister are visible to the south.

Marion Lake — Mt. Jefferson

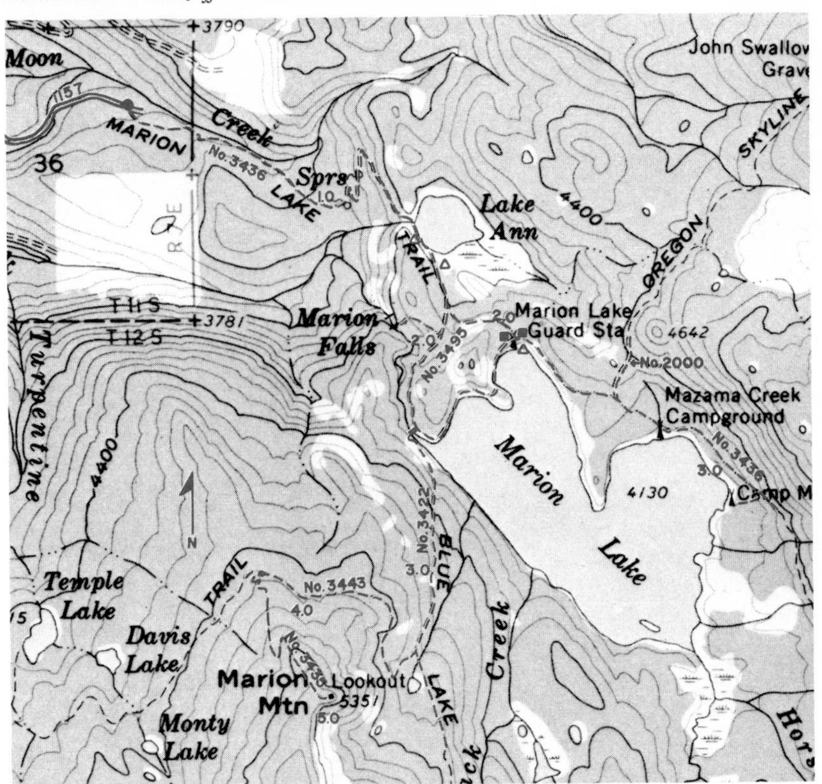

59 EIGHT LAKES BASIN CENTRAL OREGON

Backpack
Distance: 8 miles one way
Elevation gain: 1,940 feet, loss 220 feet
High point: 5,300 feet
Allow 4 to 5½ hours one way
Usually open late June through October
Topographic map:
U.S.G.S. Mt. Jefferson, Oreg.
N4430-W12145/15
1961

Little Bowerman Lake — Mt. Jefferson

Mt. Jefferson and Three Fingered Jack can be seen from points on this trail, which travels through dense forest and open country. The lakes visited are well-known for their good fishing.

Drive on Oregon State Highway 22 to Marion Forks, a small community about midway between Detroit and the junction of the North and South Santiam highways. Turn east on the Marion Creek Road, No. 1157, which is just north of the Marion Creek Bridge. Proceed for 4.5 miles to the road's end where you will find ample parking space.

The trail starts on the south side of the road near the turnaround and is marked by a sign reading Marion Lake Trail, No. 3436. It climbs gently through old growth timber until reaching Lake Ann. About one-quarter mile beyond Lake Ann is the junction of the Marion Lake Outlet Trail, No. 3495. Keep to the right on Trail 3495, where three-quarters mile further the Marion Lake Outlet Trail meets the Blue Lake Trail, No. 3422. Continue south along the Blue Lake Trail for two miles, passing the Marion Mountain Trail, to a sign which points to shallow Jenny Lake about 50 yards to the east.

Proceed on the level for one mile through several marshy areas and then climb steeply through the woods for one-half mile to the ridge crest. Hike along the trail to the east side of Blue Lake where there are several good campsites. Descend gradually for three-quarters mile to Jorn Lake. This spot is particularly scenic and there are very good places to camp along the southwest shore.

A short distance beyond Jorn Lake is the junction with the Bowerman Lake Trail. Turn to the left here and hike through flat open country for three-quarters mile to Bowerman Lake. Little Bowerman Lake is a short distance further and slightly off the trail to the left.

If you want to make a loop trip returning to Marion Lake on the Skyline Trail, hike northeast from Bowerman Lake gradually descending through increasingly dense woods. Two and three-quarter miles from Bowerman Lake come to the junction with the Minto Pass Trail, No. 3437. Keep the left, and you will continue to lose elevation while crossing several streams. Soon after crossing frothy Mist Creek, pass Camp Marion on your left where a shelter looks out across Marion Lake. One-half mile further is Mazama Campground. Walk through the northern portion of this camp, following the tree blazes, and climb up to the ridge crest about 100 feet above the shore. Keep to the left at the Skyline Trail junction and drop down to the steep boulder-strewn northeastern shore of Marion Lake. Here you will have a good view of Three Fingered Jack. Continue on to the guard station, which is manned during the summer months, and hike past it one-quarter mile to the junction of the Marion Lake Outlet Trail, the one which you took at the beginning of the loop.

Marion Lake — Three Fingered Jack

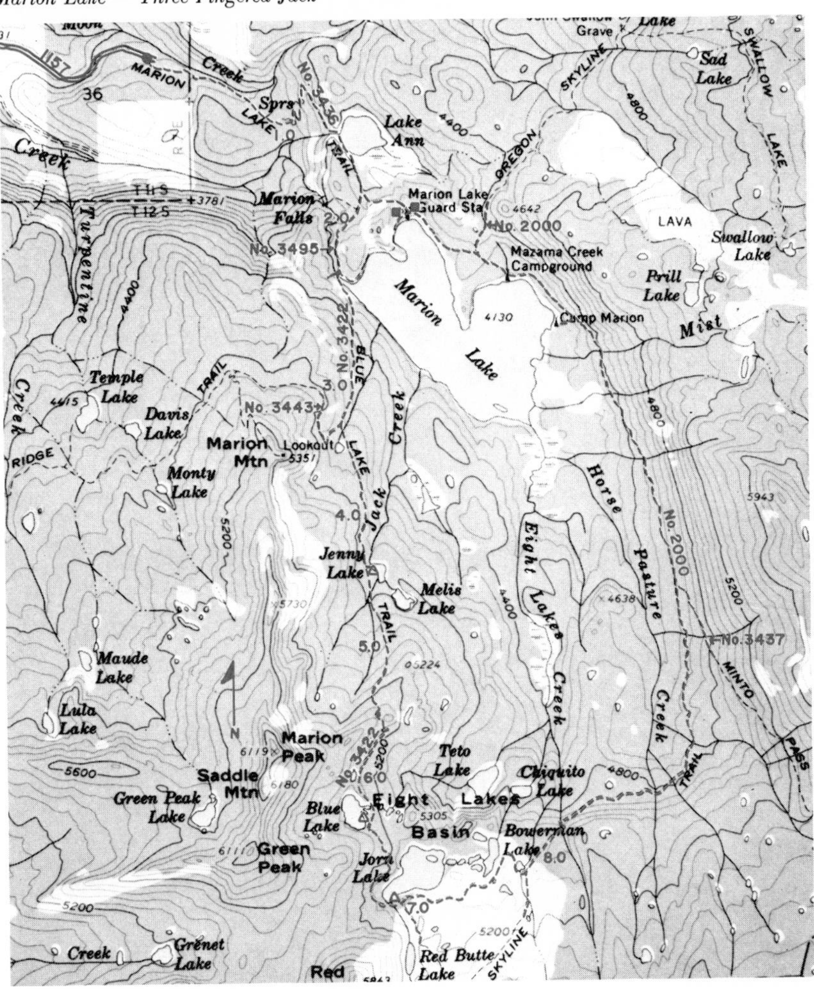

60 MAXWELL BUTTE
CENTRAL OREGON

One day trip
Distance: 4.8 miles one way
Elevation gain: 2,429 feet
High point: 6,229 feet
Allow 2½ to 3 hours one way
Usually open late June through October
Topographic map:
U.S.G.S. Three Fingered Jack, Oreg.
N4415-W12145/15
1959

Be sure to choose a sunny day for the trip to Maxwell Butte, an old cinder cone that rises almost directly west of Three Fingered Jack. From its summit, you can look toward Three Fingered Jack and see Santiam Lake, Duffy Lake, the Berley Lakes, and a host of other bodies of water surrounding the cone. Three Fingered Jack is very close on the east, and there are excellent views all up and down the west side of the Cascade Range. Carry an adequate supply of water as the creeks in this area tend to dry up rather early in the summer.

Drive east of Salem on the North Santiam Highway, Oregon 22, to a point about three miles north of the junction with the South Santiam Highway, U.S. 20. Turn east on an unmarked logging road (No. 1379) near the sign pointing west to Road No. 13002. Proceed east for one-half mile to the trail head at the east end of the clearcut. You can park your car on a spur road either north or south of the trail head. The trail sign reads, Maxwell Butte Trail, No. 3391 — Maxwell Butte 5 miles, Duffy Lake 6 miles.

Follow the trail east (actually it is an old jeep road) up a gentle grade for 1.3 miles where you will enter the Mt. Jefferson Primitive Area. Here the jeep road terminates. At two and one-quarter miles, you will meet the junction of the Lava Trail, No. 3433, to Duffy Lake. Turn right, continuing on Trail No. 3391, which circles two small ponds called Twin Lakes and climbs through country alternating between open woods and grassy slopes. At four miles the trail meets the southwestern shoulder of Maxwell Butte and begins climbing more steeply. From here it switchbacks the final 0.8 mile to the dome-shaped summit.

Maxwell Butte and Three Fingered Jack

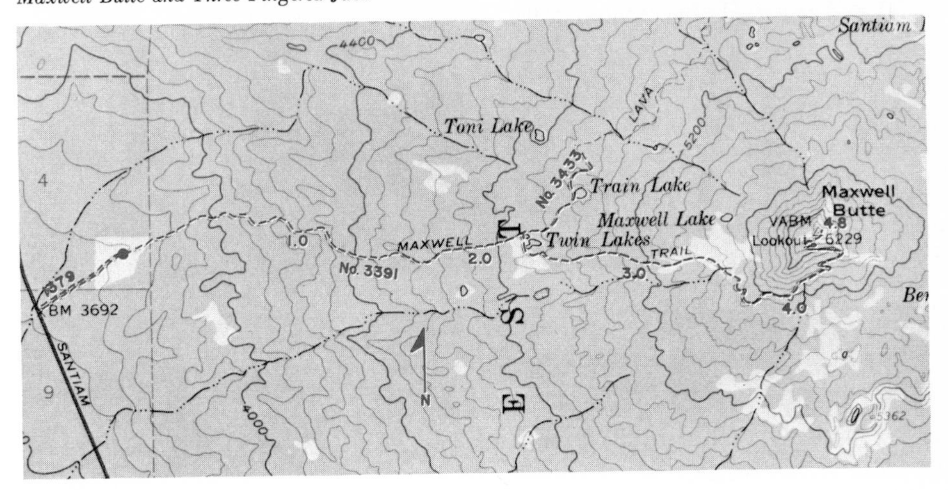

61 DUFFY LAKE CENTRAL OREGON

One day trip or backpack
Distance: 6 miles one way
Elevation gain: 700 feet, loss 647 feet
High point: 5,440 feet
Allow 3 to 4 hours one way
Usually open June through October
Topographic map:
U.S.G.S. Three Fingered Jack, Oreg.
N4415-W12145/15
1959

Three Fingered Jack from Santiam Lake

This is one of the most enjoyable hikes in the Willamette National Forest. The steep west face of Three Fingered Jack rises closely to the east as the trail travels through woods, meadows, and a few almost barren, desert-like stretches. It also passes a variety of lakes.

Take the North Santiam Highway, Oregon 22, or the South Santiam Highway, U.S. 20, beyond the junction of the two highways (now U.S. 20) to the Santiam Lodge. The lodge is located approximately three miles east of Lost Lake on the east side of Hogg Rock opposite the Big Lake junction. The Skyline Trail, No. 2000, begins at the large parking area about 50 yards east of the lodge and may be marked as the Santiam Lake Trail, No. 3491.

Climb very gradually through woods for two miles to a trail junction on your left. Keep to the right and you will immediately come to Jack Shelter at the edge of a marshy meadow. Continue over semi-open terrain to the 3.2 mile point on a rise where an unmarked trail leads off to the left about 200 yards to Lower Berley Lake. A short distance further the trail crosses a quarter-mile long open area of pebbles and volcanic ash which is almost void of vegetation. Enter the woods and descend slightly to Ruby Lake. Lose a little more elevation before coming to a large grass-covered slope where the trail forks.

Keep to the right if you wish to stop at Santiam Lake. From its shores the summit of Mt. Jefferson is visible to the north and Three Fingered Jack is nearby to the east. Take the trail around the west side of the lake to reach a well-developed campsite complete with tables. Continue to the north a few hundred feet to meet the main trail. Again descend, and in one-half mile come to a flower-covered meadow and a junction with the Dixie Lakes Trail, No. 3494 leading off to the right. Keep to the left here and continue through the remainder of the meadow and into the woods. At the six-mile point come to another trail junction and turn to the right, following the signs to Duffy Lake. There are many campsites at this large lake, which lies at the foot of Duffy Butte.

East end of Duffy Lake

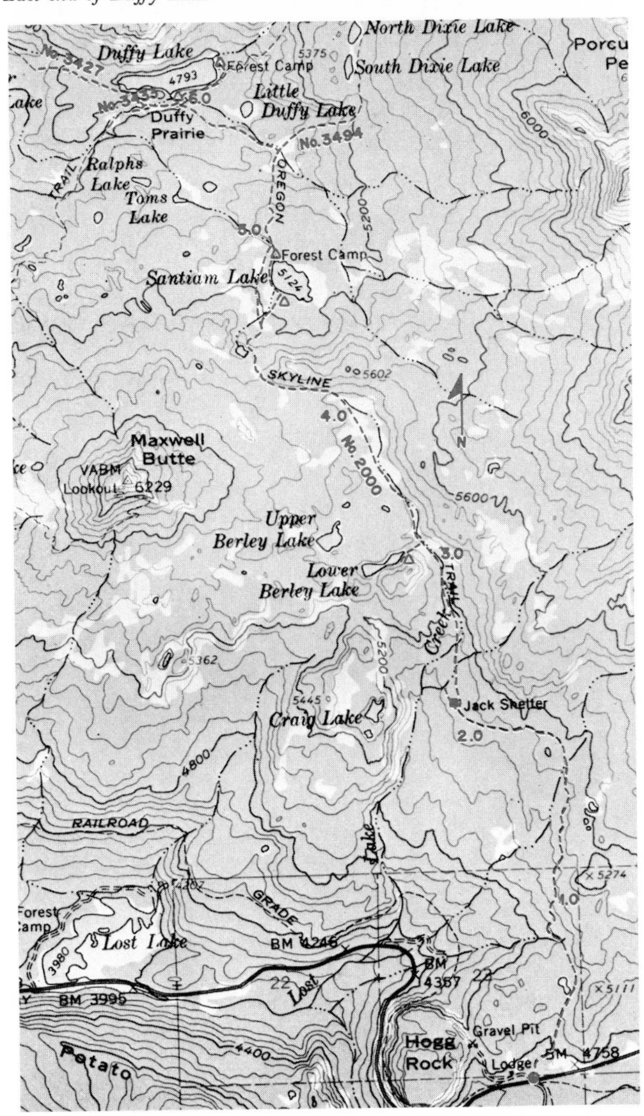

62 IRON MOUNTAIN CENTRAL OREGON

One day trip
Distance: 1.5 miles one way
Elevation gain: 1,335 feet
High point: 5,455
Allow 1 hour one way
Usually open June through October
Topographic map:
U.S.G.S. Echo Mountain, Oreg.
N4415-W12200/15
1955

The slopes below the massive pinnacle of Iron Mountain are famous for a profusion of wild flowers. Thus the ideal time for this trip is in the spring during the peak of the blooming season, although some color remains on the mountainside all summer long. Carry water as none is available on the trail.

Drive on U.S. Highway 20 (South Santiam) east of Sweet Home a short distance past the junction of the Deer Creek Road, No. 1345, to a cement foundation on the south side of the highway one-mile east of the 63-mile post. You can park your car either on the foundation or on the highway shoulder. The trail begins across from and a few feet east of the foundation and is identified by a sign reading, Iron Mountain Trail, No. 3389.

Climb gradually through deep, lush woods for one-third mile where the trail makes one long switchback through a small meadow and then comes to the junction on the left of the Iron Mountain Cut-off Trail, No. 3389A. Stay to the right, continuing up the ridge, and then begin switchbacking up the very steep, grassy slope. You will see an "eye" in the rocks about 50 feet below the lookout after you have climbed part of the way up the slope.

The lookout is manned during the summer months and an extensive amount of forested country around the South Santiam River is visible from the rocky summit.

Iron Mountain lookout

Iron Mountain

63 CRESCENT MOUNTAIN CENTRAL OREGON

One day trip
Distance: 4 miles one way
Elevation gain: 2,140 feet
High point: 5,750 feet
Allow 2½ to 3 hours one way
Usually open late June through October
Topographic map:
U.S.G.S. Echo Mountain, Oreg.
N4415-W12200/15
1955

Slash burning from Crescent Mountain

It is wise to wait for a haze-free day in the spring to make the ascent of Crescent Mountain. At this time of year wild flowers are rampant on the steep slopes below the summit, and the view is virtually unmatched by any peak on the west side of the Cascade crest.

Drive about 44 miles east of Sweet Home on the South Santiam Highway, U.S. 20, and turn north on the Lava Lake Road, No. 1349, located about one-half mile west of the junction of Highway 126 to Clear Lake and Belknap Springs. Proceed north for 1.2 miles and turn left on Road No. 1349A. Continue for one-half mile to the end of the road at the trail head where a turnaround affords parking space for several cars.

The trail, No. 3384, starts above and about 100 feet south of the turnaround, and is posted with a sign saying, Crescent Mountain 4 miles. Facing west, take the trail to the left, which goes east about one-fourth mile through considerable uncut underbrush, then across a clearing to the woods. A large white sign marks the trail's entry into the woods.

The trail is essentially level until crossing Maude Creek at 1.5 miles, when it begins to climb. At 2.5 miles a sign at the edge of an avalanche scar points west to the North Side Sheep Camp, one mile. At three miles, the trail leaves the woods and continues upward across a large, open hillside below the east peak of Crescent Mountain. At the west end of this hillside, just below the point where a saddle comes into view on the skyline, the trail appears to vanish. Continue straight ahead, climbing at the same gradient, gradually contouring right to the saddle.

From the saddle to the summit of the peak the trail is again clear. At the site of the former fire lookout you can enjoy a magnificent panorama of the western Cascades. The view to the west is marred to some extent by the many clearcuts in the H. J. Andrews experimental forest. The lake to the north of Crescent Mountain is not named.

Mt. Jefferson from Crescent Mountain

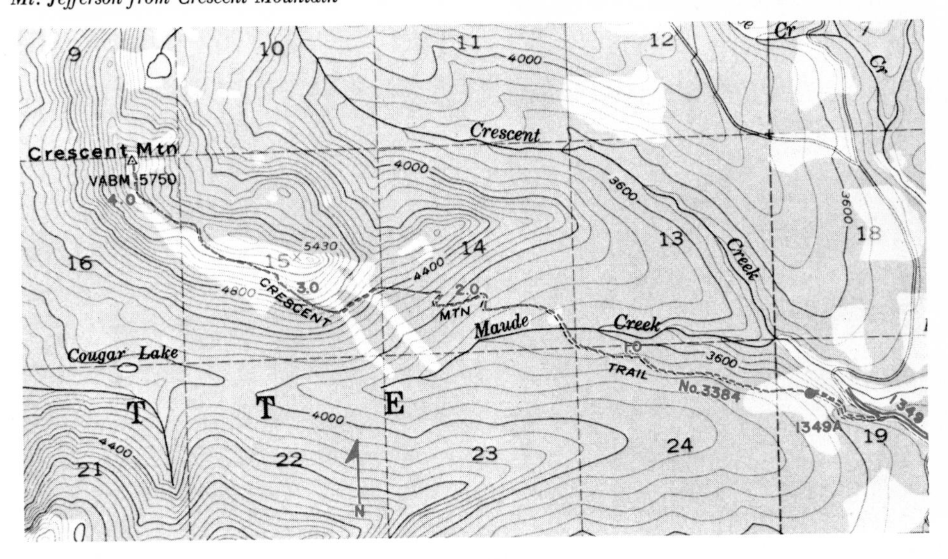

64 BLACK BUTTE CENTRAL OREGON

One day trip
Distance: 4 miles one way
Elevation gain: 2,916 feet
High point: 6,436 feet
Allow 2½ to 3 hours one way
Usually open late May through October
Topographic map:
U.S.G.S. Sisters, Oreg.
N4415-W12130/15
1959

This large and very symmetrical cinder cone is a familiar sight to those who have spent much time in Central Oregon. Since Black Butte stands well to the east of the Cascade crest, it is one of the few places commanding a broad, sweeping view of this side of the range.

If you are very quiet, you may hear marmots whistling at one another on the rocks near the lookout tower, which is manned during the summer fire season. The trail is dry so be sure to carry an ample supply of water.

Drive on U.S. Highway 20 west of the town of Sisters and turn north at the junction of Road 13048 leading to the Metolius River and Camp Sherman. Follow this road for a little over two miles and turn right on Road 113 at the sign pointing to the Black Butte Trail, one mile. Drive for 0.2 of a mile to the junction of Road 139E and turn right again. Continue for 1.2 miles being careful to follow the signs to the Black Butte Trail and keep on the road marked with a "1" symbol. Just after a short steep stretch of road you will see the trail head which is marked by a sign stating Black Butte Trail, No. 82. Here a dirt road runs perpendicular to Road 139E, and you can turn onto the side of it to park your car.

After 0.1 of a mile the dirt road narrows to a trail. Climb through open woods of pine and cedar for one-quarter mile to a logging road. The trail continues on the opposite side of the road and begins climbing again. Just before the one-mile point, the trail crosses another road and continues again a short distance to the south.

A little over a mile further you will come to a third road. Hike along it to the southeast for about 100 yards to its end and a sign pointing to the Black Butte Trail.

The trail then makes one long switchback through the woods and crosses a large open slope on the southwest side of the butte. Just before reaching the top, the trail curves around to the east side and winds through a rocky area dotted with evergreens. In addition to the lookout, several other small buildings and a weather station will be found on the summit. Black Butte Ranch is visible to the southwest at the base of the cone, and on a cloudless day you can see all the major peaks from Mt. Hood south to Broken Top.

The Three Sisters from Black Butte

Black Butte

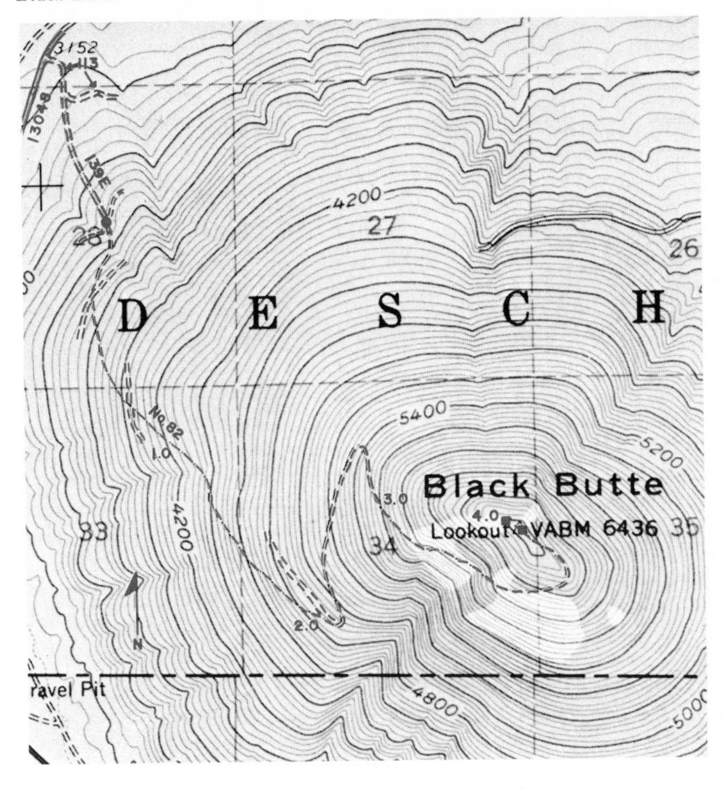

4200
27
26
28
D E S C H
5400
5200
No. 82
1.0
Black Butte
3.0
4.0
Lookout VABM 6436
33
34
35
2.0
N
ravel Pit
4800
5000

65 SMITH ROCKS CENTRAL OREGON

One day trip or backpack
Distance: 5 miles round trip
Elevation gain: 970 feet
High point: 3,480 feet
Allow 3 to 5 hours round trip
Usually open all year
Topographic maps:
- **U.S.G.S. O'Neil, Oreg. N4415-W12100/7.5 1962**
- **U.S.G.S. Gray Butte, Oreg. N4422.5-W12100/7.5 1962**
- **U.S.G.S. Redmond, Oreg. N4415-W12107.5/7.5 1962**
- **U.S.G.S. Opal City, Oreg. N4422.5-W12107.5/7.5 1962**

Smith Rocks is a cluster of spectacular formations east of the small Central Oregon community of Terrebonne, located on U.S. Highway 97, six miles north of Redmond.

Geologically, the area is a western segment of the John Day formation consisting of outcroppings of rhyolite and tuffs (fine volcanic fragments) rising above lava flows, one of which forced the Crooked River into its present circuitous course.

Smith Rocks is a virtual mecca for rock climbers. The most predominant rock is the 300-foot spire of Monkey Face, which overhangs on every side. It stands apart from the surrounding cliffs above the Crooked River on the northwestern side of the formation. Monkey Face was first surmounted by a group of climbers in January, 1960.

The five-mile long trail around the rocks is not difficult and offers many superb vistas of cliffs, farm fields, and the Crooked River, as well as the major snow capped peaks of Central and Northern Oregon.

Drive on U.S. Highway 97 to the town of Terrebonne. Turn east on B Avenue at a sign pointing to Smith Rock State Park. Cross the railroad tracks and continue east on Smith Rock Market Road. Turn left 2.4 miles from Highway 97 at a sign pointing to Smith Rock State Park. When 2.6 miles from the highway, turn right onto Lambert Road and follow it for 0.9 mile and turn left on an unpaved side road just west of the bridge crossing the main canal. Cross over the Crooked River on a narrow concrete bridge and, immediately after, turn left at the "Y" and follow the road paralleling the canal on the left. Park your car at a turnout just before the canal enters Tunnel No. 1.

To get to the trail, follow the canal road — known locally as the Burma Road — for 0.8 mile to a level area where it reaches its high point. Turn left and pick up the unmarked trail leading down to a rock knob. Here the trail turns to the right and descends behind a line of cliffs to a view point overlooking the Crooked River Gorge.

Follow the ridge crest down until you come to a barbed wire fence. Pass through the fence on its left end and move across to a ridge on the western skyline. Topping the ridge, you will see Monkey Face for the first time as it stands apart from the main row of cliffs to the south. Walk west along the ridge and drop down the steep slope which leads to the east bank of the Crooked River. Here a very clear trail follows along the bank underneath the many rock formations. It rounds the southern tip of Smith Rocks and proceeds north on the eastern side of the cliffs. You may find ducks and geese here at any time of the year, and during the spring months you sometimes will see nesting birds on the large rocks in the river. Just before the trail climbs back to the entrance to Tunnel No. 1, there is a short side trail to the right leading to several good camp sites. However, if you are planning to camp here, either bring adequate water, or chemically purify or boil the river water. During the warm months a snakebite kit would be a wise addition to your regular equipment.

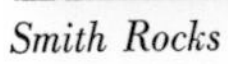

Smith Rocks

Monkey Face, Smith Rocks

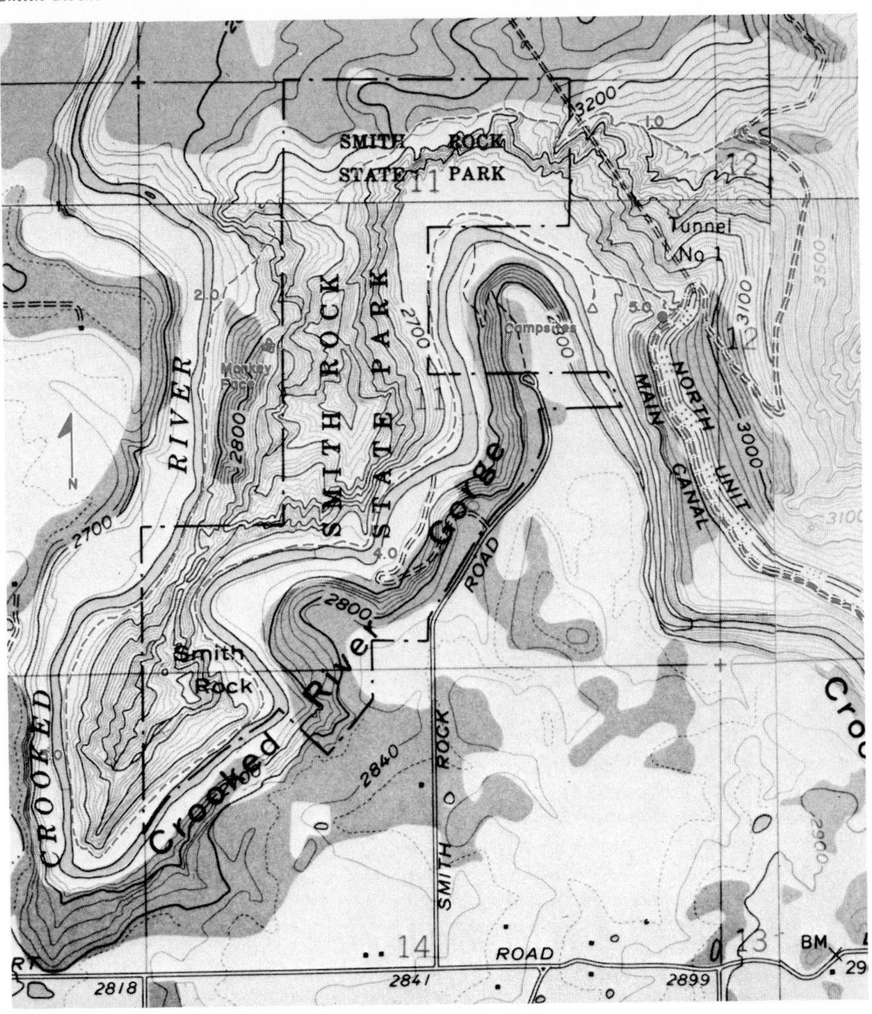

66 LITTLE BELKNAP CRATER CENTRAL OREGON

One day trip
Distance: 3 miles one way
Elevation gain: 1,155 feet
High point: 6,305 feet
Allow 1½ to 2 hours one way
Usually open July through October
Topographic map:
U.S.G.S. Three Fingered Jack, Oreg.
N4415-W12145/15
1959

This short hike to Little Belknap Crater should not be attempted without adequate boots, or thick rubber-soled shoes. The trail is carved out of the lava flow and is extremely abrasive. The volcanic throat at the crater is the source of the vast flow which covers many square miles of the McKenzie Pass region.

Drive on McKenzie Pass Highway, Oregon 242, between McKenzie Bridge and Sisters, to the Skyline Trail on the north side of the highway 0.4 mile west of the Dee Wright Observatory. A parking area is available off the highway at the trail head and will accommodate several cars. Carry an adequate supply of water as the trail is dry.

The Skyline trail, No. 2000, is marked by a sign pointing to Little Belknap Crater 3 miles, Washington Ponds 7 miles, Big Lake 13 miles, and Santiam Highway 16 miles. It starts in open woods, crosses a lava flow between two buttes, and then enters the woods again and contours around the north butte. The trail then turns sharply left and strikes out across the main lava flow and stays on it all the way up to Little Belknap Crater. During the last two miles you will see many bizarre shapes in the lava, including depressions, caves, tunnels, and a great many grotesque dead snags, which seem to have flourished for a time and then for some reason died.

At 2.5 miles, to the west side of Little Belknap Crater, a side trail to the right goes to the crater proper, site of a recent lava flow (in geologic measurement of time).

From the summit of the crater you will be able to see a close-up view of the southeastern face of Mt. Washington and also Three Fingered Jack and Mt. Jefferson to the north. To the south you can look down on the McKenzie Pass Highway and across to the Three Sisters and their numerous satellite peaks.

Dead tree near Little Belknap Crater

Mt. Washington from Little Belknap Crater

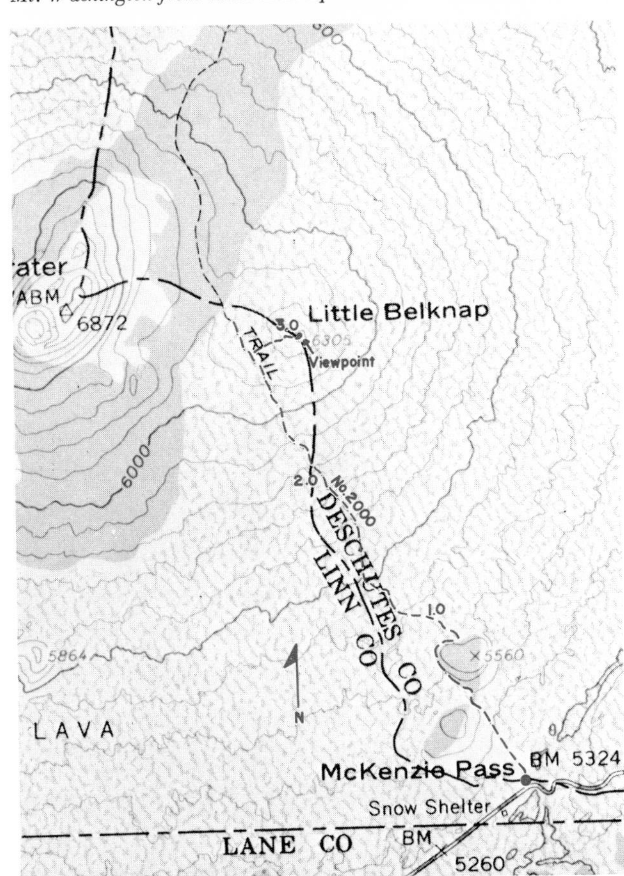

67 BLACK CRATER CENTRAL OREGON

One day trip
Distance: 3 miles one way
Elevation gain: 2,342 feet
High point: 7,251 feet
Allow 2 to 2½ hours one way
Usually open July through mid-October
Topographic maps:
U.S.G.S. Sisters, Oreg.
N4415-W12130/15
1959
U.S.G.S. Three Fingered Jack, Oreg.
N4415-W12145/15
1959

The symmetrical cone of Black Crater rises from the southeast edge of the McKenzie Lava Flow, and from its summit you can see many of the remains of Oregon's volcanic past. In addition to the massive lava beds, the once fiery summits of the Three Sisters and Broken Top stand out boldly only a few miles to the south.

Drive on the McKenzie Pass Highway, Oregon 242, east of the pass to a point 0.2 of a mile west of the 81-mile post. A sign on the north side of the highway points south across the pavement to the Black Crater Trail. Parking is available off the south side of the road on a turnaround next to the trailhead, which is marked by a sign pointing to the Black Crater Trail, No. 93. Be sure to carry water as none is to be found along the trail.

The trail climbs steadily in long switchbacks through dense forest for almost one mile, then it turns southeast and continues climbing in a more or less straight line. Frequently you will pass through small open grassy meadows. For the last one-half mile the trail switchbacks up the steep, tree-dotted rocky slopes below the summit ridge. When you come to the ridge, turn to the right (west) and walk a few hundred yards across the red volcanic rock to the site of the old lookout. From here you can look down on the north side of the mountain and see the actual crater about 700 feet below. Mt. Hood, Mt. Jefferson, Three Fingered Jack, and Mt. Washington are visible to the north, and Black Butte, Smith Rocks, and the city of Redmond can be seen to the east.

Three Sisters and Broken Top from summit of Black Crater

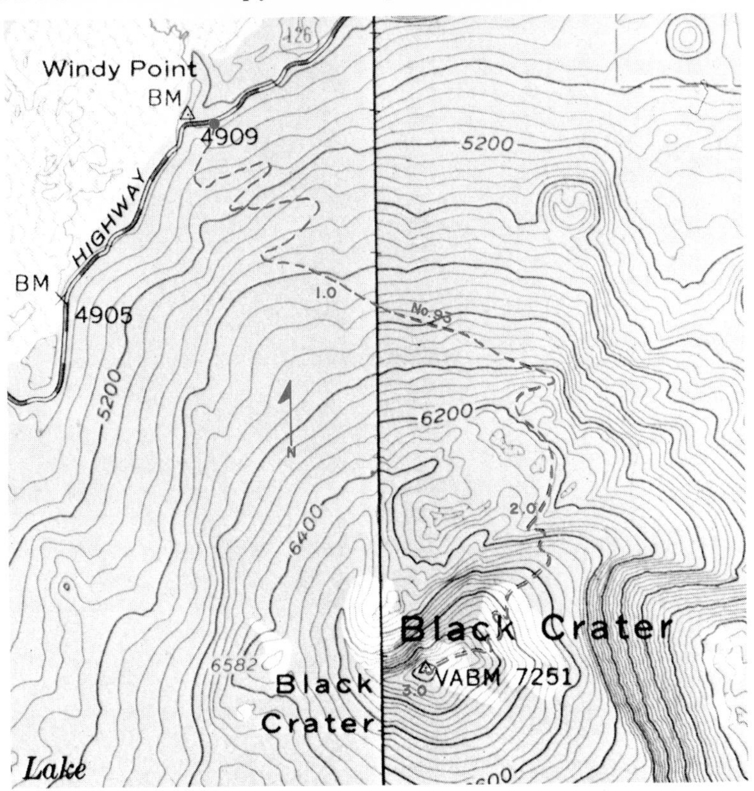

68 SCOTT MOUNTAIN CENTRAL OREGON

One day trip or backpack
Distance: 3 miles one way
Elevation gain: 1,246 feet
High point: 6,116 feet
Allow 2 hours one way
Usually open late June through October
Topographic map:
U.S.G.S. Three Sisters, Oreg.
N4400-W12145/15
1959

The trail to the wildflower-covered summit of Scott Mountain is short enough for you to have ample time to take the side trips to Benson and Tenas Lakes. From the summit is one of the best views of the west side of the Three Sisters.

Drive east of Belknap Springs on the McKenzie Pass Highway, Oregon 242, and turn west on Road 1532, one-third mile west of the 72-mile post. Follow the road for 0.9 mile past Scott Lake Camp to a fork in the road, where a sign reads Benson Trail, ¼ mile. Park here as the road to the left is not suitable for automobile travel. Carry water — there are no streams along the route.

Hike up the road about one-tenth mile to a sign on the right stating, Benson Trail, No. 3502. Turn to the right here and descend a short distance through open woods, then climb gradually for one mile to the junction of the trail to Benson Lake. The sign pointing to the lake is on the left hand side of the trail and is somewhat obscure. The path is almost level and passes several ponds and small meadows. Go around to the south shore for a view of Scott Mountain.

From the Benson Lake junction, climb gradually for three-quarters mile to the junction of the trail to Tenas Lake. The side trip to this long, narrow, rock-rimmed lake is recommended. It is deep enough for good swimming, and there is an excellent campsite on the north end. The main trail forks to the right and climbs through semi-open woods, gradually circling around to the eastern slope of the mountain. About one-quarter mile before the summit is the junction of the Hand Lake Trail, which drops steeply down to the right. Follow the trail around to the left and climb through the trees. Leave the woods and travel along open slopes around and up to the summit. The Little Brother and the Husband are visible in addition to Black, Belknap, and Little Belknap Craters and the peaks of Mt. Jefferson, Three Fingered Jack, and Mt. Washington. To the south at the base of the mountain are Scott, Benson, and Tenas Lakes.

Scott Mountain from Benson Lake

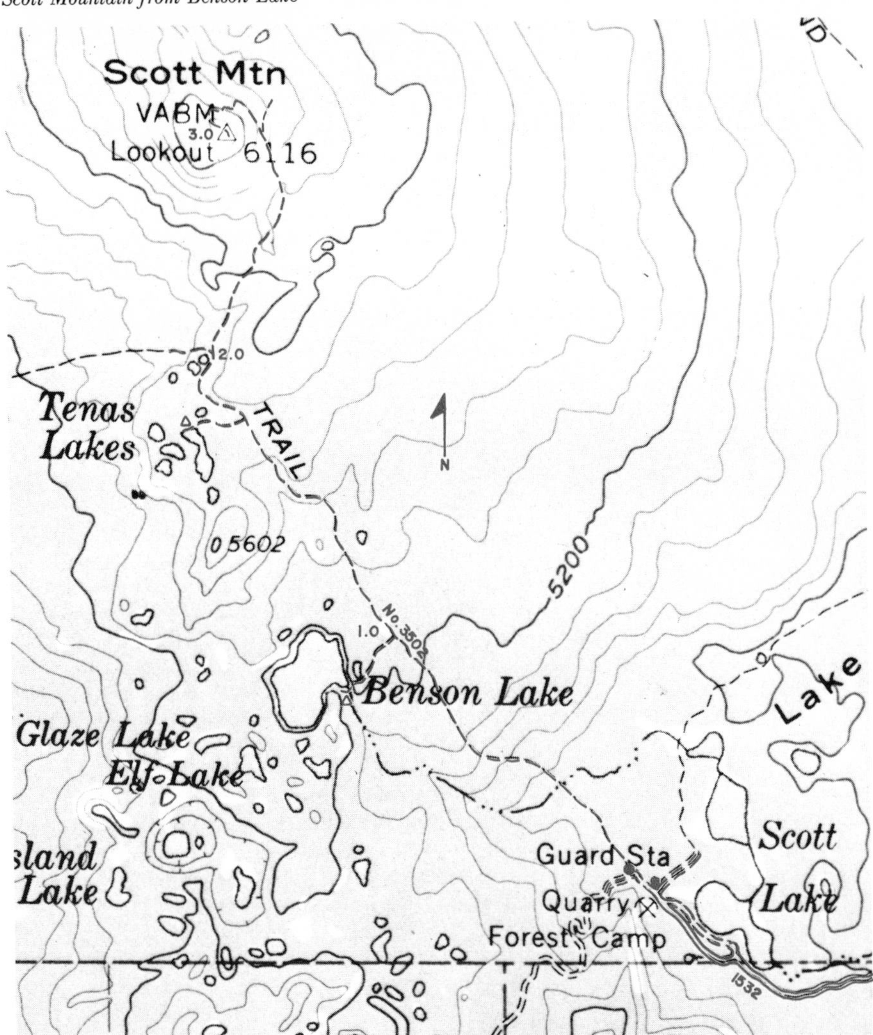

69 COLLIER GLACIER VIEW CENTRAL OREGON

One day trip or backpack
Distance: 7 miles one way
Elevation gain: 2,163 feet, loss 200 feet
High point: 7,150 feet
Allow 4 to 5 hours one way
Usually open mid-July through mid-October
Topographic maps:
U.S.G.S. Three Sisters, Oreg.
N4400-W12145/15
1959
U.S.G.S. Three Fingered Jack, Oreg.
N4415-W12145/15
1959

This part of the Skyline Trail takes you through lava fields, past small lakes, over the sides of several cinder cones, and across pumice flats to a startling view of the terminus of Collier Glacier, the largest glacier in Oregon. It originates between the North and Middle Sister, and flows north to a sink hole and a muddy lake surrounded by cliffs of dirt-covered ice.

Take the McKenzie Pass Highway, Oregon 242, to the Lava Camp Lake Road, one-quarter mile east of the Dee Wright Observatory and just west of the 78-mile post. Turn south on Road 1550 at the sign pointing to Lava Camp Lake and Millican Crater Trail and drive for 0.1 mile to the trail head where the road makes a sharp left turn. The trail sign is adjacent to the parking area and reads North Matthieu Lake 2 miles, Sunshine Shelter 9 miles, Horse Lake Guard Station 26 miles.

The trail, No. 2000, proceeds south along the east side of the lava flow, and at 1.7 miles climbs to North Matthieu Lake and a good campsite. The trail then contours along the west side of an unnamed butte to Scott Pass and South Matthieu Lake and another good camping place. Here, the Scott Trail, No. 95, drops down to Road 1535, four miles to the southeast.

From Scott Pass, continue south along the Skyline Trail which crosses a lava flow and contours around the north slopes of treeless Yapoah Center. At 5.2 miles is the junction of Trail 3531 to Scott Lake. Both trails are marked with cairns since the path crossing this sandy plain is hard to follow. Continue south, climbing gradually to Minnie Scott Springs at six miles. This is an ideal camping area, in the open next to a wide, sparkling spring which comes out of the hillside several hundred feet south of the trail.

Beyond the spring, the trail climbs to Oppie Dildock Pass at 6,890 feet. Several hundred yards down from the pass, where the trail turns west, you will see a large cairn marking the junction of the spur trail leading south to the rim of Collier Cone and Collier Glacier Viewpoint.

A grand panorama of the North and Middle Sisters and Collier Glacier awaits you at this spot. Use extreme caution if you hike down to the lake below the North Sister as quicksand may be encountered in some places due to the action of water seeping up through the volcanic sand.

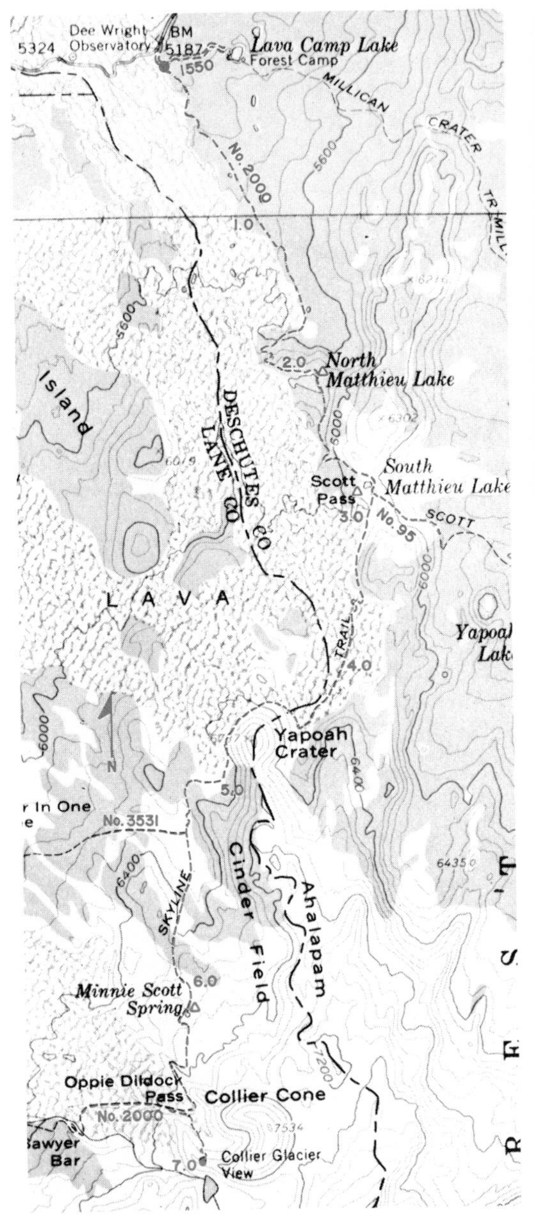

Collier Glacier from Collier Glacier View

North Sister from Collier Glacier View

70 EILEEN AND HUSBAND LAKES CENTRAL OREGON

One day trip or backpack
Distance: 9 miles one way
Elevation gain: 2,450 feet, loss 920 feet
High point: 6,700 feet
Allow 6 to 8 hours one way
Usually open July through October
Topographic map:
U.S.G.S. Three Sisters, Oreg.
N4400-W12145/15
1959

The trail to Sunshine Shelter is the standard access route to the Three Sisters area from the McKenzie Pass Highway and is used by climbers attempting the North and Middle Sister. An interesting feature of this area is the great quantity of obsidian, a volcanic, glass-like material found between the lava flow on the north and Lane Plateau on the south.

Drive along the McKenzie Pass Highway (U.S. 126) to the Frog Campground Road, No. 1634, located on the east side of the highway about six miles southwest of the pass.

The trail, No. 3528, begins one-quarter mile from the highway at the south end of the campground. For the first few miles it rises gently through the forest. At 1.5 miles, a way trail to the right leads to Lupine Spring, the only water source on this portion of the route. At three miles, the trail winds through a quarter-mile wide lava flow originating in the vicinity of Collier Cone. On the southern side of the flow, at 3.5 miles, is White Branch Creek, another water source. At this point Trail 3528 becomes the Skyline Trail, No. 2000.

Side Trip: On the south side of White Branch Creek, the unmarked trail follows the creek east to Oppie Dildock Pass and Collier Glacier view point.

Sunshine Shelter at 6,000 feet, is reached at four miles on the Skyline Trail. This shelter is a rather large, open-ended structure and out buildings are provided. Excellent campsites may be found here and also at Scott Camp, one-third mile up the trail. At Scott Camp, adjacent to Glacier Creek, there are open meadows with numerous timbered hillocks where tents can be placed for some wind protection.

From Scott Camp, the Skyline Trail, No. 2000, is marked by a large cairn on top of a bluff to the right (southwest). The trail can be reached also directly from Sunshine Shelter. It passes several small tarns near Sister Spring and then leads to another camping area at the top of Obsidian Falls, a good subject for photographers.

A descent of about 200 feet is made to Obsidian Camp near a small butte, elevation 6,543 feet. Follow the sign marked Linton Meadows Trail 4 miles. The trail turns left, climbs to a ridged plateau on the western shoulder of the Middle Sister. At the 7.2 mile point, turn right at a sign saying "Trail Abandoned" and descend one mile with an elevation loss of 560 feet to Linton Meadows. At the edge of the meadows the Eileen Lake Trail is marked by cairns on the right. Follow this trail to the Linton Creek crossing, then up to the lake, which is situated at 6,200 feet on a bench between the Husband and a small butte on the north.

To get to Husband Lake, continue across the meadows on the Linton Meadows Trail for almost a mile where a way trail to the right follows a clear area to the lake at an elevation of 6,060 feet. Both of these lakes are in semi-open meadows, offering several camp sites and excellent views of the Husband and the Three Sisters.

Scott Camp

Obsidian Falls

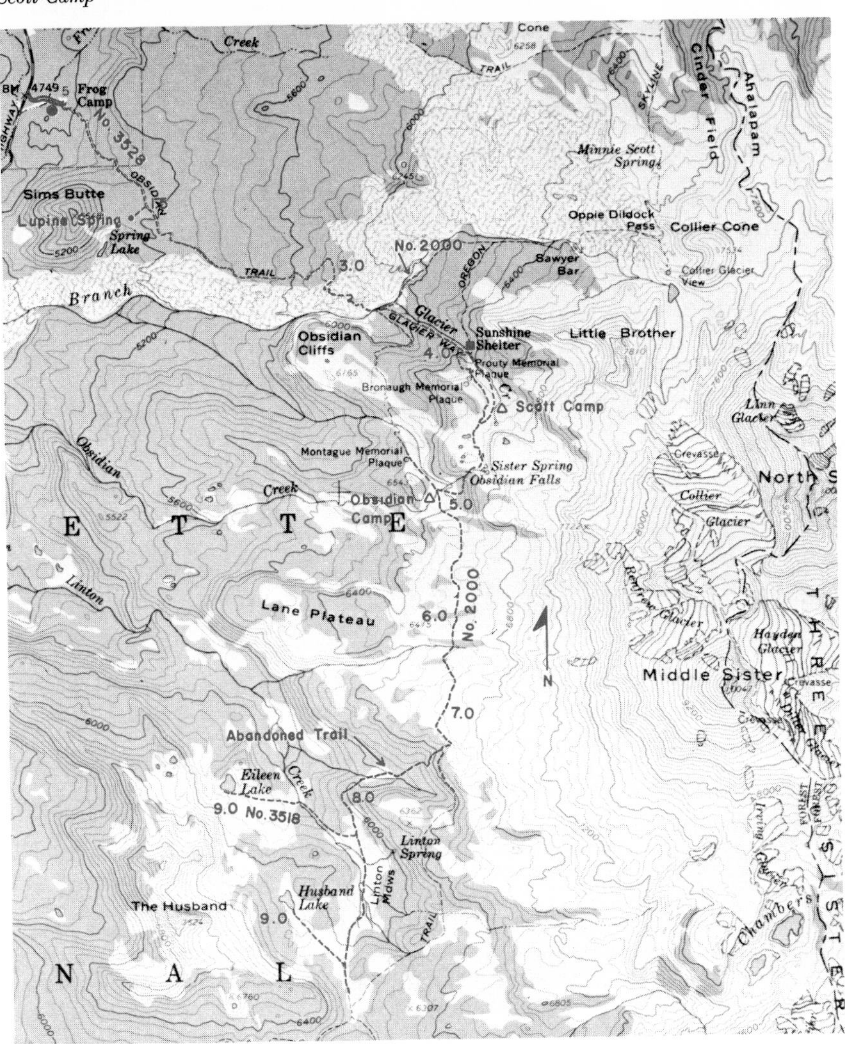

71 HORSEPASTURE MOUNTAIN CENTRAL OREGON

One day trip or backpack
Distance: 5.5 miles one way
Elevation gain: 3,180 feet, loss 240 feet
High point: 5,660 feet
Allow 4 to 5 hours one way
Usually open late June through October
Topographic map:
U.S.G.S.McKenzie Bridge, Oreg.
N4400-W12200/15
1955

Rows of iris and a crumbling rock fence surround the foundation of the lookout which once stood on the summit of Horsepasture Mountain. Black, Belknap, and Little Belknap Craters and peaks from Mt. Jefferson south to Broken Top can be seen from the top.

Take the McKenzie Highway, U.S. 126, to the community of McKenzie Bridge. Near the center of town turn south onto the North Bank Road and just after crossing the McKenzie River turn south again at the Willamette National Forest Work Center onto Horse Creek Road. Cross a covered bridge over Horse Creek and turn left onto Road 161. Continue past Horse Creek Campground to a junction, and turn right here onto Road 1667, following the signs to Olallie Trail. Drive three miles to the trailhead on the right side of the road, which is marked by a sign that reads, Olallie Trail, No. 3529. Carry water as there is none west of Horsepasture Pass.

The trail climbs steadily, but gradually, switching from one side of the ridge to the other. The difference in vegetation as you cross from the north to south slope is remarkable. On the south slope there is little undergrowth and madrone trees mix with a few evergreens to create the appearance of a dry, brown-colored forest. The more moist northern side, however, is a lush green and the large trees and abundant ground cover combine for a cool, shaded effect. As you gain elevation through the woods, both sides of the ridge become uniformly dense. One mile before coming to Horsepasture Pass the trail traverses along heavily brush-covered slopes where you can look east to Horsepasture Mountain.

Of the network of trails leading from Horsepasture Pass, the one to Horsepasture Mountain is the only trail that climbs. It is marked by a yellow "Closed to Motor Vehicles" sign. Climb gradually along the slope, crossing many logs, and come to a small spring about one-quarter mile from the shelter. (The spring may be dry in the late summer.) A short distance further the trail leaves the woods and climbs along a brushy slope. Although obscure in some places, the trail is generally discernible and switchbacks several times before coming to the open summit ridge where it turns north. To facilitate locating the trail on your return trip, be sure to note the place where it meets the ridge.

Remains of storage cave, Horsepasture Mountain

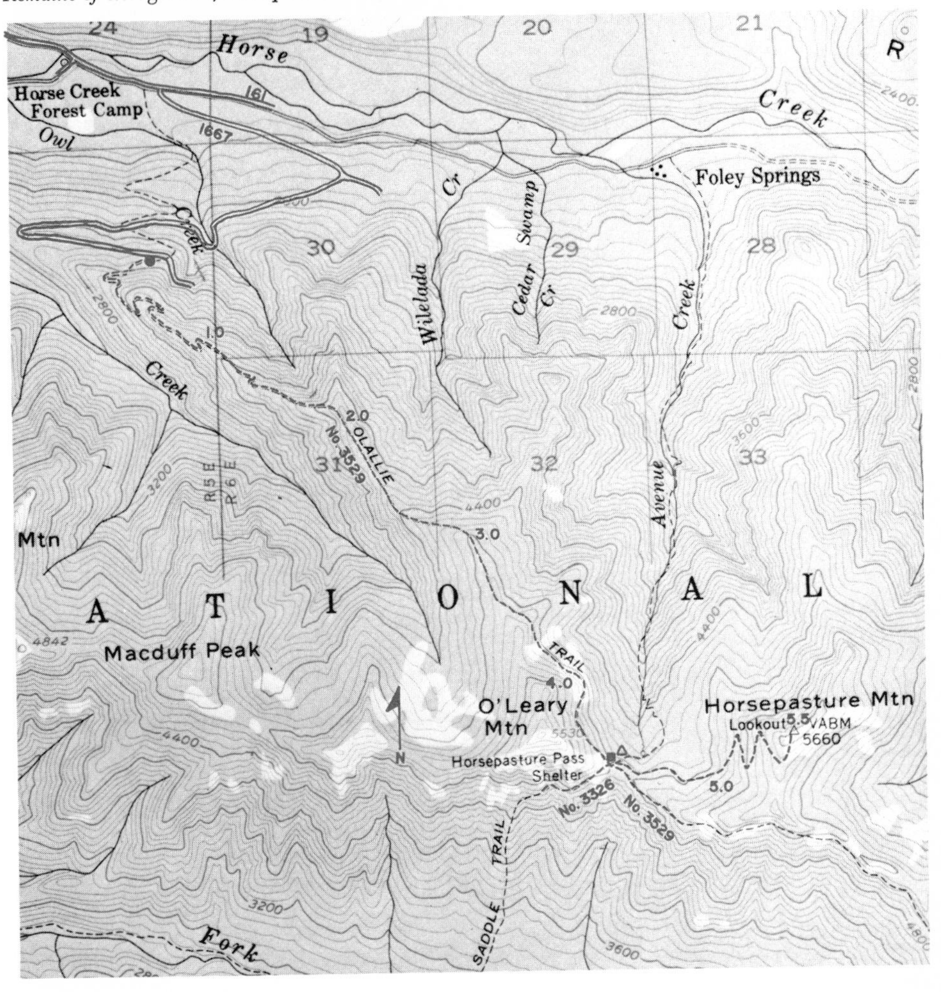

72 GREEN LAKES CENTRAL OREGON

One day trip or backpack
Distance: 6 miles one way
Elevation gain: 1,110 feet
High point: 6,550 feet
Allow 3 to 4 hours one way
Usually open from mid-July to mid-October
Topographic map:
U.S.G.S. Broken Top, Oreg.
N4400-W12130/15
1959

This is one of the most popular trails in the Three Sisters Area. The lakes border the eastern slopes of the South Sister at an altitude of 6,500 feet in a beautiful setting of scattered trees, meadows, and pumice fields. When the wind is calm, South Sister's early morning reflection in the lakes is a magnificent sight.

Drive westward from Bend 28 miles along the Cascade Lakes Highway (formerly Century Drive) past Bachelor Butte to the Fall Creek Bridge just north of Sparks Lake. A sign on the west side of the bridge points north to a side road leading to the Green Lakes Trail, No. 17. Turn right and proceed 0.2 mile to a parking area at the start of the trail where a sign reads Green Lakes, 6 miles.

For most of its distance the trail follows Fall Creek, and numerous falls and rapids are almost constantly in view. About one-third mile up the trail a sign points to an unnamed 30-foot falls 300 feet to the right. A path leads to the bottom of the falls, 50 feet below the main trail.

At three miles a side trail, No. 17B, leads off to the left two miles to Moraine Lake. Shortly thereafter the trail crosses a small side stream and Fall Creek on separate foot bridges and then approaches a large lava flow on the left. At the edge of the lava flow it climbs in switchbacks about 300 feet to a meadow alongside Fall Creek.

On a rise at the north end of the meadow a sign shows Green Lakes, one-half mile to the right. However, since the trail completely encircles the two largest lakes, you can proceed in either direction.

On the northeast side of Lower Green Lake (elevation 6,550 feet), is a trail south to Todd Lake and Crater Canal, five miles away.

The best camping sites are on the eastern shore of the large lake on high ground where there is abundant water. Fishing is good here, although most trout are rather small.

The area is often used as a base camp for climbers attempting South Sister and Broken Top.

South Sister and Green Lake

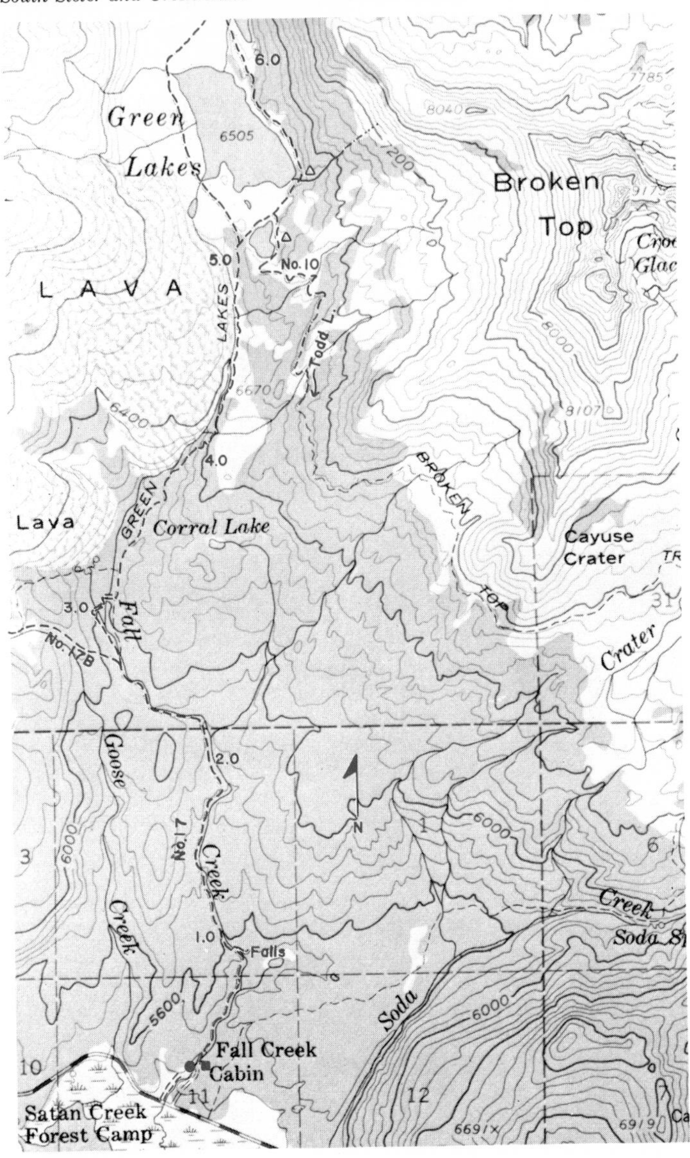

73 SISTERS MIRROR LAKE CENTRAL OREGON

One day trip or backpack
Distance: 5 miles one way
Elevation gain: 520 feet, loss 240 feet
High point: 6,120 feet
Allow 3 hours one way
Usually open from mid-July through October
Topographic map:
U.S.G.S. Three Sisters, Oreg.
N4400-W12145/15
1959

Sisters Mirror Lake is located a few miles southwest of the South Sister on a rolling plain that alternates between woods, meadows, and lakes. Within an area of less than a square mile are 29 lakes varying in size from a few feet to several hundred yards in diameter. Most of the lakes are shallow and afford good swimming in the late summer. The summit of the South Sister is visible from as far north as Sisters Mirror Lake.

Proceed west from Bend on the Cascade Lakes Highway (formerly Century Drive) past Bachelor Butte to Devils Lake. At the west end of the lake the highway turns to the southwest. Almost through the turn on the right side of the road is a dirt road and a sign that reads Wickiup Plains 3 miles, Skyline Trail 4 miles, and Mirror Lake 5 miles. Turn right and follow the dirt road a short distance to the turnaround at the trailhead, where you will find ample parking. The trail crosses Tyee Creek on a board bridge and climbs steadily on an abandoned road bed. (Tyee Creek is the only water source between the highway and Mirror Lake.)

One mile from the highway turn right at a sign marking the Elk Lake junction (Trail 12A). The trail continues to climb until it reaches the eastern end of Wickiup Plain. Here a side trail (12B) to the right goes behind Kaleetan Butte to Moraine Lake 4 miles and Green Lakes 9 miles.

Continue across the plain to the base of The House Rock where Trail 12 joins the Skyline Trail, No. 2000. Turn left and follow the Skyline Trail. At 4.5 miles you will reach the trail to Nash Lake, No. 3527. Stay to the left on the Skyline Trail and continue on to the edge of the next meadow where it joins the Mirror Lake Trail, No. 20. Stay to the right and continue one-half mile to Sisters Mirror Lake, the first of a cluster of lakes.

Good campsites can be found almost anywhere, and ample firewood and horse pasturing areas are available.

Sisters Mirror Lake

74 BACHELOR BUTTE CENTRAL OREGON

One day trip
Distance: 2 miles one way
Elevation gain: 2,580 feet
High point: 9,065 feet
Allow 2 to 3 hours one way
Usually open mid-July through October
Topographic maps:
U.S.G.S. Bachelor Butte, Oreg.
N4352.5-W12137.5/7.5
1963
U.S.G.S. Broken Top, Oreg.
N4400-W12130/15
1959

Bachelor Butte is best known as a prime ski area, for its winter and spring climate provides some of the best ski conditions in Oregon. Although the altitude and the scrambling over rocks to reach the summit make this seem more like an easy mountain climb than a short hike, there are no technical problems and the view is superb. The dominant features to the north are the Three Sisters and the crater of Broken Top. To the south you will be able to see Waldo Lake, Wickiup Reservoir, Davis Lake, and many of the other lakes that are so plentiful in this area.

Remember that the weather can deteriorate quickly on a peak this size so carry adequate protection against wind, rain, and cold. Also, carry water as there is none along the trail.

Drive on the Cascade Lakes Highway (formerly known as Century Drive) about 22 miles west of Bend and turn left at the sign pointing to the Bachelor Butte Ski Area. When the road forks, take the left branch to the upper parking lot.

Follow the cat road, which begins near the lower terminal of the chair lift, for one mile as it winds up the mostly open slope. Continue along this road to its end past the poma lift towers some distance above the chair lift. From here scramble up the rocks along the ridge to the west of the permanent snowfield. Just before the summit you will come to a flat area from where the trail to the top can be spotted easily.

For a better view of the lakes to the south as well as a sheltered place from the prevailing southwest wind, walk east along the summit and drop down slightly to a bench and continue a short distance further to a second flat area.

Bachelor Butte from Sparks Lake

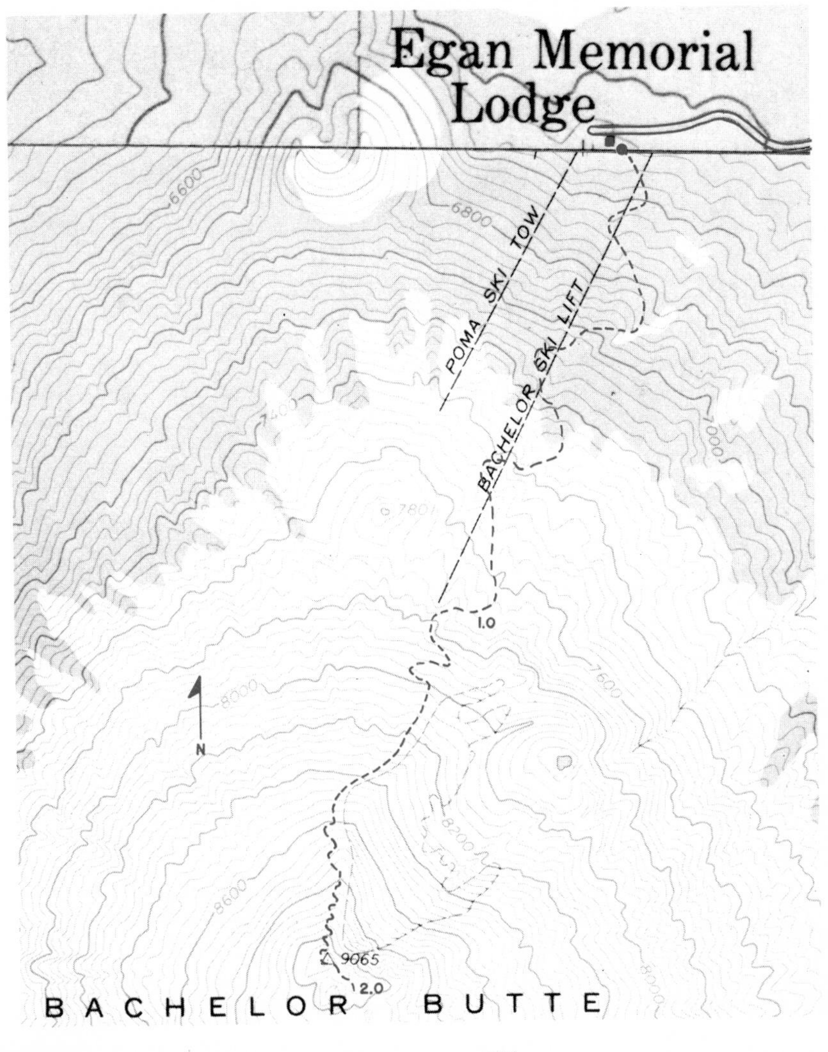
Egan Memorial
Lodge
6600
6800
POMA SKI TOW
BACHELOR SKI LIFT
7400
7000
7801
1.0
7600
8000
N
8200
8600
9065
2.0
8000
BACHELOR BUTTE

75 MINK LAKE BASIN CENTRAL OREGON

Backpack
Distance: 8 miles one way
Elevation gain: 1,650 feet, loss 1,035 feet
High point: 5,820 feet
Allow 3½ to 4½ hours one way
Usually open from late June through mid-November
Topographic maps:
U.S.G.S. Elk Lake, Oreg.
N4352.5-W12145/7.5
1963
U.S.G.S. Packsaddle Mtn., Oreg.
N4352.5-W12152.5/7.5
1963

Several large lakes and numerous ponds accent this generally level trail which travels through both the Deschutes and Willamette National Forests. There are large, well-maintained shelters at two of the lakes.

From Bend take the Cascade Lakes Highway (formerly Century Drive) past Bachelor Butte and Sparks Lake to the south end of Elk Lake. A parking area is on the west side of the road at the trailhead by a large sign stating, Six Lakes Trail No. 14, Blow Lake 1 mile, Doris Lake 3 miles, Senoj Lake 5 miles.

Hike through open timber along a level trail for one mile to the Blow Lake junction. Turn left here and cross a bridge, following the Trail 14 signs. Continue through more dense woods past Blow Lake to a junction just before reaching Doris Lake. Turn to the left here, again following the Trail 14 marker.

Climb gradually for one-half mile before coming to a level, lightly timbered area. Just beyond the three-mile point is the Senoj Lake junction (Trail 14B). Keep to the right here, on Trail 3534, and climb gradually through the woods to the ridge crest which forms the boundary between the Deschutes and Willamette National Forests. Then descend for a mile to the junction with the Skyline Trail, No. 2000, near Ledge Lake.

Turn to the left and continue on the level trail, No. 2000, past many small meadows and two small lakes. About one-fourth mile past the second lake is a rock-slide which marks another junction. Signs at this point state Mink Lake Loop Trail, Mink Lake Side Trail 1 mile, Mink Lake Shelter 1 mile. An unofficial sign indicates that Cliff Lake is 150 yards to the south. There is a good shelter at this scenic lake.

From this junction take the downslope trail, No. 3526, to Mink Lake. Do not take the Skyline Trail. Descend steeply and go past Porky Lake and continue one mile beyond to Mink Lake. Turn to the right at the junction just before the lake to reach an excellent shelter. All water must be obtained from the lakes.

Mink Lake Basin from the southwest

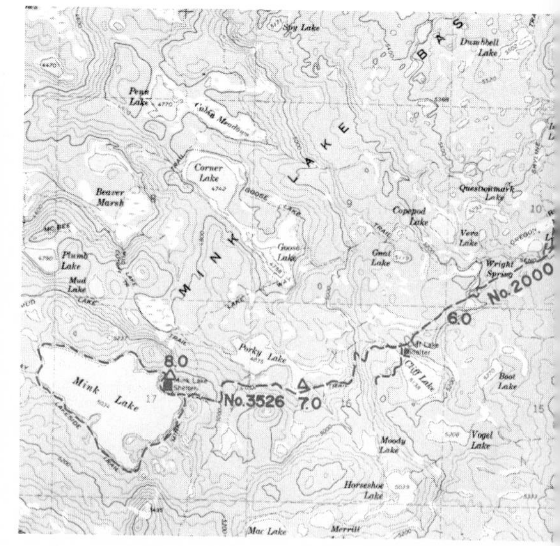

Mink Lake

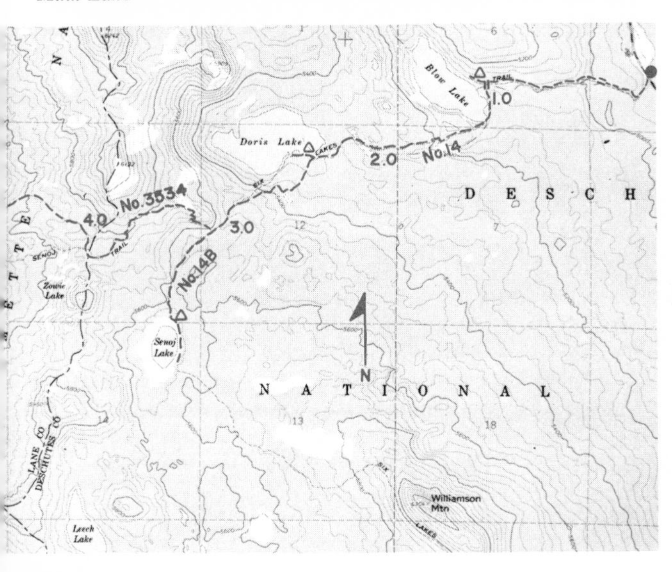

Blow Lake
1.0
Doris Lake
2.0
No.14
D E S C H
No.3534
4.0
3.0
No.14B
Zowie Lake
Senoj Lake
N
N A T I O N A L
LANE CO
DESCHUTES CO
Williamson Mtn
Leech Lake

76 ERMA BELL LAKES CENTRAL OREGON

One day trip or backpack
Distance: 3 miles one way
Elevation gain: 330 feet
High point: 4,780 feet
Allow 1½ hours one way
Usually open late June through October
Topographic map:
U.S.G.S. Chucksney Mt., Oreg.
N4345-W12200/15
1955

Lower and Middle Erma Bell Lakes

This region of five large lakes lies on a bench above the North Fork of the Willamette River and is a favorite among fishermen. The wide, well-maintained trail is quite short with very little gain in elevation. All of the lakes have been stocked with rainbow trout. In the fall, large flocks of ducks may be seen on the lower and middle lakes. Excellent campsites are available at each lake.

Drive 36 miles east of Eugene on the Willamette Pass Highway, Oregon 58, and turn north at the Westfir junction across the highway from the Oakridge Ranger Station. When you reach the lumber mill at Westfir, keep to the left at the green covered bridge and take the gravel road under the railroad bridge, on the far side of which the pavement begins again. You are now on the North Fork Road, No. 196. Drive north and then east on this road for about 31 miles to the junction of Road 163 at Box Canyon. Turn right and follow Road 163 south for 3.7 miles to the Skookum Creek Forest Camp. The Erma Bell Trail, No. 3563, starts on the south end of the large parking area and is marked by a sign that provides mileages to the various lakes.

The trailhead also can be approached from the north by taking the McKenzie Highway (U.S. 126) to Road 1663, five miles west of McKenzie Bridge. Turn south on Road 1663 and follow the signs to Cougar Dam. Continue to the south end of Cougar reservoir, where the road number changes to 163, and remain on that road past Box Canyon Guard Station to Skookum Creek Campground.

Cross a footbridge over Skookum Creek and continue on the level trail for three-quarters mile where you will pass the junction of the Otter Lake Trail, No. 3588, on your left. Otter Lake is only one-half mile from this junction and offers good fishing and good places to camp. The trail leading southeast from the lake has been abandoned.

Lower Erma Bell Lake is reached at one and three-quarter miles. The trail then crosses the outlet creek on a bridge and climbs about 200 feet to the middle lake. The upper lake is three-quarters mile further, and a faint trail on the right leads down to its shore.

Middle Erma Bell Lake

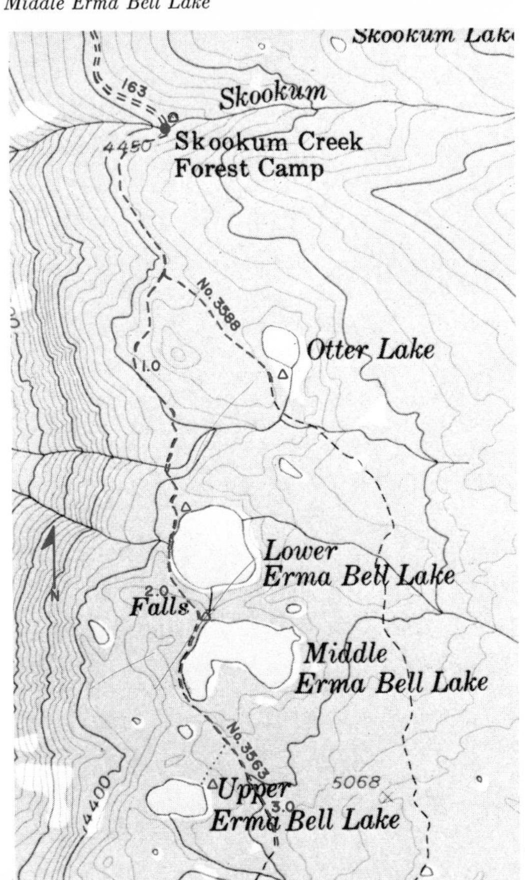

77 HARDESTY MOUNTAIN CENTRAL OREGON

One day trip
Distance: 3.8 miles one way
Elevation gain: 3,263 feet
High point: 4,273 feet
Allow 3 to 4 hours one way
Usually open June through November
Topographic map:
U.S.G.S. Hardesty Mtn., Oreg.
N4345-W12230/15
1955

Lush rain forest and views of Lookout Point Reservoir highlight this hike, which is only about 30 miles southeast of Eugene. There are a few steep places, but overall the trail grade is moderate as it climbs along the crest of a ridge. Be sure to carry water as there are no creeks along the trail.

Take the Willamette Pass Highway (Oregon 58) to a large parking area on the south side of the road between the 20 and 21-mile markers at the reservoir backwater at Goodman Creek. The trailhead is a dirt road bordering the eastern side of the parking spot and is identified by a sign reading, Hardesty Trail No. 3469.

Hike south along this road, which goes straight for a short distance and then turns left and begins climbing. Continue straight ahead at the second turn to the left. A large blaze marks the beginning of the actual trail, which leads off to the right.

The trail climbs gradually through rain forest for about three-fourths mile. Then, for one-half mile, it becomes quite steep, but after coming to a bench, it follows the ridge crest at a more moderate grade. (NOTE: the mile markers seen periodically on the trees were put there when the trail began at the north side of what is now the reservoir, and are therefore inaccurate.) At three miles the trail begins to switchback. At 3.5 miles a sign on the downslope side of the trail states, Eula Ridge Way, Willamette Highway 4 miles. After one more switchback the trail winds through an open grassy area. Just after re-entering the woods there is a second junction. A sign here states, Eagles Rest Trail 8½ miles, Mt. June Way 2½ miles, Willamette Divide Trail 1/7th mile. Keep to the left and proceed through a clearing and a few feet beyond to the summit.

Diamond Peak dominates the eastern view and Lookout Point Reservoir can be seen below to the north.

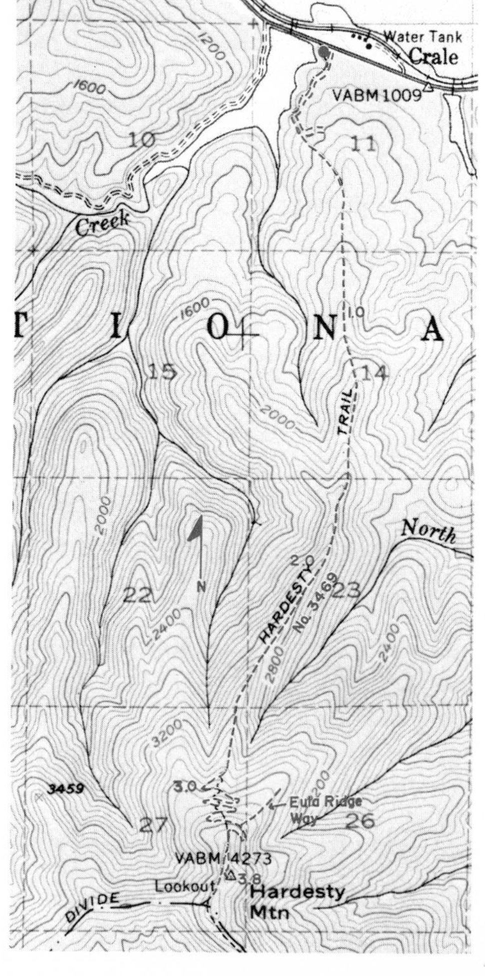

Rain Forest on Hardesty Mountain Trail

78 FUJI MOUNTAIN CENTRAL OREGON

One day trip or backpack
Distance: 5.5 miles one way
Elevation gain: 2,314 feet
High point: 7,144 feet
Allow 3 to 3½ hours one way
Usually open late June through October
Topographic map:
U.S.G.S. Waldo Lake, Oreg.
N4330-W12200/15
1956

Unlike its Japanese namesake, Oregon's Fuji Mountain is not symmetrical and has rocky cliffs on the north side of the summit. A side trip to the Island Lakes, so named because of the two tree-dotted islands, offers a good place to camp if you wish to make this a two-day trip.

Drive east of McCredie Springs on the Willamette Pass Highway (Oregon 58) and about five miles east of the tunnel turn north onto Road 223 at the sign pointing to Gold Lake and the Gold Lake Ranger Station. Continue along this road past the trail heads to Marilyn Lake and Maiden Peak. Go through the Gold Lake Campground and cross over a bridge. A few hundred feet further you will come to a sign stating that the road is closed beyond that point. There is ample space here to park your car.

Walk along the road about 100 yards beyond the closure sign and come to a sign marking the beginning of the Gold Lake Trail, No. 3677. Just before this sign is an unmarked trail leading off to the left. Follow this path a short distance to the Waldo Lake Road (no parking space here). Cross the pavement and walk to the northwest (right) a short distance to a sign that reads Fuji Mountain Trail, No. 3674.

Lily pads, Fuji Mountain Trail

The trail climbs steeply through the woods for the first quarter mile then ascends very gradually, passing several ponds, to the junction of the South Waldo Trail, No. 3586, at the three-mile point. If you wish to make the short side trip to the Island Lakes, be sure to continue on to Upper Island Lake where you can see the summit of Fuji Mountain.

Keep to the left and when the trail forks, about 100 feet after the junction, keep to the right, following an unofficial sign pointing to Fuji Mountain. Continue through the woods, periodically contouring around open and rocky slopes. At the four-mile point come to the junction on the left of the David Douglas Trail, No. 3661. Veer to the right and then step down a few feet and turn right. The trail climbs gradually, curving around a bowl-like slope and then switchbacks up to the rocky summit. This is one of the few accessible high points from which you can look down upon Waldo and Odell Lakes. The major peaks from Mt. Jefferson south to Mt. Thielsen are visible, and Diamond Peak is nearby to the south.

Waldo Lake from Fuji Mountain

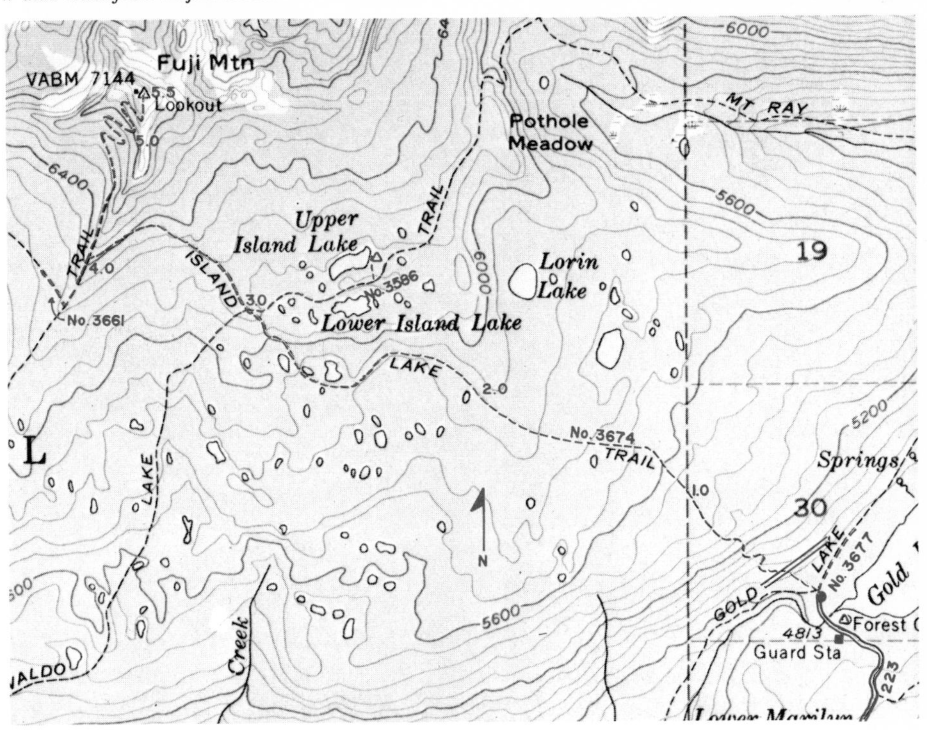

79 MAIDEN PEAK CENTRAL OREGON

One day trip
Distance: 5.5 miles one way
Elevation gain: 2,748 feet
High point: 7,818 feet
Allow 3 to 4 hours one way
Usually open July through October
Topographic maps:
U.S.G.S. The Twins, Oreg.
N4337.5-W12152.5/7.5
1963
U.S.G.S. Waldo Lake, Oreg.
N4330-W12200/15
1956

The crater of Maiden Peak is alongside the trail so you will be able to examine the source of this large cinder cone. The last one-half mile of the trail is obscure, adding a particular challenge to the final portion of the climb. Many major peaks and large lakes are visible from the summit.

Drive east of McCredie Springs on the Willamette Pass Highway (Oregon 58) and about five miles east of the tunnel turn north on Road 223 at the sign pointing to Gold Lake and Gold Lake Guard Station. Continue along this road for 1.6 miles to the trail head, which is marked by a sign.

The trail, No. 3681, climbs through the trees for a short distance and then contours along wooded slopes for one and three-quarter miles to Skyline Creek. This is the only water on the trip so be sure and fill your water bottles here. Just beyond the creek you will reach the junction of the Oregon Skyline Trail, No. 2000 and Wait Here Camp. Continue straight ahead coming to an open area and then begin climbing steeply as you re-enter the woods. The trail eventually becomes less steep and winds through a boulder-strewn forest.

Mushrooms on Maiden Peak Trail

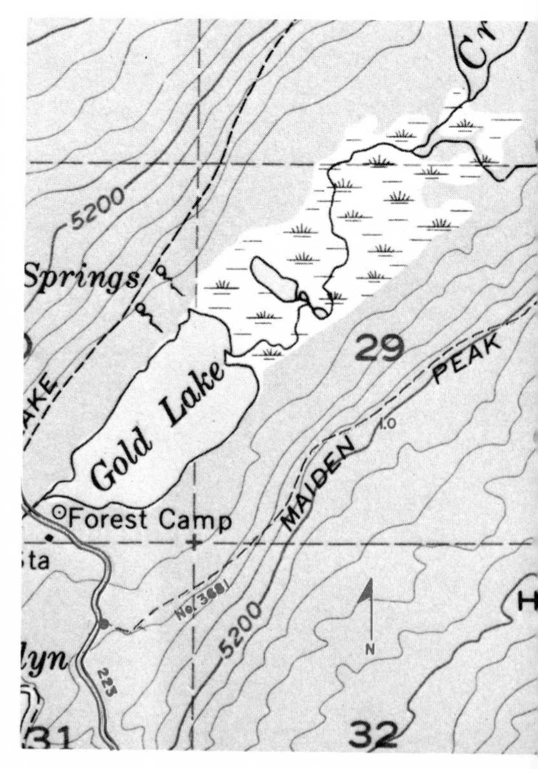

After the four-mile marker, begin climbing steeply again. The trail is faint in some places, but the trees are well blazed. You will come to a bench where there is a small, open, sandy area scattered with very small evergreens. Head for a big snag on the right where the trail again becomes obvious. Contour along the semi-open slope, and about one-quarter mile past the five-mile marker, turn to the left and head for the summit. If you have trouble keeping on the trail there are several wires coming down from the former lookout station which can be used as guides. However, be sure and note prominent landmarks so you will be able to find the route on the return trip.

The crater of Maiden Peak is just below the summit, at the beginning of the first switchback. The summit is quite large and flat; if you need a windbreak you can descend a short distance down to the east slope to some large rocks. Waldo Lake, Wickiup Reservoir, and Davis Lake — the large one below the peak to the east — can be seen from the summit.

Davis Lake from the north slope of Maiden Peak

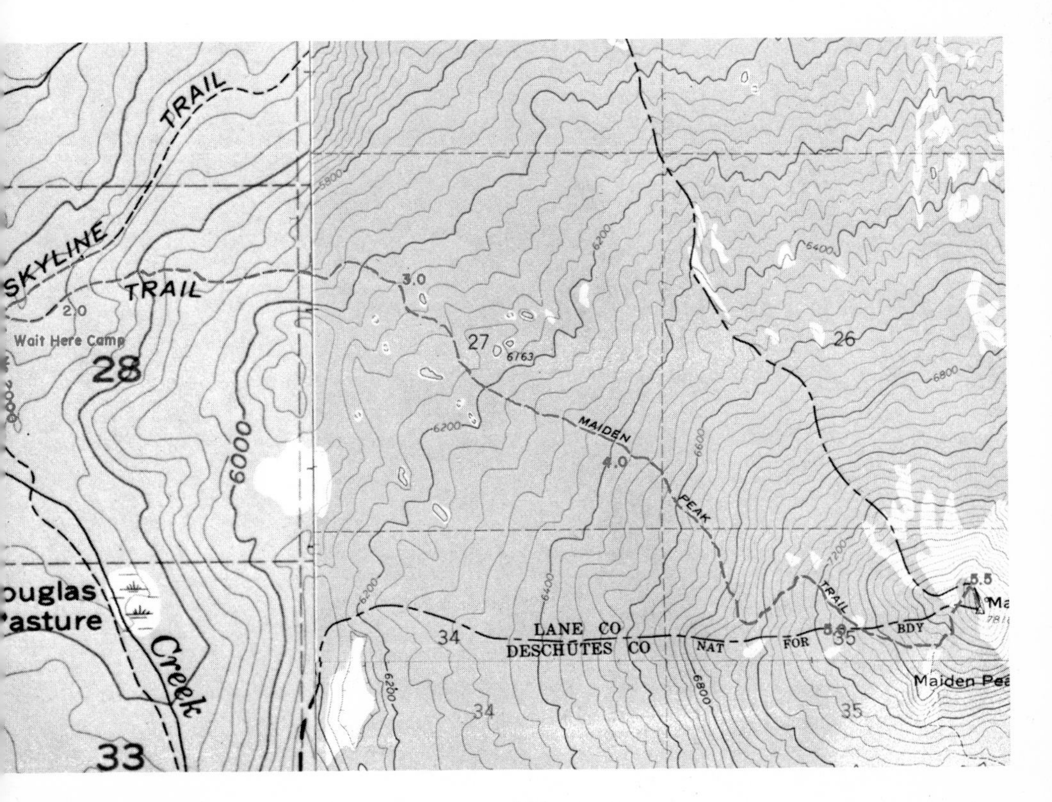

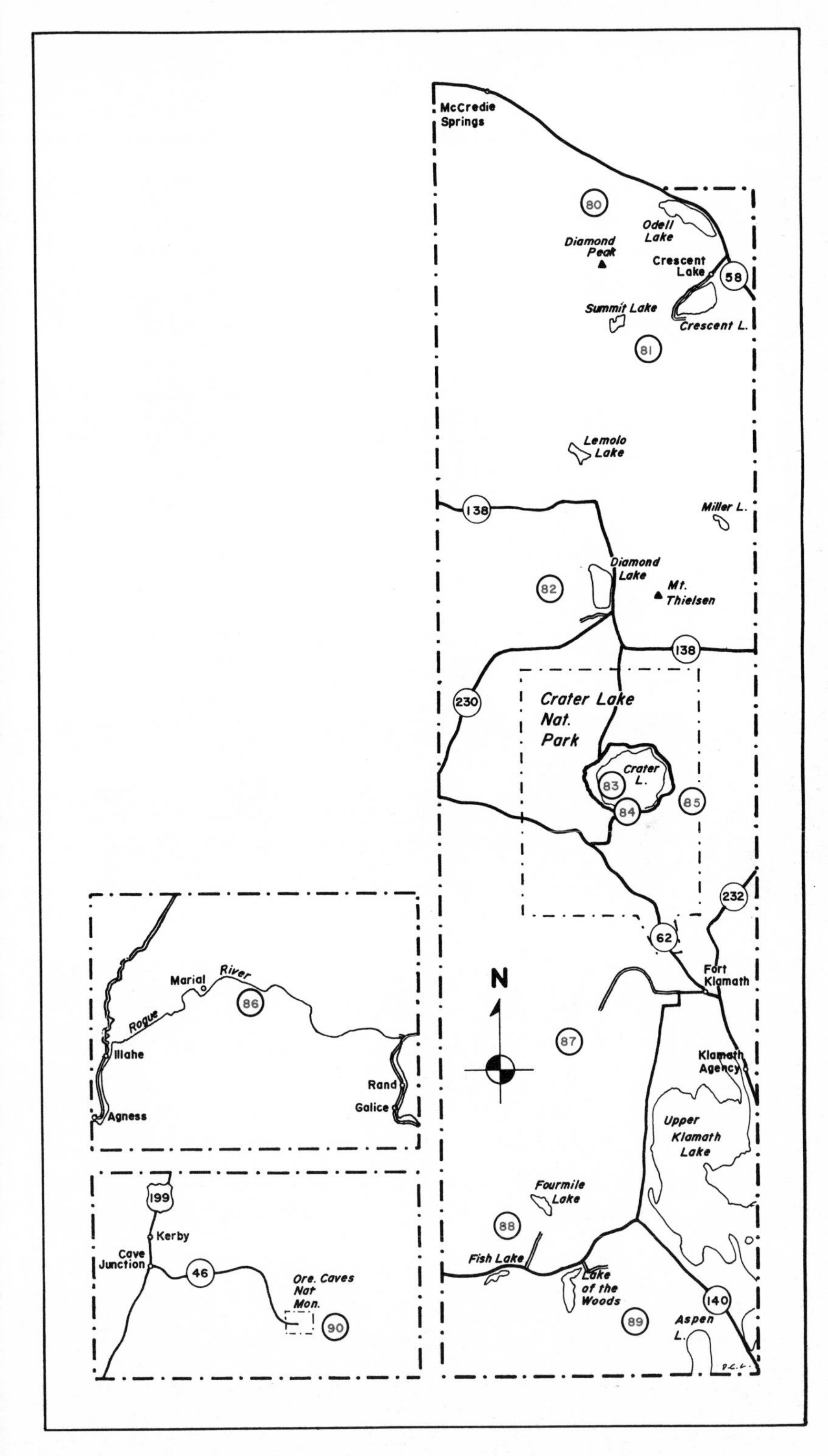
McCredie Springs
80
Odell Lake
Diamond Peak
Crescent Lake
58
Summit Lake
Crescent L.
81
Lemolo Lake
138
Miller L.
Diamond Lake
82
Mt. Thielsen
138
230
Crater Lake Nat. Park
Crater L.
83
84
85
232
62
Fort Klamath
N
87
Klamath Agency
Upper Klamath Lake
Fourmile Lake
88
Fish Lake
Lake of the Woods
140
89
Aspen L.
Marial
River
Rogue
86
Illahe
Rand
Galice
Agness
199
Kerby
Cave Junction
46
Ore. Caves Nat Mon.
90

SOUTHERN OREGON

Despite the fact that most of Southern Oregon is somewhat arid and has few streams in the higher mountains, the vegetation is quite dense in places such as the Mountain Lakes Wild Area, the lower slopes of Mt. McLoughlin, and the Seven Lakes Basin, all of which are served by trails described in this book.

The southern part of the state is a mixture of scenic attractions, probably the most famous being Crater Lake, the only national park in Oregon. This impressive feat of nature was once a massive volcano called Mt. Mazama, which rose to a great height as estimated from the presence of many volcanic dikes that cross radially through the rim of the crater. According to one theory, the summit exploded and then caved in to form a six-mile diameter depression which now contains the clear, deep blue lake. Wizard Island, near the west rim, was formed by volcanic action after the depression had been created. Several other cinder cones were formed, but do not extend above the surface of the lake. The level of the lake remains almost constant as the annual snow and rainfall equals the moisture lost by evaporation and seepage.

There are enough attractions in Crater Lake National Park to warrant a stay of several days. Accommodations are available at Crater Lake Lodge, or you may wish to use one of the many campgrounds. (These are very crowded at the peak of the tourist season.) Informative lectures about the area are given by the park rangers during the day in the Sinnot Memorial on the rim near the lodge, and evening activities include illustrated lectures and fireside talks. Boats make several scheduled trips daily to Wizard Island and other trips take you around the rim of the lake. On all routes, which travel close to the crater rim, a ranger points out geologic examples as he discusses the formation of the lake.

One of the trails described in this section climbs one mile to the summit of Wizard Island and you are urged to take a day to make this interesting circuit. Two other trails in the park are detailed in this section. The one to Mt. Scott, the highest point in the park, affords an extensive panorama of the lake and surrounding country. From the summit of Garfield Peak you will have good views of Wizard Island, the Phantom Ship, and Dutton Cliff.

Another of Oregon's famous natural phenomena where you may wish to stay overnight is the Oregon Caves National Monument. Although no camping facilities are available close by, there is a charming chateau with lodging and a restaurant within the monument. As at Crater Lake, fireside talks are given in the evening in addition to other social activities. Guided tours are conducted into the caves and you may wish to spend one day exploring them and the other special features of the monument, and a second day taking the trail to Lake Mountain which is described in the text. From this peak on a clear day you can just barely see the ocean along the California-Oregon border.

This section contains the longest trail in the book, the 40-mile backpack along the Rogue River. It has the highest, too — the climb to the summit of 9,495-foot Mt. McLoughlin. The Rogue, one of Oregon's most famous rivers, is notable for its scenery, excellent fishing, and reminders of the past, particularly the abandoned cabins and old relics of former gold mining days. This is a thoroughly enjoyable trek which should be done in the spring of the year at a leisurely pace.

80 DIAMOND PEAK TRAIL SOUTHERN OREGON

One day trip or backpack
Distance: 6.5 miles one way
Elevation gain: 2,020 feet, loss 520 feet
High point: 5,980 feet
Allow 3½ to 4 hours one way
Usually open late June through October
Topographic map:
U.S.G.S. Waldo Lake, Oreg.
N4330-W12200/15
1956

This is an adventurous trip that takes you across railroad tracks, through abandoned campgrounds, near high waterfalls, up huckleberry bush-covered slopes, and past one large lake and several ponds to long and narrow Notch Lake. Mt. Yoran, a small but horrendous-looking mountain that is usually dwarfed by the bulk of Diamond Peak, is seen from several points along the trail.

Drive east of McCredie Springs on the Willamette Pass Highway (Oregon 58) to Salt Creek Campground, one-third mile east of the tunnel. Turn south and continue a few hundred feet to a number of signs just before the road curves to the left. There is plenty of parking space here and throughout the campground.

The trail begins by crossing Salt Creek on a fallen log north of the bend in the stream. On the opposite side, trails go to both the right and left. The one to the right climbs a short distance to Too Much Bear Lake and a viewpoint over Salt Creek Falls.

Take the trail which climbs to the left and continue through lush woods for one mile to a sign just below the Southern Pacific Railroad tracks identifying this as the Diamond Peak Trail, No. 3662. The trail continues directly opposite the tracks and goes through the woods for one-quarter mile before coming to a dirt road. Turn right here and follow the dirt road for about one-half mile, crossing two creeks and passing an abandoned campground.

Turn south at the sign on the left side of the road at the 1.5 mile point stating, Vivian Lake Trail (actually the Diamond Peak Trail). The trail soon begins to climb steeply. Just before the three-mile point you will see a waterfall on your left. It is not Fall Creek Falls which is a short distance further on. Beyond Fall Creek Falls, the trail climbs less steeply among huckleberry bushes that grow thickly on the slopes.

At the four-mile point you will come to a sign pointing to a path leading right to Vivian Lake. From the grassy shore on the west side of the lake you can look southeast to the summit of Mt. Yoran. Continue on the level through semi-open forests past several ponds and begin climbing steeply the heavily wooded slopes. All of Mt. Yoran's northwest side is visible at various points through the trees. After reaching the pass on the ridge top, begin descending the opposite side. Come to the junction with the Pinto Mountain Trail, No. 3684, just after the six-mile point. Keep to the left and descend gradually for one-half mile to the junction of the Mt. Yoran Trail, No. 3683, on the left. Keep to the right, and continue the short distance to Notch Lake where there are several good campsites.

Fall Creek Falls

Small lake, Diamond Peak Trail

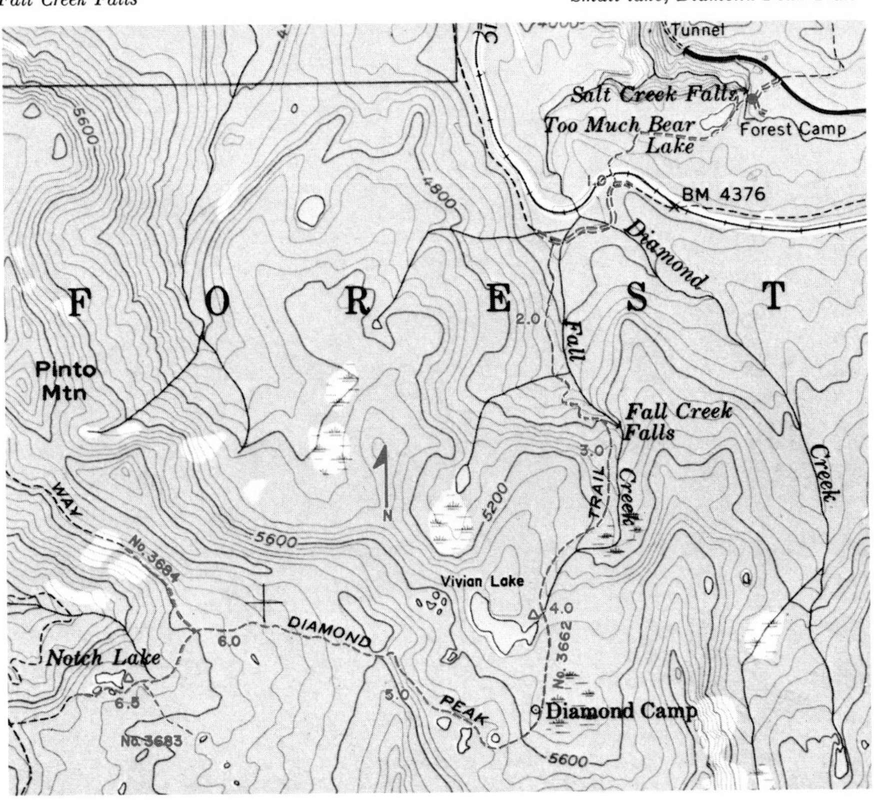

81 WINDY LAKES SOUTHERN OREGON

One day trip or backpack
Distance: 4.5 miles one way
Elevation gain: 1,380 feet
High point: 6,270 feet
Allow 2 hours one way
Usually open July through October
Topographic map:
U.S.G.S. Summit Lake, Oreg.
N4315-W12200/15
1956

The Windy Lakes are located below the northwest shoulder of Cowhorn Mountain several miles south of Crescent Lake. The jagged summit of Diamond Peak is visible from the most northerly of the three lakes. If you wish, you can also take a side trip to emerald-colored Bell Lake, hidden one-quarter mile off the trail.

Drive east of Willamette Pass on Oregon 58 just past Odell Lake to the Crescent Lake Junction. Turn south and proceed for two miles crossing the railroad tracks just before coming to the community of Crescent Lake. Turn right on the road at the south end of the town following the sign to Organization Camp, 6 miles. Continue to the camp, on the southwest end of Crescent Lake, which consists of a number of buildings to the north of the road. The unmarked trail (No. 50) begins on the south side of the road across from the camp about 30 yards west of a water tank.

The trail starts in open timber, but the forest becomes more dense as you gradually gain elevation. Just before the three-mile point, an unofficial sign points east to Bell Lake, one-fourth mile. To make a side trip to this beautiful, green lake, follow the blazes cross-country to the east since there is no path as such. Beyond the Bell Lake junction, you will pass through a meadow area before coming to the junction on the left of Trail 46 which leads east to Suzanne and Darlee Lakes. One-quarter mile further is the junction again of Trail 46 which this time leads west (right) to Summit Lake.

You will come to the south shore of the first of the Windy Lakes in another one-quarter mile. The trail continues for one-half mile, reaching both of the other two lakes. All three are shallow and the most southerly is rimmed by the steep slopes of the ridge below Cowhorn Mountain.

Windy Lakes and Cowhorn Mountain

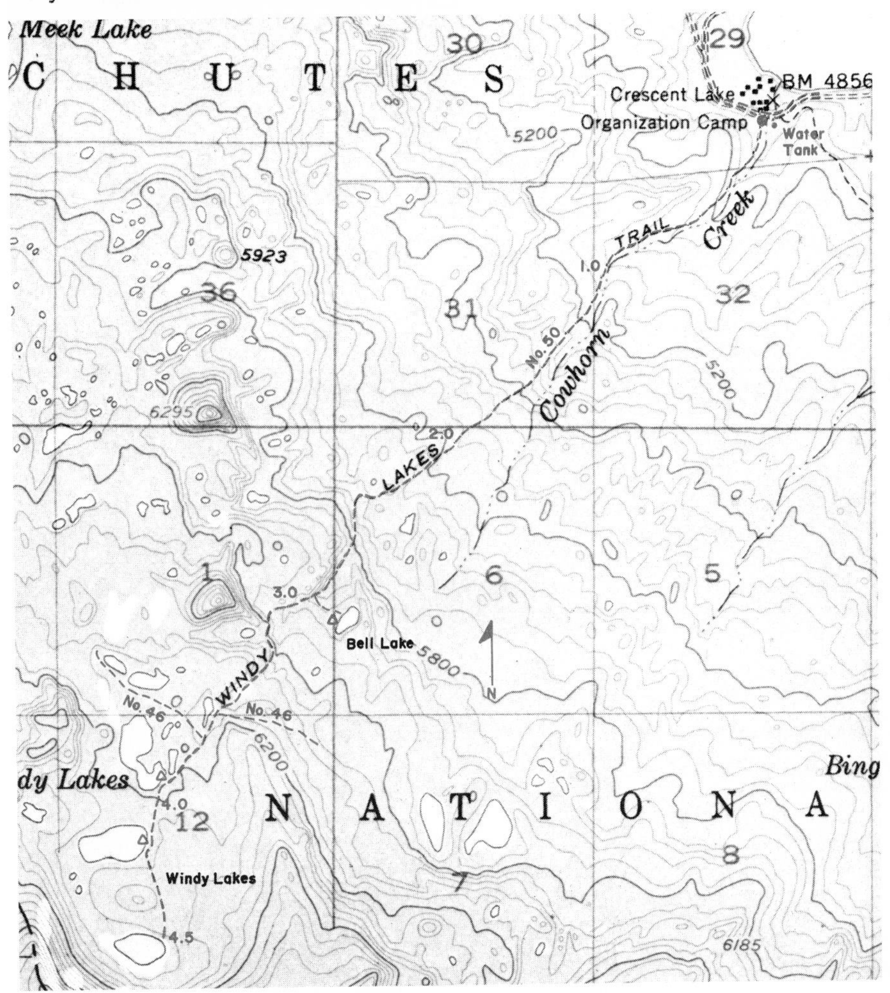

82 MT. BAILEY SOUTHERN OREGON

One day trip
Distance: 4 miles one way
Elevation gain: 3,083 feet
High point: 8,363 feet
Allow 3 to 4 hours one way
Usually open late July through mid-October
Topographic map:
U.S.G.S. Diamond Lake, Oreg.
N4300-W12200/15
1956

Mt. Bailey rises several miles to the west of Diamond Lake to an 8,363 foot summit. This is a fairly strenuous hike with an elevation gain of over 3,000 feet. With the exception of late summer, it is wise to carry an ice axe for assistance in contouring across the western side of the summit ridge, which is blocked from direct ascent by several rock pinacles. Be sure to carry water as there are no creeks near the trail.

The best approach to Mt. Bailey is to take State Highway 138 to its junction with Oregon 230 just south of Diamond Lake. Then proceed southwest on Highway 230 for a short distance and turn right (northwest) on the Three Lakes Road. One-half mile later turn left onto Road 271 at the sign pointing to Organization Camp and Summer Homes. Follow Road 271 for less than a mile and turn left onto Road 284 at the sign pointing to the Mt. Bailey Trail, Three Lakes, and Old Man Camp. Four-tenths of a mile later, you will see the trail sign on your right. On the opposite side of the road there is an open area among the trees where several cars can be parked. A sign by the beginning of the trail requests hikers to register at the Diamond Lake Guard Station, which is off Highway 138 on the east side of Diamond Lake.

The trail, No. 1451, proceeds through open forest climbing very gradually. At one mile it begins contouring around the north side of twin-peaked Hemlock Butte. However, the forest is so thick that the butte is not at all obvious. Once past the butte the trail crosses a level plain of scattered timber and downed logs. It crosses a logging road at one and three-quarter miles.

Beyond the logging road the trail begins to climb sharply, switchbacking up the steep, wooded slopes. It is well-marked with red-painted blazes on the trees. At three miles you will leave the trees and come out into the open, climbing up several ridges and then passing a deep crater on the south side of the mountain. The crater usually is filled with snow.

After reaching the south summit, the trail contours to the west around several gendarmes, then switchbacks up to the summit ridge and continues on up the crest to the north and highest peak. The latter portion of the hike can be rather dangerous if snow still covers the western side of the summit ridge.

A lookout once stood on the north peak, but all that remains today is the concrete foundation bearing the date of its construction — 1923.

Summit of Mt. Bailey

Mt. Thielsen from Mt. Bailey Trail

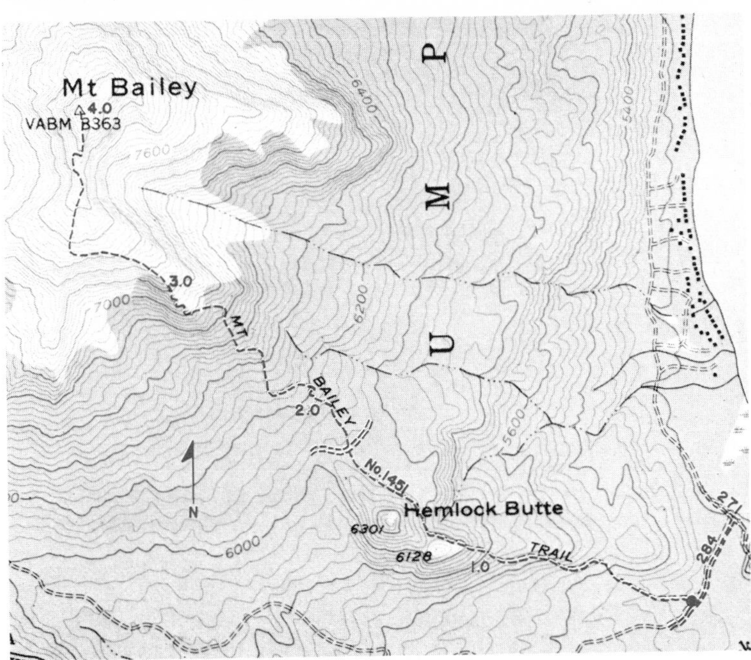

83 WIZARD ISLAND SOUTHERN OREGON

One day trip
Distance: 3 miles one way
Elevation gain: 764 feet, loss 774 feet
High point: 6,950 feet (rim of Cleetwood Cove)
Allow up to 7 hours round trip (see text)
Usually open July 15 through September 10
Topographic map:
U.S.G.S. Crater Lake
National Park and Vicinity, Oreg.
N4243-W12155/26X25
1956

It is a fun and informative day to take the boat to Wizard Island inside Crater Lake, hike up to the crater rim, stroll back down to the dock, and catch the return boat before dark. If you don't spend too long on the summit, you will have enough time before the trip back for a hike to the west end of the island and a swim in usually warm Emerald Pool.

Take one of the several highways to Crater Lake National Park and follow Rim Drive to Cleetwood Cove on the northeast side of the lake where a large sign marks the trail to the boat landing. Much parking space is available on the north side of the road. The wide trail switchbacks for one mile down to the moorage.

Boats for Wizard Island leave the moorage at 9:30 a.m., 12:00 noon, 1:30 p.m., and 3:00 p.m. Unless you wish to make the longer trip around the rim of the lake, be sure to get the boat that goes only to Wizard Island and back. The launch leaves Wizard Island for the return trip at 12:30 p.m., 2:00 p.m. and 3:30 p.m. If possible, plan to take the 9:30 a.m. boat and return on the last scheduled departure. (If the last boat is full, you will have to wait until 4:15 p.m. for a special run that is sent out to retrieve anyone left on the island.)

The fare is $2.50 round trip per person and the boats operate from July 15 through September 10 in a year of normal snowfall. On the way to the island, a National Park ranger explains how Crater Lake was formed. The boat passes close to the rim so the various layers of lava, volcanic dikes, and other geologic formations can be distinguished clearly.

The trail to the summit of Wizard Island starts directly from the dock and winds through the lava to the left of the outbuildings. Keep to the right after 0.1 of a mile where the trail forks. The branch on the left goes part way to Emerald Pool which you will be able to see from the rim of the cone. Switchback up the wooded slope to the summit. A short trail goes around the rim of the crater which is about 80 feet deep. Water from the lake is quite safe to drink when away from the docks and is of far greater purity than most city reservoirs.

Boat dock at northern end of Crater Lake

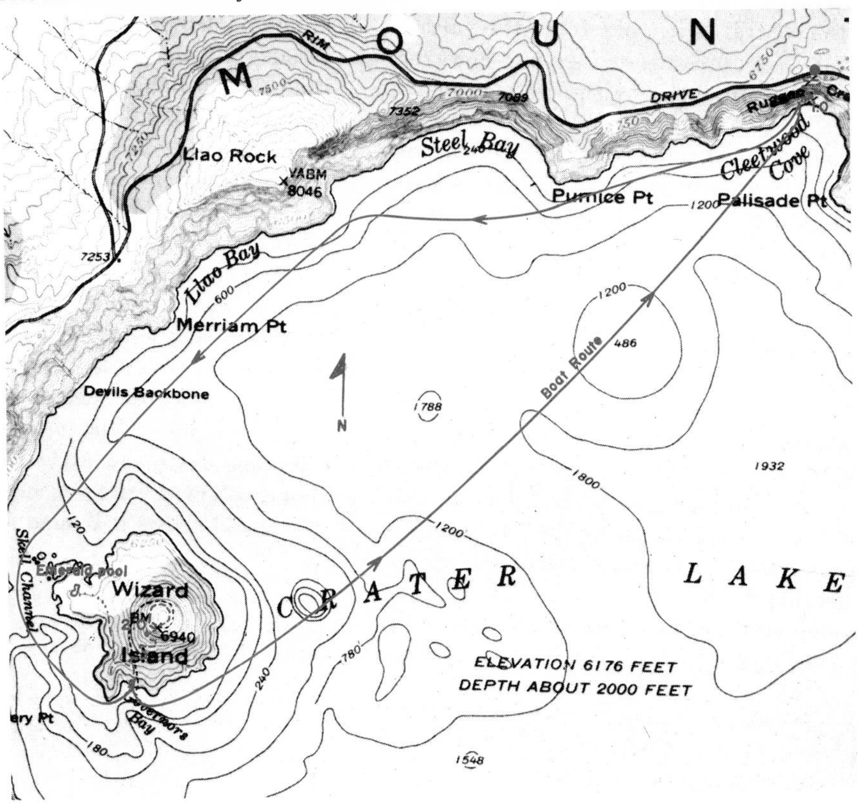

84 GARFIELD PEAK SOUTHERN OREGON

One day trip
Distance: 1.7 miles one way
Elevation gain: 984 feet
High point: 8,060 feet
Allow 1 hour one way
Usually open mid-July through September
Topographic map:
U.S.G.S. Crater Lake
National Park and Vicinity, Oreg.
N4243-W12155/26X25
1956

One of the best views of Crater Lake can be found along the rim from the 8,060 foot summit of Garfield Peak, a hike of less than two miles from the Crater Lake Lodge.

Drive to Crater Lake National Park and follow Rim Drive to the Crater Lake Lodge. Park here, and walk to the east end of the Lodge where you will see a sign that indicates the trail to Garfield Peak, 1.7 miles distance.

The trail proceeds east, dropping slightly, and upon reaching the edge of Castle Crest switchbacks up for the next 1.5 miles to the dome-like summit of Garfield Peak. Benches are spotted at strategic viewpoints along the way so that those who wish may sit down in comfort and admire the view.

From the summit of Garfield Peak you can see the volcanic cone of Wizard Island and the Watchman to the west, and to the east the Phantom Ship lies seemingly at anchor just off spectacular Dutton Cliff. Mt. Scott is the large cinder cone on the horizon above the Phantom Ship. To the south the double summit of Mt. Shasta seems to be suspended above the haze.

The Phantom Ship and Mt. Scott from Garfield Peak

Wizard Island from Garfield Peak

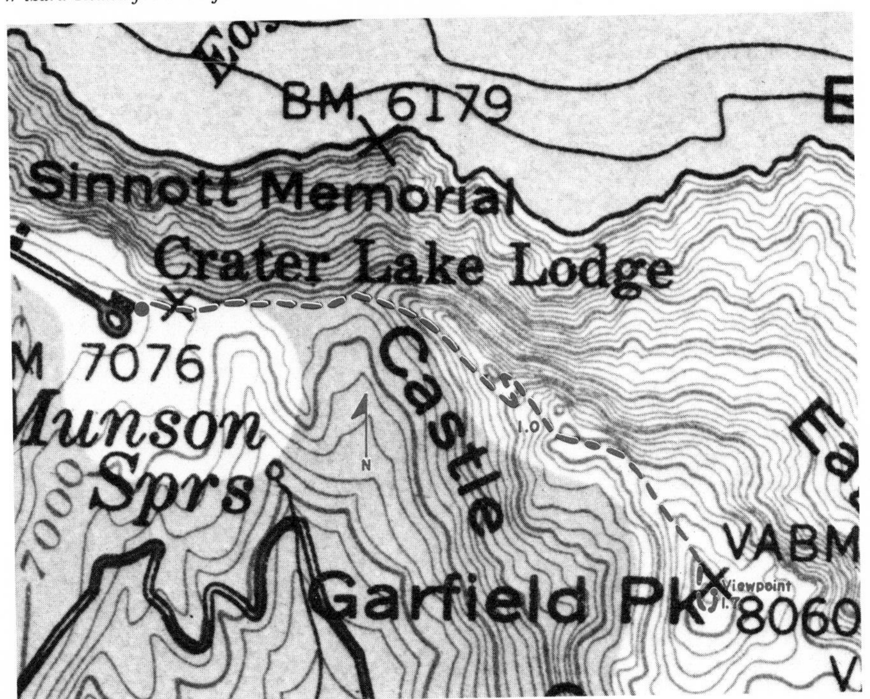

85 MT. SCOTT SOUTHERN OREGON

One day trip
Distance: 2.5 miles one way
Elevation gain: 1,230 feet
High point: 8,926 feet
Allow 1 to 1½ hours one way
Usually open mid-July through September
Topographic map:
U.S.G.S. Crater Lake
National Park and Vicinity, Oreg.
N4243-W12155/26X25
1956

Mt. Scott, at 8,926 feet, is the highest point in Crater Lake National Park, and from the summit you can get a bird's eye view of almost the entire extent of this geological wonder. You also can see Klamath Lake and its surrounding marshlands and the summit of Mt. Shasta to the south; Mt. Thielsen and the Three Sisters are visible on the northern horizon.

Drive to Crater Lake National Park and take Rim Drive to the east side of the lake. The trail to Mt. Scott starts just east of The Cloudcap Viewpoint junction, and is marked by a sign. There is plenty of parking space on the shoulder of the road. Take along water as none is available along the trail.

Follow a dirt road across the flat pumice field at the foot of the mountain. After a few hundred yards it narrows to a trail and enters the woods. Climb gradually along the western slope. Just before the one-mile point the trail turns and travels in an easterly direction. From this point the tree cover becomes sparse and you can observe the surrounding country easily. At about 1.5 miles, the trail begins switchbacking and continues climbing until reaching the summit ridge. From here hike on the level for one-quarter mile to the lookout, which is manned only during periods of extreme fire danger.

Mt. Scott from the west

Summit of Mt. Scott from the trail

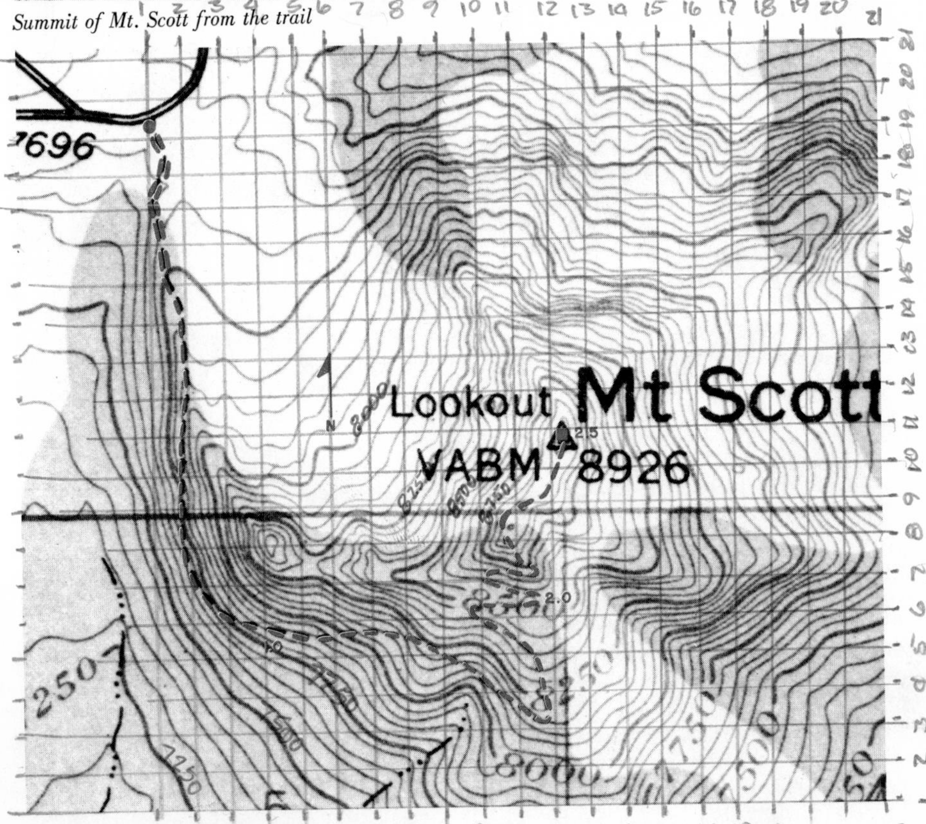

86 ROUGE RIVER TRAIL SOUTHERN OREGON

Backpack
Distance: 40 miles one way
Elevation gain: 2,000 feet (est.)
High point: 800 feet
Allow 4 to 5 days one way
Usually open all year round
Topographic maps:
U.S.G.S. Agness, Oreg.
N4230-W12400/15
1954
U.S.G.S. Galice, Oreg.
N4230-W12330/15
1946
U.S.G.S. Marial, Oreg.
N4230-W12345/15
1954

The Rogue, one of Oregon's most famous, most fabled rivers, offers an unusually glamorous hiking trip. And, if you are a fisherman as well as a hiker, disregard the times given here, for you will wish to spend more time near this legendary water.

Backpacking along the 40-mile Rogue River Canyon Trail offers an interesting contrast to the less arid regions of the Cascade Mountains. The trail follows the river closely several hundred feet above the water, affording spectacular views of the canyon.

Flowers and animals are varied and plentiful. Evergreens and live oak forests are common, and during early May, wild iris is especially prominent. Grey squirrels scamper through the woods and almost every pool abounds with salamanders. Bear and elk tracks are seen frequently on sandy beaches along the river.

Spring is the best time to make this trip as it becomes very hot later in the season, and drinking water is less easily found. Carry a snake bite kit when traveling after the warm weather has begun. Drinking water is available at regular intervals except in the vicinity of Quail Creek. (Be sure to use Halizone tablets if you obtain drinking water from the Rogue River.) Poison oak is prevalent all along the trail, sometimes growing head high.

Generally, the trip is made eastward from Illahe, and the trail mileage is numbered in that direction. The most efficient car shuttle is to drive two or more cars to the confluence of Graves Creek and the Rogue River at the eastern terminus of the trail. It is reached by proceeding on Interstate 5 to the town of Wolf Creek, 43 miles south of Roseburg. From Wolf Creek, drive on the only road going west for 15 miles to the Rogue River Bridge. Here, at the end of the trail, is a boat landing with room for many vehicles. Leave one or more empty cars here for the return trip and drive the other(s) loaded with hikers and gear back to Interstate 5 and travel north 38 miles to the Winston turnoff. Continue west on Oregon 42 for 51 miles to the Powers junction. Turn left and proceed through Powers following the signs to Illahe.

The official (mile 0) trailhead starts 0.6 mile to the south of the Illahe Lodge entrance. However, a more logical place to begin the hike is just east of the lodge. Proceed down the driveway past the lodge proper and across a bridge. Park off the road in the open area. Permission to leave the car(s) here should first be obtained at the lodge.

To get to the trail, follow the road north for about one-fourth mile. The Rogue River Trail, No. 1160, begins on the left hand side of the road at a wooden post. The trail contours through the woods for about one-half mile until it meets an old road. Turn left here and follow the road uphill and around a bend to the right where the road then narrows to a trail once again.

The first good stopping place for the night or for lunch is a grassy area about 2.5 miles from Illahe Lodge. Since it takes many hours to make the car shuttle, traveling this short distance and establishing a camp for an early start the following day is actually very practical. The spot is about 50 feet down from the trail next to the river and is reached by a path which leads diagonally down from the main trail in a southwesterly direction. Water is available from a small creek several hundred yards to the west.

Another very interesting way to reach this grassy spot is to travel along the river's edge. Instead of turning left one-half mile beyond the beginning of the trail, continue to the right down the road until it reaches the water, and follow the riverbank to the camp spot, about one-fourth mile to the east of Hicks Creek and a gravel island.

From the campsite, the trail travels through woods of oak, generally above the river. About one-fourth mile before the six-mile marker is a sign for the Clay Hill Trail, No. 1191. It points to Panther Ridge Trail, 4 miles and Upper Staley Place, 1 mile. From here, two houses can be seen near the river.

Rogue River near Illahe

Approaching Bushy Bar

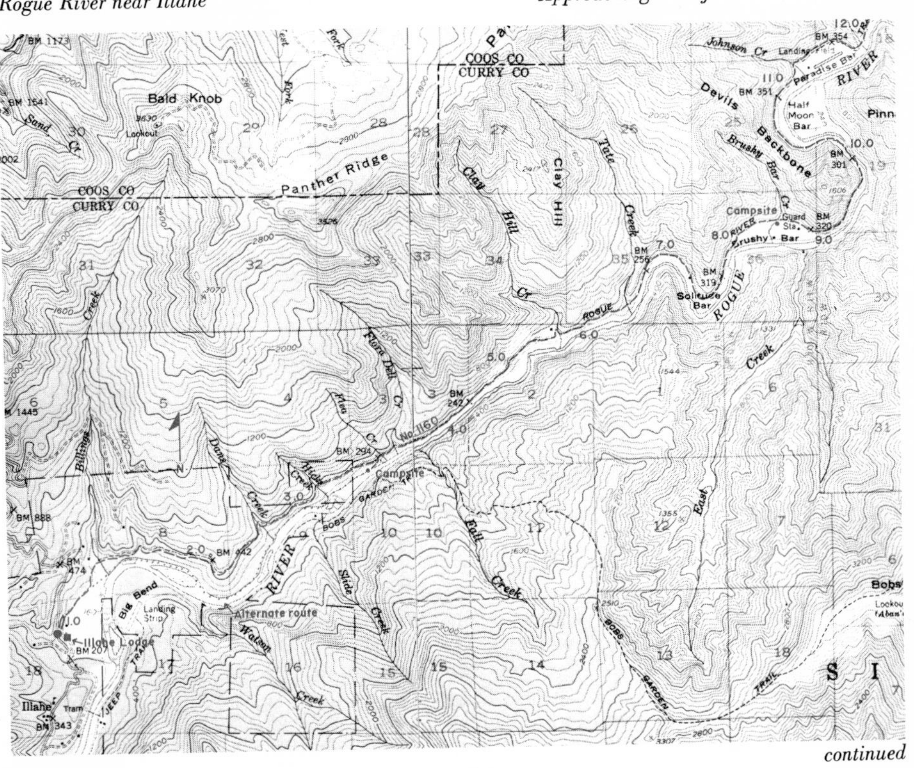

continued

86. ROGUE RIVER TRAIL

Soon the trail enters a more open and rocky area. A lovely meadow is passed above Solitude Bar just beyond Camp Solitude, but there is no water. An ideal lunch or camping spot is among the tall evergreens at Brushy Bar Creek.

Two and one-quarter miles further is another stopping place and a potential camping site at Johnson Creek. (The sign says Jackson Creek.) Just beyond this crossing is a home and airstrip. The last good campsite before Marial is west of Blossom Bar Creek. The trail continues high above the river and at Inspiration Point there is a good view of Stair Creek Falls.

At 15 miles the trail comes to a road and a sign which points south to Stair Creek Falls 1 mile, Paradise Bar 3 miles, Illahe Road 15 miles, and Agness 24 miles. Marial Lodge is located a few hundred feet beyond the fire station. The community of Marial is made up of a number of summer homes, the lodge, and a ranch.

Continue along the road, crossing a bridge, and rounding a bend. A sign here points to a road leading left uphill to Tucker Flat campground. This is the largest and most developed facility on the trail and is equipped with tables, fireplaces, tap water, and outbuildings.

To again pick up the Rogue River Trail, continue south along the road for a few hundred yards to a side road descending to the right to Anderson Ranch. At this junction an aluminum sign reads, Alemeda Road 22 miles, Black Bar Ranch 14 miles, Horseshoe Bend 10 miles, and suspension bridge ¼ mile. Continue down this road for about 200 feet to the trail which leaves the road and contours along the left (uphill) bank. Go through a gate and follow the path around the slope of the hill above the ranch. Shortly thereafter the path is joined by a road from below. Continue left around the hill and take the high (left) route when the road forks. Further on, turn right and follow the trail at the point where the road heads uphill.

Continue through the wooded area. Just beyond the 20-mile marker, take the high trail above the slide. Although the slides are subject to seasonal change, there are always paths that go above the obliterated portions of the trail.

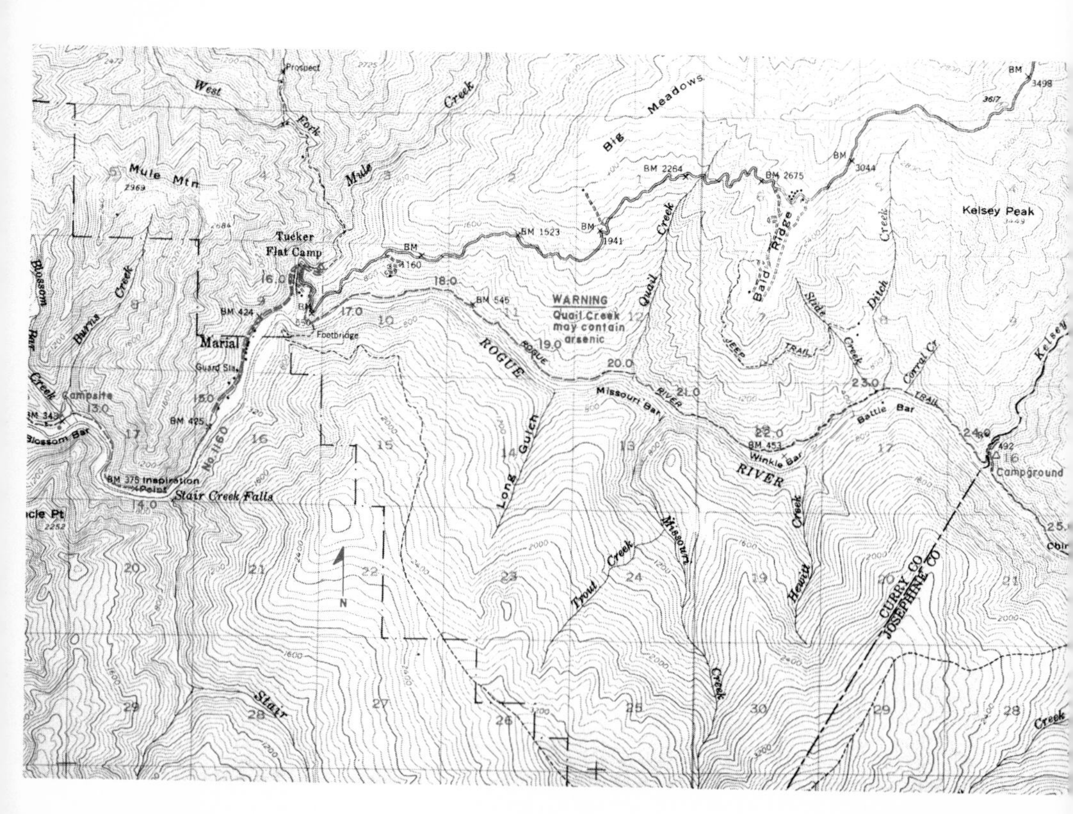

Do not drink water from Quail Creek as it has been found to contain traces of arsenic. In the Winkle Bar area an old flume parallels the trail downslope. It is sometimes obscure and is eventually crossed by the trail.

A good stopping place for lunch is the grassy slopes across from Battle Bar. On April 27, 1856, Battle Bar was the scene of the Battle of the Rogue River fought during the Indian Wars of 1855-56. Several buildings, apparently abandoned, can be seen across the river. In fact, the whole trip is punctuated with abandoned cabins, summer homes, and year-around residences.

There are tables, fireplaces, and outbuildings at Kelsey Creek. However, a much more pleasant camping spot is just two miles beyond, to the west of Meadow Creek. This is a large open flat area with fireplaces and tables, and is an excellent location for an overnight stay — the last for many miles.

The next 11 miles represent the only appreciable elevation gains and losses on the entire trip. Views of the canyon, wooded slopes, and the swift moving river are often very spectacular. As you progress eastward, you will notice increasing evidence of aridity by the changing types of animal and plant life.

At 30 miles a trail drops down to a point opposite Black Bar Ranch, clearly visible across the river. A good stopping place is Russian Creek, where you will find a fireplace, table, and outbuildings. After crossing Alder Creek, there appear to be two trails. Take the lower one on the east side of the creek.

At 35.7 miles is Big Slide Camp. This is a large, well-developed area with tables and fireplaces. Just around the bend, after you cross Whiskey Creek on a pole bridge, is an alternate trail which climbs up to the Alemeda road. In times past, the upper road junction formed the eastern terminus of the Rogue River Trail, but it is now seldom used. For the last three miles the trail follows the river 20 to 50 feet above its banks, at one point traversing a wide band of scree.

Near the end of the trail a sign commemorates the high water mark of 55 feet above mean summer level which occurred in the flood of December 1964.

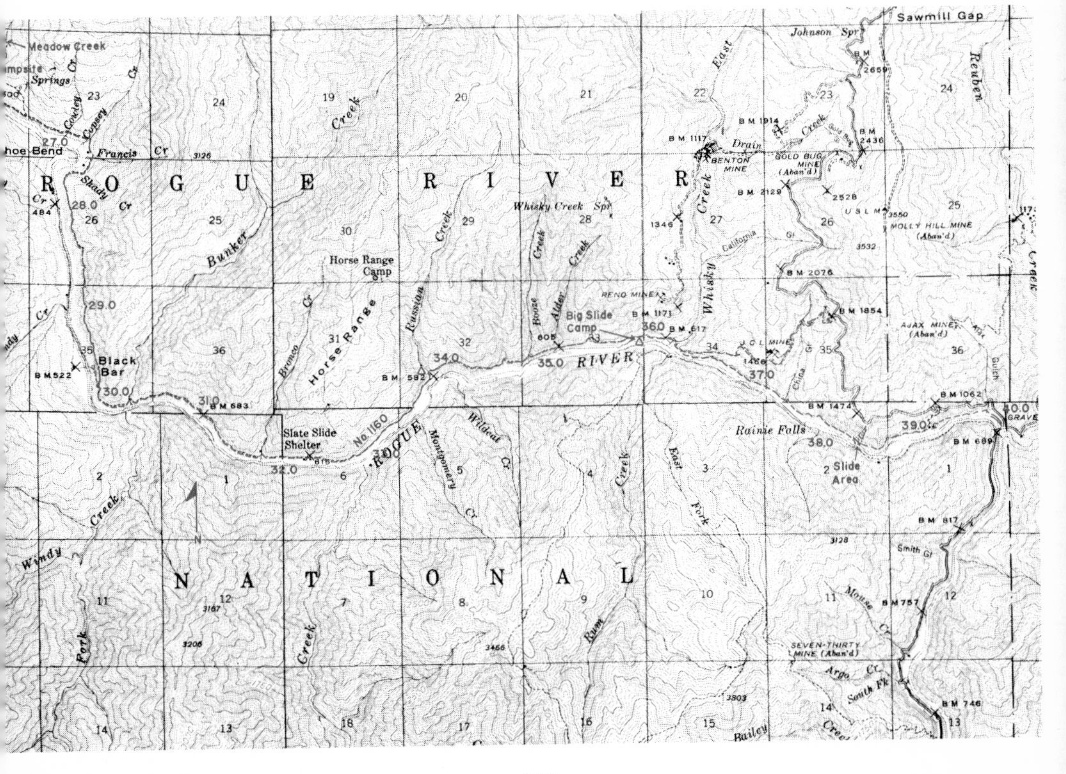

87 SEVEN LAKES BASIN SOUTHERN OREGON

Backpack
Distance: 8.5 miles one way
Elevation gain: 2,102 feet
High point: 7,582 feet
Allow 5 to 6 hours one way
Usually open July through October
Topographic map:
U.S.G.S. Pelican Butte, Oreg.
N4230-W12200/15
1955

This trip, a portion of which is on the Skyline Trail, takes you near the source of the Middle Fork of the Rogue River, past the Seven Lakes Basin to the summit of 7,582-foot Devils Peak.

Take Oregon State Highway 62 to Fort Klamath and follow the signs to the Seven Mile Guard Station on the road that leads west from this community. One-half mile west of the guard station turn right at the junction of Road 334, and follow the sign reading Seven Lakes Trail, 5½ miles. A few hundred feet before the trail head the road forks to the right and goes downhill. Turn right here and you will come to a creek-side picnic area with tables and outbuildings. The beginning of the trail is marked by a sign saying, Sevenmile Trail, No. 3703.

Cross a footbridge and travel for 1.5 miles to the first junction. The Sevenmile Trail ends at this point and you will now be traveling on the Skyline Trail, No. 2000, which comes in from the north. Continue straight ahead and in one-half mile you will come to the junction of what is probably an old portion of the Skyline Trail. Keep to the left and continue climbing gradually through the woods.

At five miles is the junction with the Seven Lakes Trail, No. 981. Keep to the left and traverse up the slope from where you can look down onto Grass Lake. Three-quarters mile further is the Spur Trail, No. 981A, to the Seven Lakes Trail. Again keep to the left and continue climbing. You soon will cross a stream by a good camping spot. At the 7.5-mile point you will be at the base of the cirque below Devils Peak. Follow the ridge along the edge of the cirque and then switchback up the rocky slope to the sign that reads Cascade Summit, Elevation 7,300 feet. Take the trail to the right which climbs the short distance to the summit of Devils Peak. From the remains of the old lookout, you can see Mt. Bailey, the rim of Crater Lake, Klamath Lake, Mt. Shasta, and several of the lakes to the north which you may wish to visit.

If you would like to make a loop trip, drop down off the summit on the path which goes in a southwesterly direction back to Trail 984. Turn right when you meet Trail 984 and continue along a ridge crest for one-eighth mile to a trail that joins from your left (southwest). Keep to the right and traverse the open and rocky northern slope of Lucifer. Descend into the woods and come to the junction of the Seven Lakes Trail, No. 981. Keep to the right and after a few hundred yards meet the junction of the Alta Lake Trail, No. 979. Again keep to the right and continue through the trees, passing South and Cliff Lakes. Just beyond the latter is the junction with the Spur Trail, the other end of which you passed on the journey up to Devils Peak. Keep to the left and on the northeast shore of Middle Lake is the last junction on this trip, the Lake Ivern Trail, No. 984, leading off to the left. Veer to the right and continue on to Grass Lake where there is a shelter and several excellent campsites.

Seven Lakes Basin

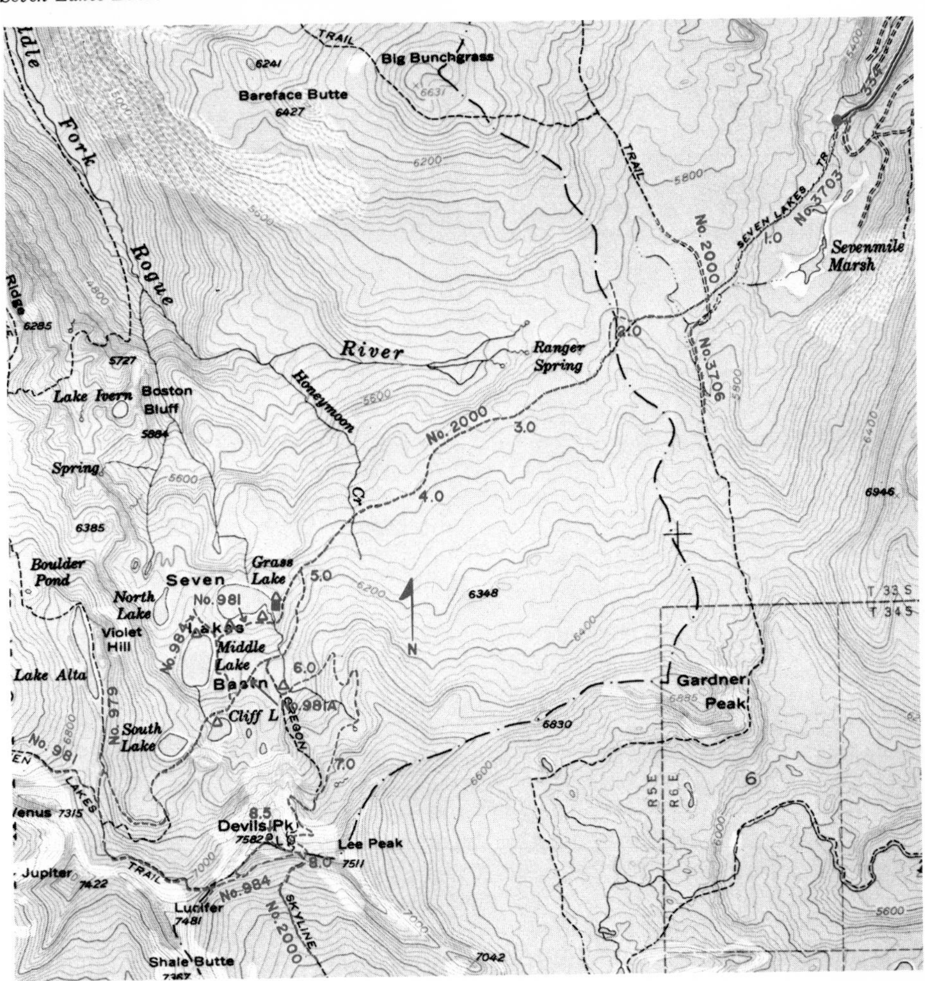

88 MT. McLOUGHLIN SOUTHERN OREGON

One day trip or backpack
Distance: 6 miles one way
Elevation gain: 3,930 feet
High point: 9,495 feet
Allow 4 to 5 hours one way
Usually open mid-July through mid-October
Topographic map:
U.S.G.S. Mt. McLoughlin, Oreg.
N4215-W12215/15
1955

Dead trees, Mt. McLoughlin

The word mountain is appropriate here because, with its elevation of 9,495 feet, Mt. McLoughlin is among the major peaks in the Oregon Cascades. Although not demanding technically, you will be hiking at an altitude which will make the going a little slower. Be sure to carry water as there is none along the trail.

Take Oregon 140 to the Four Mile Lake Road, No. 350, just west of the 31-mile post, about 33 miles west of Klamath Falls. Turn north here and proceed for 2.5 miles over rough road to the trail head located on the left hand side and marked by a sign reading, Mt. McLoughlin Trail, No. 3716. There is ample parking in a turnaround next to the trail.

After a few feet the trail crosses over the Cascade Canal, which probably will be empty late in the summer. Go through an open area with a small campsite on the right and then begin climbing gradually through the woods. At one and one-quarter miles and just after a ridge crest and level stretch, you will come to the sign marking the trail that leads to the right to Freye Lake. It is only a short side trip to this lake, from which you can see the summit of Mt. McLoughlin. There is also a very good campsite here among tall trees.

As you continue climbing on the main trail, follow the paint marks. The grade becomes steeper and the vegetation more sparse. At timberline, the 4.5-mile point you will come to the summit ridge that overlooks the steep, bowl-like northeast face. Although the summit looks close from here, it will actually take about one hour to reach. The trail leads to the left, traveling on the level around the southwest side of the ridge for about one-half mile before turning and climbing up to the ridge again. From here, you must scramble over large boulders up to the summit, keeping to the left side of the ridge where there is less exposure. The high rock foundation of the former lookout still remains on the peak. On a clear day the view is most impressive.

On the return trip, if there is no snow on the southeastern face of the mountain, you can make an easier descent by following the path that cuts diagonally down across the loose scree to the point where the trail begins contouring around the southwest slope. Taking this route on the way up would be exhausting but following it down is an interesting change of pace. Be observant the first two miles below the summit as the trail is easy to lose in some places.

Foundation of former lookout cabin, Summit of Mt. McLoughlin

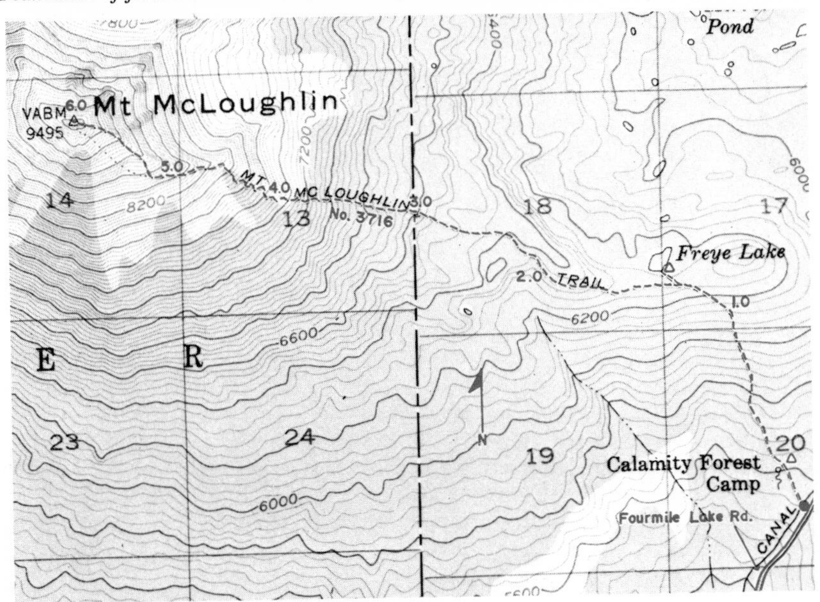

89 MOUNTAIN LAKES WILD AREA SOUTHERN OREGON

Backpack
Distance: 9 miles one way
Elevation gain: 2,750 feet, loss 820 feet
High point: 7,420 feet
Allow 6 to 7 hours one way
Usually open July through October
Topographic map:
U.S.G.S. Lake O'Woods, Oreg.
N4215-W12200/15
1955

The Mountain Lakes Wild Area is a good place to spend several days hiking, fishing, swimming, or horseback riding. Both Klamath Lake and Mt. McLoughlin can be seen from several points along the trail, and several large and many small lakes are visited. A loop trip is possible for part of the hike, enabling you to see more of this forested region. Be sure to take suitable rain wear as thunderstorms are frequent in the latter part of the summer.

Drive on State Highway 140 between Klamath Falls and Medford to the Dead Indian Road junction at the northeast end of Lake of the Woods. Proceed south on the Dead Indian Road for about 100 yards and turn left onto Road 3660 following it for 0.7 of a mile to the junction of Road 361. Turn left on Road 361 and follow it for one-fourth mile to the trail head on the east side of Seldom Creek. A sign here locates the Mountain Lakes Trail, No. 3721.

The path climbs gently through the woods for one mile to a small clearing at the junction of the Mountain Lakes Spur Trail, No. 3721B. Continue straight ahead and re-enter the woods. A short distance further you will pass through a large meadow, and at the 3.5 mile point you will come to an unmarked trail leading off on the right to shallow, grass-bordered Lake Waban. The main trail continues climbing and at one of the switchbacks there is a good view of Mt. McLoughlin. At five miles you will come to the junction of the Mountain Lakes Loop Trail, No. 3721A. (This number may have been changed to 3727).

Turn to the left here and hike around Whiteface Peak, then switchback down a scree slope from which you can see a portion of Klamath Lake. Enter the woods and continue on the level past good campsites at Eb and Zeb Lakes. At the seven-mile point, at Trail 3718, turn right and begin climbing. You will pass Como, Silent, and Zephyr Lakes, all of which are a short distance off the trail. After one short uphill pitch, the trail comes to a saddle and drops down by a boulder slope to Lake Harriette where good campsites can be found along the western shore.

If you wish to make the loop trip, continue on the trail around the northwest side of the lake and keep to the right at the junction of Trail 3719 at the nine-mile point. Climb steeply up the ridge to the southeast of the lake passing side Trail 3720 on your left. After traveling on the level for a short distance, begin descending. Turn right at the junction of Trail 3722, just beyond which you will find good places to camp at Clover Lake and the surrounding ponds. Beyond Clover Lake the trail climbs to the saddle below Whiteface Peak where the loop trail originates.

Lake Harriette

Campground at Lake Harriette

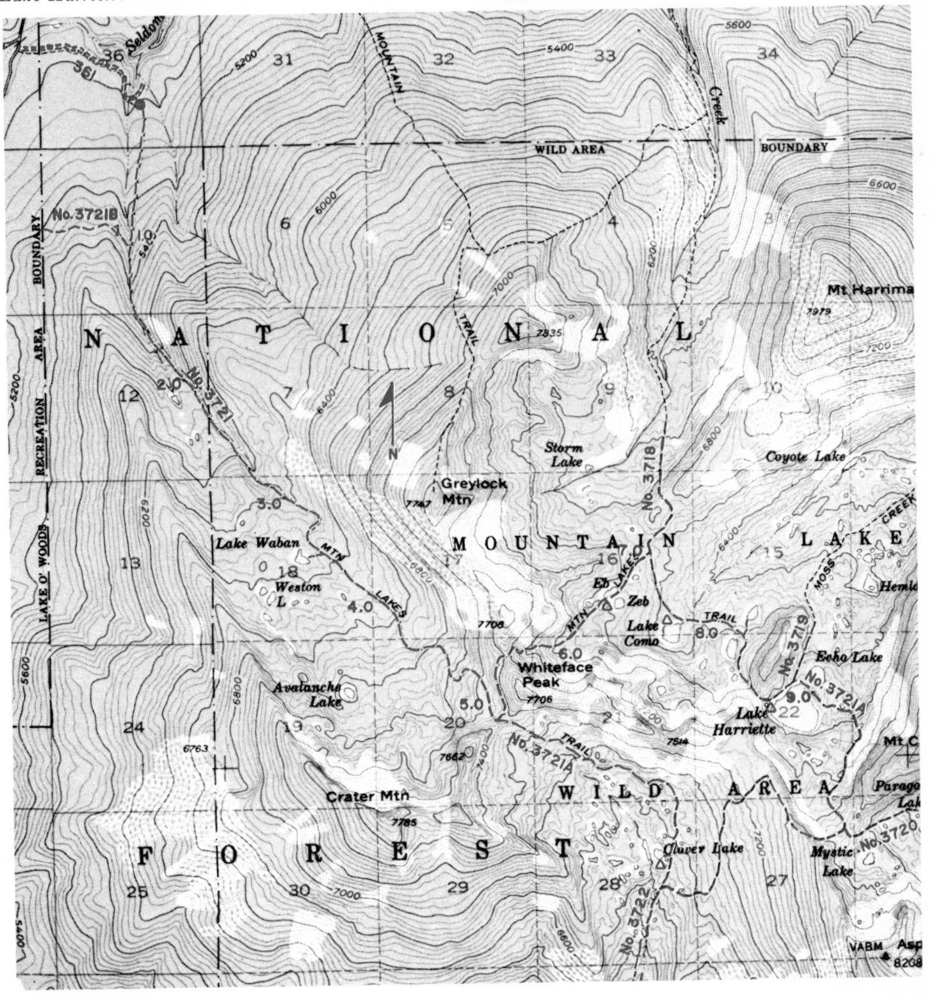

90 LAKE MOUNTAIN SOUTHERN OREGON

One day trip
Distance: 5 miles one way
Elevation gain: 3,280 feet, loss 100 feet
High point: 6,649 feet
Allow 3 to 4 hours one way
Usually open mid-June through October
Topographic map:
U.S.G.S. Oregon Caves, Oreg.-Calif.
N4200-W12315/15
1954

The Oregon Caves National Monument is the starting point for this trail which will take you over two mountain tops. Although the woods on the lower slopes are very lush, the two summit areas are treeless and from them you can see, in addition to peaks in the Siskiyou National Forest, the Pacific Ocean and Mt. Shasta, both of which are visible on clear days.

Follow U.S. Highway 199 to a point 30 miles south of Grants Pass, turn left on Oregon 46 and drive for 18 miles to the Monument. Ample parking is available in the large lot outside the main entrance.

The trail, No. 1206, begins as a paved path just east of the information building, through the archway. It passes to the left of several cabins and then switchbacks above them. Three-tenths of a mile from the beginning, you will come to the junction of the Cliff Nature Trail. Stay left and continue through deep woods. Water is available downslope from the trail just before a long switchback. Walk through a grassy, open slope at the one-mile point and a short distance later, re-enter the trees, and come to a cutoff trail climbing steeply upslope. Do not take this trail, but continue a few hundred feet further to the marked junction. Turn right here following the sign to Lake Mountain and climb gradually for 0.3 of a mile to the ridge top at the junction with the Limestone Trail, No. 1235. Keep to the left and hike along the level, semi-open ridgetop to the Cedar Camp junction on the right. Again keep to the left and climb gradually through the trees and small grassy clearings. At the three and one-quarter mile point, you will reach the open rocky slopes of Mt. Elijah, known locally as Mt. "E." When the trail forks, stay right. This fork goes up to the summit, from which you can see Mt. Shasta to the southeast and Lake Mountain to the northeast.

Follow the trail down the northeast side of Mt. Elijah and merge with the trail that traverses the north side of the summit ridge. At the sandy saddle continue across its upslope side heading for a blazed tree. The junction of the Boundary Trail, No. 1207, is in the southwest downslope corner. Just after entering the woods is the junction with the Meadow Mt. Trail, No. 1214, which drops down to the lily pad-covered Bigelow Lakes. Keep to the right, following the sign to Lake Mountain Lookout, and climb very gradually along the western side of the peak. After one-quarter mile, the trail disappears in an overgrowth of manzanita. Turn right and make your way up to the rocks on the summit ridge and scramble north across these to the blown over lookout cabin.

If you wish, you can make a small loop trip on your return. When you come to the junction just beyond the one-mile point, turn to the right, following the sign to Big Tree. This botanical wonder is 12 feet 4 inches in diameter, 182 feet 6 inches high and from 1,200 to 1,500 years old. Keep left at the junction of the trail to Panther and Lake Creeks and return to the parking area.

Lake Mountain from Mt. Elijah

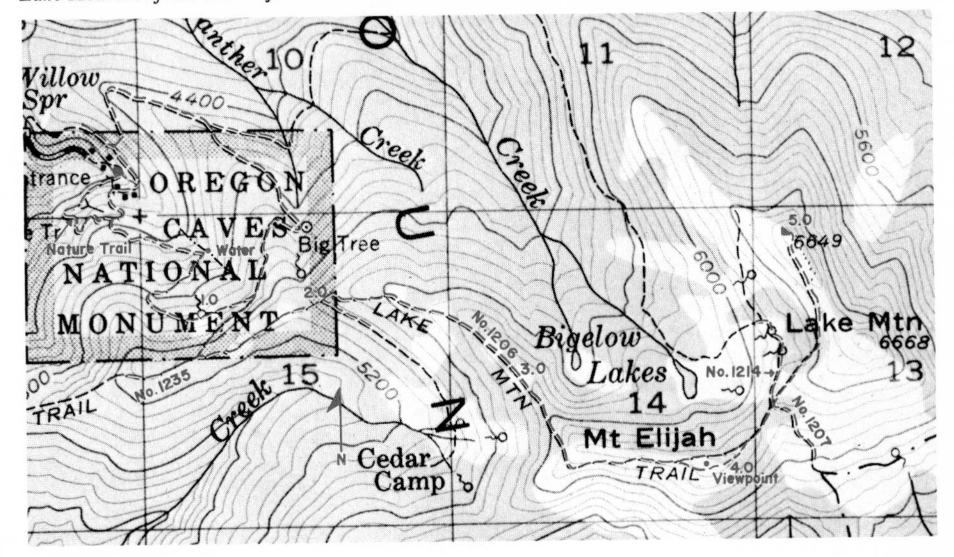

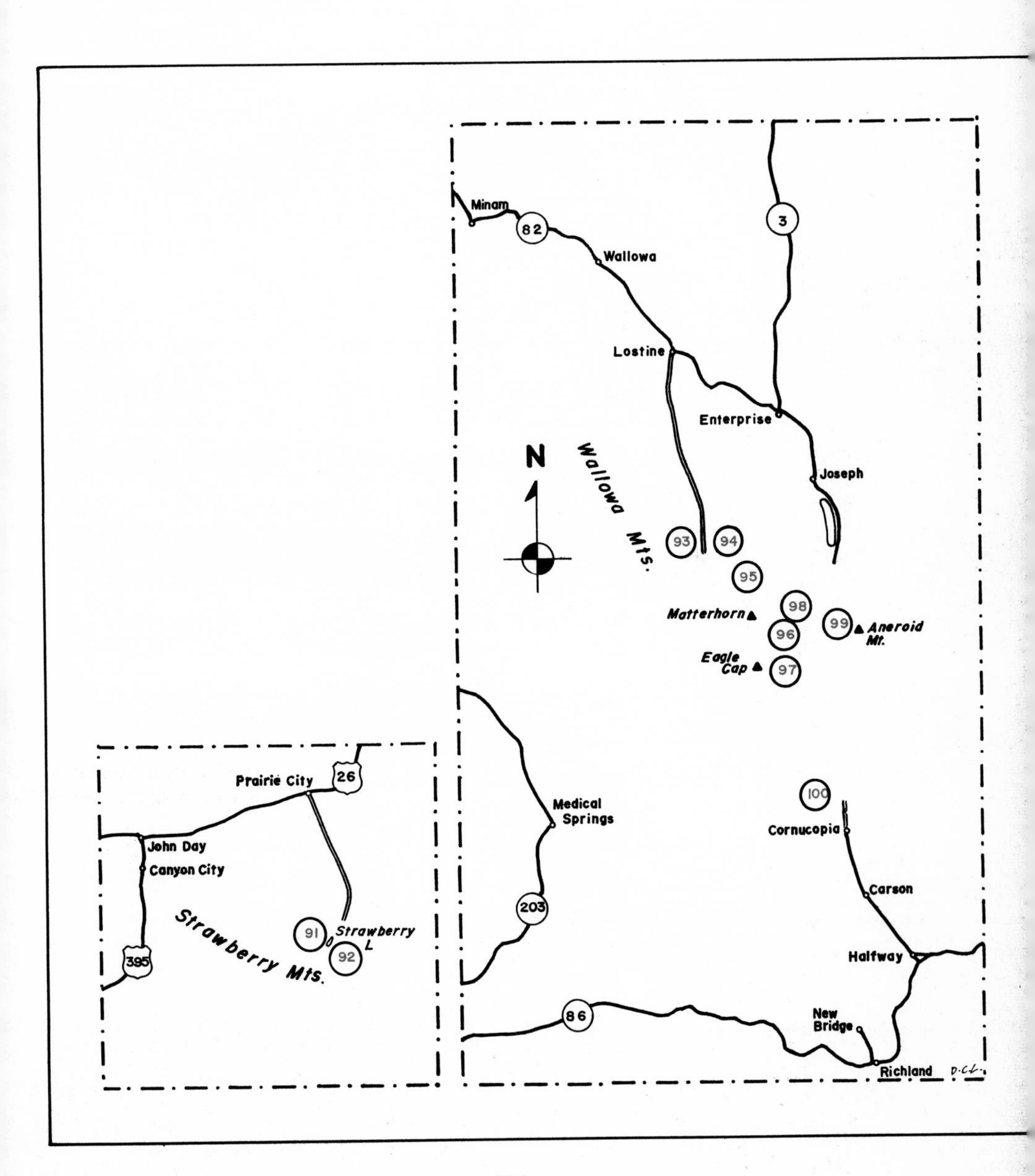

Minam
82
Wallowa
3
Lostine
Enterprise
Joseph
N
Wallowa Mts.
93
94
95
98
Matterhorn
99
Aneroid Mt.
96
Eagle Cap
97
Medical Springs
100
Cornucopia
203
Carson
Halfway
86
New Bridge
Richland
Prairie City
26
John Day
Canyon City
Strawberry Mts.
91
Strawberry L
92
395

The mountains rising steeply along the southern edge of the Wallowa River Valley afford little hint of the majestic country that lies beyond, where massive granite cliffs and peaks tower over the many high, alpine meadows and sparkling lakes. Rushing streams wind down U-shaped valleys carved by massive glaciers during the Ice Age. Of the many lakes scattered about the range, the largest is Wallowa Lake, just south of Joseph. The glaciers, which once came out of the valleys of the West and East Fork of the Wallowa River, deposited a terminal and two lateral moraines which now form the shores of the lake.

There is so much to savor in the Wallowas that you are urged to spend as many days as possible exploring this region. If you don't want to do a lot of packpacking, several rental cabins are available on private land at Aneroid Lake. You will not have to pack food to the lake since there is a small store adjacent to the cabins which handles most staples. An excellent lodge is located at the southern end of Wallowa Lake, and there are many good car camping facilities on Hurricane Creek and the Lostine River.

Hikers who are also fishermen will want to allow additional time for trying their luck in the many lakes. Often you will be lured from the trail to scramble over boulders or roam through lush meadows. Another delightful distraction is the number of less common animals that inhabit the Wallowas. Conies make their homes in rock slides at lower elevations. These furry little rock rabbits have a distinctive whistling sound and with a little patience you may be able to see them. All woods support chipmunks and squirrels, but not usually as many as the number that scamper around in the forested valleys of the Wallowas. Gophers and prairie dogs can be seen running in and out of homes they have burrowed in grass-covered ground. Deer are seen frequently; viewed less often are the coyotes which roam the upper meadows. The hiker who sees one of the rare mountain goats that inhabit the highest peaks is fortunate indeed. Many of the bear that once were native to the Wallowas were killed after eating poison bait set out for coyotes.

All of the trails, with the notable exception of the one to Echo Lake, climb very gradually as the grades have been designed for horse travel. It is suggested that each be done as an overnight hike. Like most other mountain areas, the trails in the Wallowas are covered with snow during the late fall, winter, and spring. Although skies are generally clear during the summer, the mountain range is extensive enough to create its own weather patterns, so be prepared for possible wet and windy conditions — particularly short but drenching thunderstorms. Nights are cold in the Wallowas.

Although less grandiose than the Wallowas, the Strawberry Mountains possess the same sort of terrain — deep valleys and lakes well-stocked with fish. Mountains rise to the south of a wide valley and from a distance offer little evidence of the rugged nature of the interior. This wild area is not too well known, probably because people do not think that such an alpine setting could exist in this arid and sometimes barren part of the state.

The trails have been graded for horse use so the angle is very moderate. Remember — HORSES HAVE THE RIGHT OF WAY, so step well off the trail on the downslope side when you meet them. Also, avoid sudden movement which will often startle a horse.

91 STRAWBERRY MOUNTAIN NORTHEASTERN OREGON

One day trip or backpack
Distance: 6 miles one way
Elevation gain: 3,265 feet
High point: 9,038 feet
Allow 3½ to 5 hours one way
Usually open July through October
Topographic map:
U.S.G.S. Prairie City, Oreg.
N4415-W11830/15
1959

Strawberry Mountain is the highest point in the wild area of the same name. This region, with its rugged cliffs, open slopes, large meadows, and numerous lakes often seems to be a miniature version of the Wallowas.

Drive on U.S. 26 to Prairie City, 12 miles east of John Day. At the east end of the town turn south on Main Street, following the sign to Logan Valley, Blue Mountain Springs, and Strawberry Lake. One-half mile south, turn right on Bridge Street at the sign pointing to Strawberry Lake. Continue on this unpaved road for 12 miles, past two campgrounds and the Onion Creek trailhead to Strawberry Camp where there is ample parking space. If you wish to camp here, tables, fire grates, running water, and outbuildings have been provided.

The trailhead can be found on the southeast side of the campground and is marked by a sign reading Strawberry Trail, No. 375 — Strawberry Lake 1½ miles, Little Strawberry Lake 3 miles.

You will follow a recently constructed trail for one mile, climbing gradually through the woods to the junction of the Slide Creek Trail, No. 372. Continue straight ahead as indicated by the signs pointing to Strawberry Lake. One-quarter mile further you will come to the second junction of the Slide Creek Trail. Keep to the right and when you come to the lake's edge, take the trail to the left and follow along the east shore for about 100 yards to a sign pointing to Strawberry Falls 1 mile, and Little Strawberry Lake 2 miles. Beyond this point there are level places for campsites at the edge of the lake. A fisherman's trail circles the lake.

Upon leaving the lake, the trail climbs gradually along the slope above the lake to the foot of 75-foot high Strawberry Falls and then switchbacks to the top of the falls, crossing Strawberry Creek and meeting the junction of the Little Strawberry Lake Trail. This small lake is at the base of a rocky cirque one-half mile east. The main trail continues to climb through woods, curving around the head of the Strawberry Valley giving a view of Strawberry Lake and a small portion of the John Day Valley.

Climb across the face of a grassy hillside in two long traverses and continue along semi-open slopes to a ridge crest and follow the trail through a very lush but swampy meadow. The trail is obscure near the west end, but the trees are well blazed. Next to a spring at the west end of the meadow is an old log cabin. Just beyond the cabin, the trail turns to the south and goes through a small, rocky canyon before switchbacking up the slope to the saddle just south of Strawberry Mountain. Here you will meet the junction of the trail to Indian Springs Road, which is 1.5 miles to the south. Continue north up the ridge crest for a short distance before contouring along the open slope on the east side of the peak. Just as the trail turns to the left towards the summit you will meet the junction of the Onion Creek Trail, No. 368. Continue south for one-quarter mile to the top of Strawberry Mountain. From this height (9,038 feet) you can see most of the Strawberry Mountain Wild Area plus the Blue Mountains, the John Day Valley, and in the far distance the Wallowa Mountains, barely visible.

Old miner's cabin near Strawberry Mountain

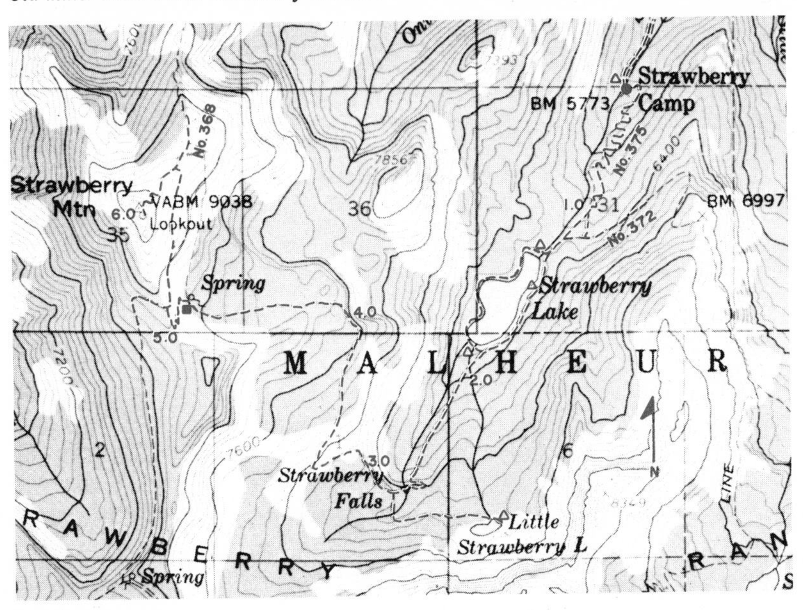

92 HIGH LAKE NORTHEASTERN OREGON

One day trip or backpack
Distance: 6.5 miles one way
Elevation gain: 2,399 feet, loss 672 feet
High point: 8,172 feet
Allow 4½ to 6 hours one way
Usually open mid-July through October
Topographic map:
U.S.G.S. Prairie City, Oreg.
N4415-W11830/15
1959

Several high points along this trail provide extensive views of the eastern section of the Strawberry Mountain Wild Area. Two large lakes are visited and a side trip can be made to a third smaller one.

Drive on U.S. Highway 26 to Prairie City, 12 miles east of John Day. At the east end of the town turn south on Main Street, and follow the sign to Logan Valley, Blue Mountain Springs, and Strawberry Lake. One-half mile south, turn right on Bridge Street at the sign pointing to Strawberry Lake. Continue on this unpaved road for 12 miles past two campgrounds and the Onion Creek trailhead to Strawberry Camp, where you will find fire grates, running water, and outbuildings.

The trailhead can be found on the southeast side of the campground and is marked by a sign reading Strawberry Trail, No. 375 — Strawberry Lake 1½ miles, Little Strawberry Lake 3 miles.

Follow a recently constructed trail for one mile, climbing gradually through the woods, to the junction of the Slide Creek Trail, No. 372. Turn left here and continue climbing through the woods in two long switchbacks. At two miles, you will come onto a semi-open area on the ridge crest. Take the upper, improved trail around to the east side of the ridge and contour along the open slope several hundred feet above the valley floor. Just after meeting the old trail and rounding a corner, you will see a sign pointing to Slide Falls, across the valley. At four miles a sign points to the left to Slide Lake ¼ mile. This is a good stopping place and water can be obtained from the lake outlet creek. Continue south along this side trail if you wish to visit Little Slide Lake.

From the four-mile point, the trail to High Lake zigzags through timber west of Slide Lake to a level clearing at the base of a steep slope. Here the trail forks. The branch to the right is a horse grade and less steep than the one on the left. If you take the steeper trail you will come to a junction with Mud Lake Trail, No. 379, upon reaching the saddle. Keep to the right. The main trail joins the alternate one a few hundred yards beyond this junction. Continue climbing to the ridge crest where you can look down on High Lake. To get a view of Slide Lake, scramble up the slope above the trail just beyond the viewpoint.

The trail drops down to High Lake in long switchbacks. Lake Creek Trail, No. 378, junctions with the High Lake Trail at the outlet creek. Ample campsites surround the lake and creek water is available a short distance up the trail.

Slide Lake

High Lake, Strawberry Mountains

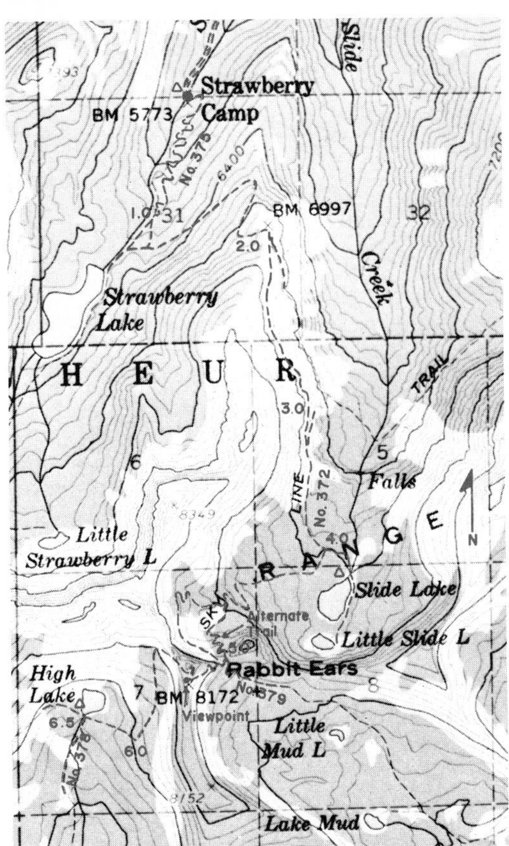

93 CHIMNEY LAKE NORTHEASTERN OREGON

One day trip or backpack
Distance: 5 miles one way
Elevation gain: 2,610 feet
High point: 7,610 feet
Allow 3 to 3½ hours one way
Usually open July through October
Topographic map:
U.S.G.S. Enterprise, Oreg.
N4515-W11715/15
1957

Chimney Lake is a good place to establish a base camp for further exploration of the high country separating the Lostine River, Bear Creek, and the North Minam River in Wallowa-Whitman National Forest. The best overall view can be obtained by hiking to Hobo Lake and climbing directly up an open rocky south ridge to the summit of 8,831 foot Lookout Mountain.

Drive on Oregon Highway 82 to the community of Lostine, 35 miles east of Elgin. Turn right at the sign pointing to the Lostine River and Irondyke Camp. Proceed south along this road for 14.5 miles to the trailhead on the right side of the road just beyond Irondyke Forest Camp where parking is available for several cars. A sign here marks the Bowman Trail, No. 1651, and reads, Chimney Lake 5 miles, John Henry Lake 6 miles, North Minam Meadows 10 miles.

The trail crosses over the Lostine River on a bridge and shortly thereafter crosses Bowman Creek on another bridge, which is for pedestrian travel only. A sign instructs horsemen to use the ford. At one-half mile the trail forks and switchbacks to the right. Stay right and climb several more switchbacks, then contour around the north side of a ridge and re-cross Bowman Creek and the stream from the Laverty Lakes. At 3.2 miles you will enter the Eagle Cap Wilderness Area at a broad meadow which goes all the way to the Brownie Basin, one mile south.

South of this sign the trail climbs up above Bowman Creek and at 3.5 miles meets the junction of the Chimney Lake Trail, No. 1659. (The mileages shown on the trail sign are incorrect.) Turn right here and climb along the slope below the Laverty Lakes, crossing its outlet creek and the creek from Chimney Lake. At both Chimney Lake and Hobo Lake, one mile beyond, you will find good campsites. However, the shore of Chimney Lake is more sheltered and usually less windy.

Side trips can be made north to Wood Lake, south to the Brownie Basin, John Henry Lake, and down into the beautiful valley of the North Minam Meadows.

Early winter snow on Chimney Lake Trail

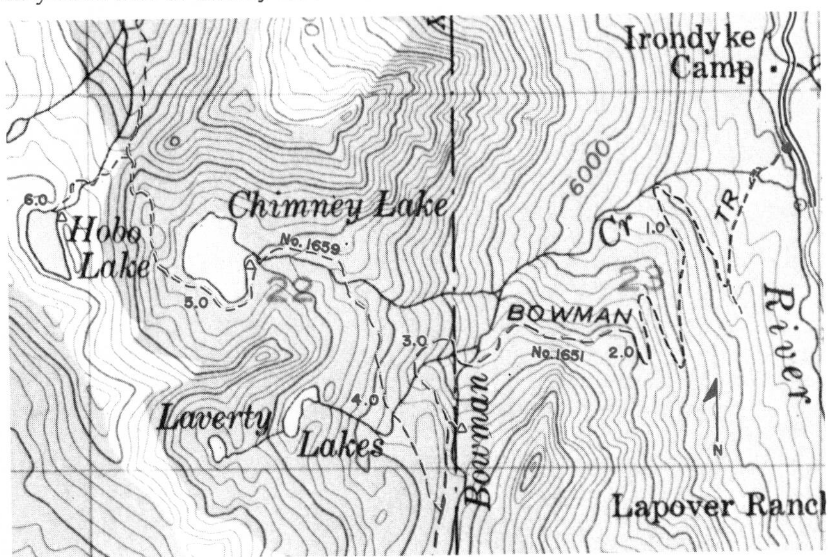

94 FRANCES LAKE NORTHEASTERN OREGON

Backpack
Distance: 9 miles one way
Elevation gain: 3,250 feet, loss 800 feet
High point: 8,480 feet
Allow 5 to 6 hours one way
Usually open July through October
Topographic map:
U.S.G.S. Enterprise, Oreg.
N4515-W11715/15
1957

Frances Lake and the chain of small ponds at its northern end are visible about two miles before you actually reach their shores. While climbing to the ridge above the lake you will enjoy views of the Lostine River Valley and the rugged peaks surrounding the Lake Basin area. Although not steep, the trail gains a great deal of elevation in numerous switchbacks to a high ridge separating Frances Lake and the Lostine River. From the Lostine Valley, the ridge looks very close, but it is a full seven miles and more than 3,000 feet to the crest.

Take Oregon Highway 82 to Lostine, 35 miles east of Elgin. Turn right at the sign pointing to the Lostine River and Irondyke Camp. Proceed south along this road for 15.5 miles, passing Irondyke and Lillyville Forest Camps, to the trail head 0.3 mile beyond King Forest Camp. A sign on the left side of the road marks the Frances Lake Trail, No. 1663. There is a turnaround on the road a few yards further south where limited parking space is available.

This new trail, built to accommodate horses, switchbacks through the woods while climbing in a very consistent but gentle grade. At three and three-quarter miles the trail leaves the woods and comes to a creek that usually is dry. The trail then switchbacks gradually up semi-open slopes affording grand vistas of the surrounding mountains. At about 6.5 miles, the trail travels in a northerly direction just below the ridge crest. For your first view of Frances Lake, leave the trail and walk up the slope a few feet to a saddle. Another good stopping place to admire the scenery is at the seven-mile point just before the trail twists for two miles down to the lake. Good camping spots can be found on the northwest shore near several small streams. Frances Lake is an ideal place to establish a base camp if you wish to either hunt, photograph, or just try to see the rare mountain goats that inhabit the high peaks to the south.

Frances Lake

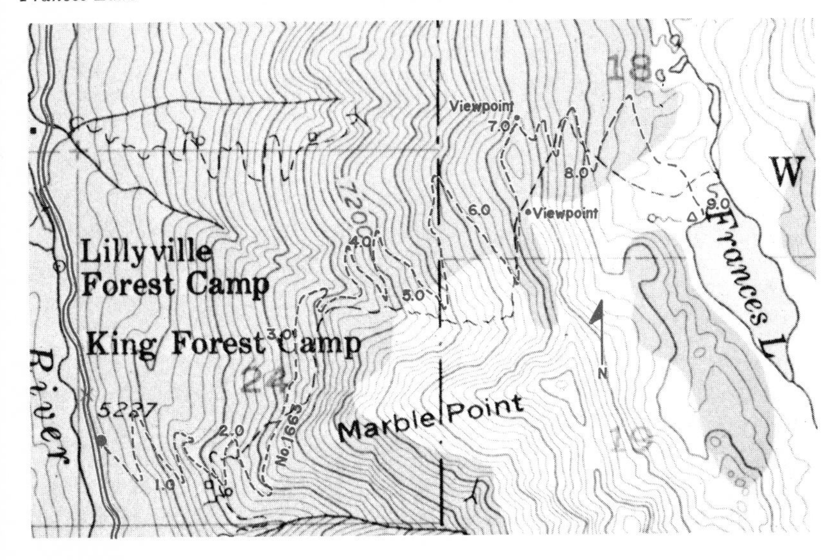

95 ECHO LAKE NORTHEASTERN OREGON

Backpack
Distance: 7 miles one way
Elevation gain: 3,334 feet
High point: 8,360 feet
Allow 4½ to 6 hours one way
Usually open mid-July through October
Topographic map:
U.S.G.S. Enterprise, Oreg.
N4515-W11715/15
1957

The trail to Echo Lake is surely one of the most beautiful trips in the Wallowas, even though the hike between Hurricane Creek and the meadow below Echo Lake is on the steepest trail in the Eagle Cap Wilderness Area. Across the valley to the southeast, you will see the fluted white granite walls of the Matterhorn rising almost vertically to its dome-like summit. It more nearly resembles the face of El Capitan in Yosemite Valley than its European namesake.

Drive east on Oregon Highway 82 to the town of Enterprise. From the center of town, turn south on the road to Hurricane Creek and follow it to the end of the pavement at the Hurricane Grange. Continue south on the gravel road, No. S-218, for three miles to its end at Falls Creek Forest Camp. There is ample parking space in this well-developed campground.

The trail begins at the southwest side of the turnaround and is marked by a sign reading Hurricane Creek Trail, No. 1807.

Climb for about 0.1 mile where you will come to the junction of a path on the right leading to Falls Creek Falls. Keep to the left and after one-quarter mile, cross Falls Creek. The trail then travels alternately through woods and open slopes. The avalanche damage at the deep narrow gorge just before Slick Creek is particularly interesting. At 4.5 miles, you will come to a campsite and the junction of the Billy Jones Lake Trail, No. 525. (The trail actually goes to Echo Lake.)

The trail turns to the right here, and is level for a few hundred yards. Then it begins to climb steeply with a few level stretches until 5.5 miles, where the grade becomes very steep. But, it is well worth the climb when you reach the top and look out across a large meadow rimmed with trees and surrounded by high granite walls.

Hike through the meadow keeping to the right of Granite Creek and head for a large *round* tree just beyond the upper end. The trail is not distinguishable in the grass, but becomes quite obvious as you enter the strip of woods which separates the large lower meadow from the small upper one. Hike up the middle of the second meadow until just before a scree slope and then turn to the left, cross the creek and follow the trail for one-half mile as it climbs through boulder-strewn slopes. At the seven-mile point, turn left at the sign pointing to Echo Lake. It is stocked and is certainly one of the highest fishing lakes in Oregon.

Meadow near Echo Lake

96 LAKE BASIN NORTHEASTERN OREGON

Backpack
Distance: 11 miles one way
Elevation gain: 2,754 feet
High point: 7,400 feet
Allow 6 to 8 hours one way
Usually open July through October
Topographic maps:
- **U.S.G.S. Cornucopia, Oreg. N4500-W11700/15 1954**
- **U.S.G.S. Eagle Cap, Oreg. N4500-W11715/15 1954**
- **U.S.G.S. Joseph, Oreg. N4515-W11700/15 1957**

This area contains six major lakes, the deepest and most scenic of which is Moccasin Lake. A short hike past this lake up towards Glacier Pass affords a good view of the entire basin. The sheer western face of the Matterhorn and nearby Eagle Cap can be seen from several places in the basin. Good campsites are available by all of the lakes.

Take Oregon Highway 82 to Joseph and follow the signs to Wallowa Lake State Park, six miles south of the town. Proceed past the park on the Powerhouse Road. At the fork, bear left where a sign points to "Mountain Trails." The road terminates in a large parking area adjacent to well-developed picnic grounds. At the southeast end of the pavement near the powerhouse is a large sign that reads in part: West Fork of Wallowa River Trail, No. 1820 — Lake Basin 9 miles, Moccasin Lake 11 miles. The trail begins as a gravel road at the southwest end of the parking area. After a few yards it crosses a stream emanating from the powerhouse, where a small sign points to the West Fork Trail. The beginning of the trail is identified by a large bulletin board bearing Forest Service circulars.

Climb for about one-eighth mile to a viewpoint overlooking Wallowa Lake, then turn south and follow the trail as it rises very gently for the next 2.5 miles. Just before the three-mile marker is the junction of Trail 18 to Ice Lake. Continue straight ahead and climb very gradually through the woods and occasional open slopes. At six miles, in the middle of a large meadow, is the junction of Trail 1810 to the Lake Basin. Good campsites can be found on the edge of the meadow by the West Fork of the Wallowa River.

Take Trail 1810 and continue through the meadow. Cross, via bridges, the West Fork of the Wallowa River and Lake Creek a few feet further on. Then climb in switchbacks through the woods for about two miles and level off before coming to Horseshoe Lake. Just after hiking around the end of the lake you will come to a junction marked by a sign saying Trail No. 1821, Unit Lake 1 mile. Keep to the left here and continue around Horseshoe Lake. On the north side of the lake, just across a bridge, is another junction with a sign pointing to Razz Lake, 2 miles. Lee Lake is just a short distance beyond this junction. Here you will switchback up a slope to the north of Lee Lake and then level off for about one-half mile. Just before Douglas Lake you will reach the Crescent Lake junction. Keep left for the most direct route to Moccasin Lake.

The trail proceeds past Douglas Lake and climbs in switchbacks for about one-half mile to where it again becomes level. It meanders through several small rocky canyons and traverses along open slopes above the northwest shore of Moccasin Lake. At the end of the lake keep to the left and cross a small bridge. The best campsites are on the southeast shore.

Moccasin Lake, Matterhorn in distance

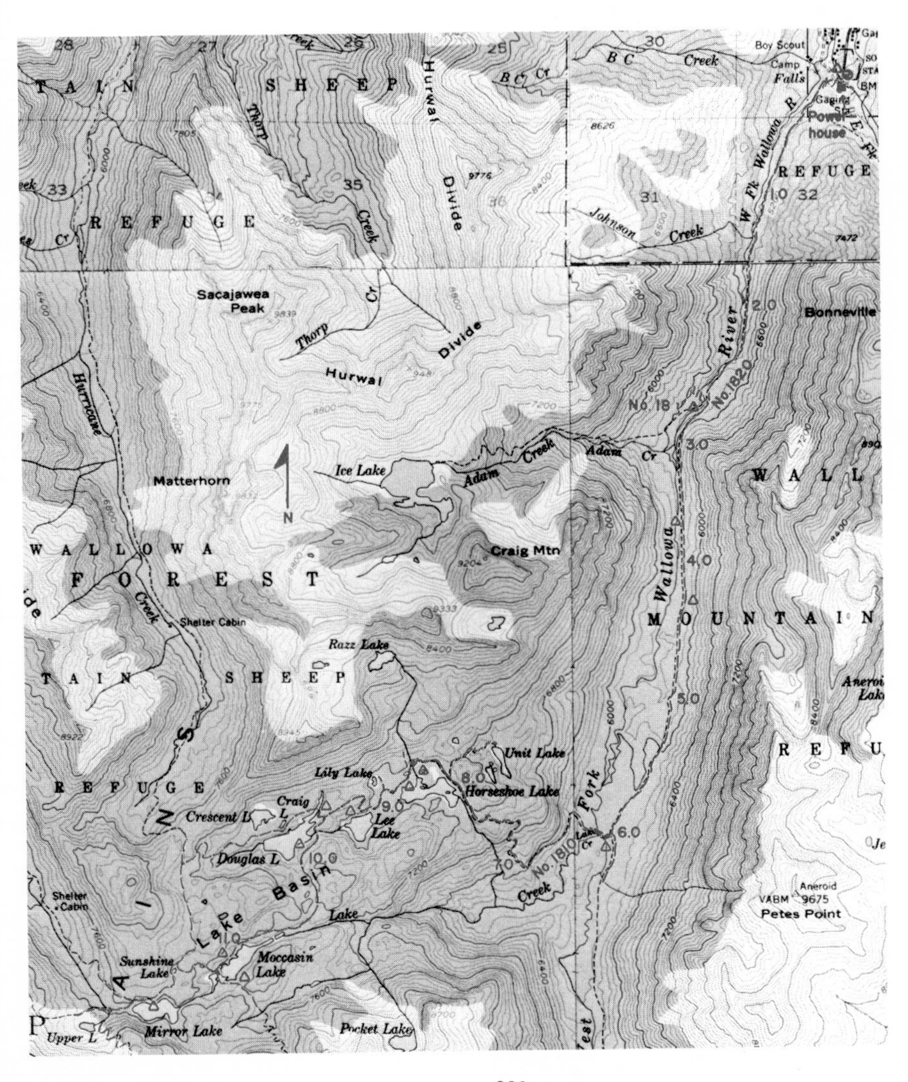
Sacajawea Peak
Matterhorn
Hurwal Divide
Ice Lake
Adam Creek
Craig Mtn
Razz Lake
Unit Lake
Lily Lake
Horseshoe Lake
Crescent L
Craig L
Lee Lake
Douglas L
Lake Basin
Sunshine Lake
Moccasin Lake
Mirror Lake
Upper L
Pocket Lake
Shelter Cabin
Petes Point
Aneroid
Bonneville
Boy Scout Camp
Falls
Power house
No. 1820
No. 1810
No. 18
Wallowa River
W Fk Wallowa R
Johnson Creek
BC Creek
Thorp Creek
Hurricane Creek
West Fork Wallowa
WALLOWA FOREST
MOUNTAIN SHEEP REFUGE

97 GLACIER LAKE NORTHEASTERN OREGON

Backpack
Distance: 11 miles one way
Elevation gain: 3,854 feet
High point: 8,500 feet
Allow 7 to 9 hours one way
Usually open July through October
Topographic maps:
- **U.S.G.S. Cornucopia, Oreg.**
  N4500-W11700/15
  1954
- **U.S.G.S. Eagle Cap, Oreg.**
  N4500-W11715/15
  1954
- **U.S.G.S. Joseph, Oreg.**
  N4515-W11700/15
  1957

Island-dotted Glacier Lake is certainly one of the most spectacular spots in Oregon. A short hike from the lake up to Glacier Pass affords a sweeping view of the Lake Basin area and the beginnings of the Lostine River and Hurricane Creek Valleys.

Take Highway 82 to Joseph and follow the signs to Wallowa Lake State Park, six miles south of the town. Proceed past the park on the Powerhouse Road. At the fork bear left where a sign points to "Mountain Trails." The road terminates in a large parking area adjacent to well developed picnic grounds. At the southeast end of the pavement near the powerhouse a large sign reads in part: West Fork of Wallowa River Trail, No. 1820 — Glacier Lake 11 miles, Frazier Lake 9 miles. The trail begins as a gravel road at the southwest end of the parking area. After a few yards it crosses a stream emananting from the powerhouse, where a small sign points to the West Fork Trail. The beginning of the trail is identified by a large bulletin board bearing Forest Service circulars.

Climb for about one-eighth mile to a viewpoint overlooking Wallowa Lake, then turn south and follow the gently-rising trail for the next 2.5 miles. Just before the three-mile marker is the junction of Trail 18 to Ice Lake. Continue straight ahead and climb very gradually through the woods and occasional open slopes. At six miles in the middle of a large meadow is the junction of Trail 1810 to the Lake Basin. Good campsites can be found on the edge of the meadow by the West Fork of the Wallowa River.

Continue south along the main trail through woods and open hillsides. At eight miles you will begin to switchback. Just before the head of the valley, a side trail leads steeply up towards Sentinel Peak. This is the newly-constructed Polaris Trail to Aneroid Lake. Continue south on the Glacier Lake Trail through a small stand of dense timber and then contour above the river through a small gorge before dropping down into a grassy valley. Cross the river and begin switchbacking up to a ridge about one-fourth mile upstream. Frazier Lake is just around this ridge. Here there are ample campsites and water is available from several creeks a short distance up the trail. Since Glacier Lake can be very windy and cold, it may be desirable to establish a camp at Frazier Lake if there is any doubt about the weather.

Continue along the trail west of Frazier Lake and follow the West Fork of the Wallowa River for a few hundred feet. Just after crossing the river you will find the junction of the Hawkins Pass Trail, No. 1820. Keep to the right, now following Trail No. 1806, which climbs to a charming, meadowed valley. The trail follows the river closely, crossing it twice. Climb again and cross a large open level area. Glacier Lake is reached after one last climb along a boulder-strewn side hill.

Weather permitting, you can find many fine campsites here. Interestingly, the impressive mountain across the lake is an unnamed peak and is not Eagle Cap, which is on the same ridge but farther to the northwest. Glacier Pass, less than one-half mile up the trail, offers panoramic views of the Lake Basin area to the northwest and back to Glacier and Frazier Lakes.

Glacier Lake

Trail from Frazier to Glacier Lake

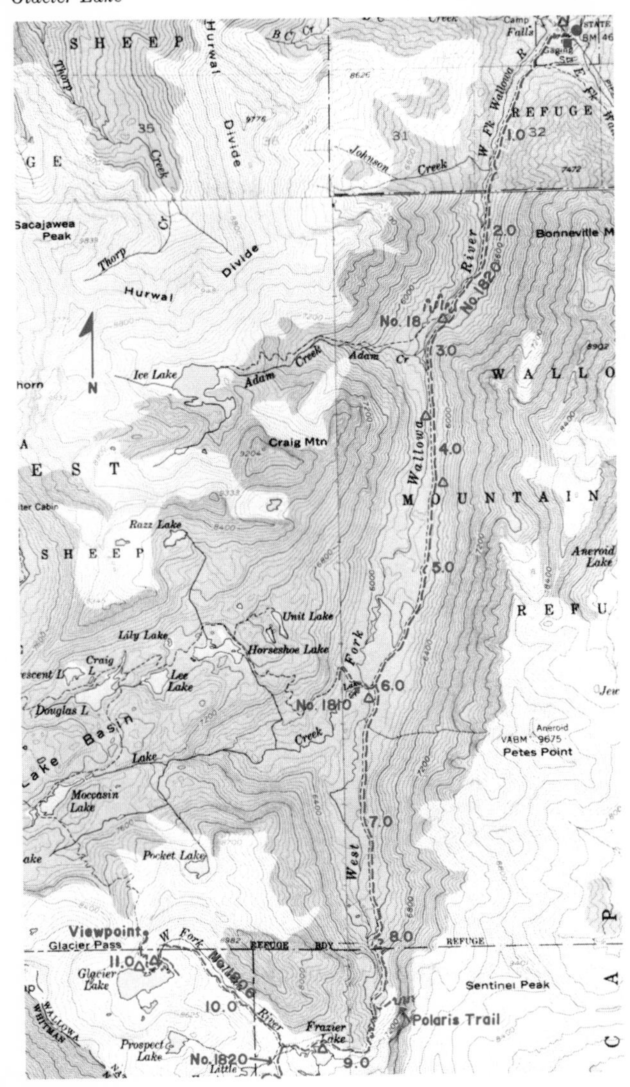

98 ICE LAKE NORTHEASTERN OREGON

Backpack
Distance: 8 miles one way
Elevation gain: 3,254 feet
High point: 7,900 feet
Allow 4 to 5 hours one way
Usually open July through October
Topographic maps:
U.S.G.S. Cornucopia, Oreg.
N4500-W11700/15
1954
U.S.G.S. Eagle Cap, Oreg.
N4500-W11715/15
1954
U.S.G.S. Joseph, Oreg.
N4515-W11700/15
1957

The more gentle eastern slopes of the Matterhorn, one of the highest peaks in the Wallowas, are seen from Ice Lake. Climbers attempting both the Matterhorn and Sacajawea usually make their approach from this large alpine lake.

Take Oregon Highway 82 to Joseph and follow the signs to Wallowa Lake State Park, six miles south of the town. Proceed past the park on the Powerhouse Road. At the fork bear left where a sign points to "Mountain Trails." The road terminates in a large parking area adjacent to well-developed picnic grounds. At the southeast end of the pavement a large sign reads in part: West Fork of Wallowa River Trail, No. 1820 — Ice Lake 7 miles. The trail begins as a gravel road at the southwest end of the parking area. After a few yards it crosses a stream emanating from the powerhouse, where a small sign points to the West Fork Trail. The beginning of the trail is identified by a large bulletin board bearing Forest Service circulars.

Climb for about one-eighth mile to a viewpoint overlooking Wallowa Lake, then turn south to follow the gently-rising trail for the next 2.5 miles. Just before the three-mile marker is the junction of the Ice Lake Trail, No. 18. Ice Lake is five miles from this point. Take this trail to the right (west). After a few hundred yards cross a bridge over the West Fork of the Wallowa River, then switchback gently for about one mile through semi-open grassy slopes and rock slides. The switchbacks then will become steeper as you zigzag up the face of a slope overlooking Adam Creek Gorge and several waterfalls. At 5.3 miles you will level off as the trail travels through a meadow. The creek crossing near the far end of the clearing offers a good campsite.

Beyond the creek the trail switchbacks up a steep, wooded slope, climbing steadily but gradually. After about a mile it becomes nearly level and heads in a westerly direction until coming to the lake.

Good campsites are plentiful. An open, grassy spot at the far end of the lake can be reached by continuing along the trail, which follows the north shore. To get to other more sheltered campsites, cross the bridge at the outlet of the lake and continue south along the trail to the level peninsula on the east shore.

Ice Lake

Falls on Adam Creek

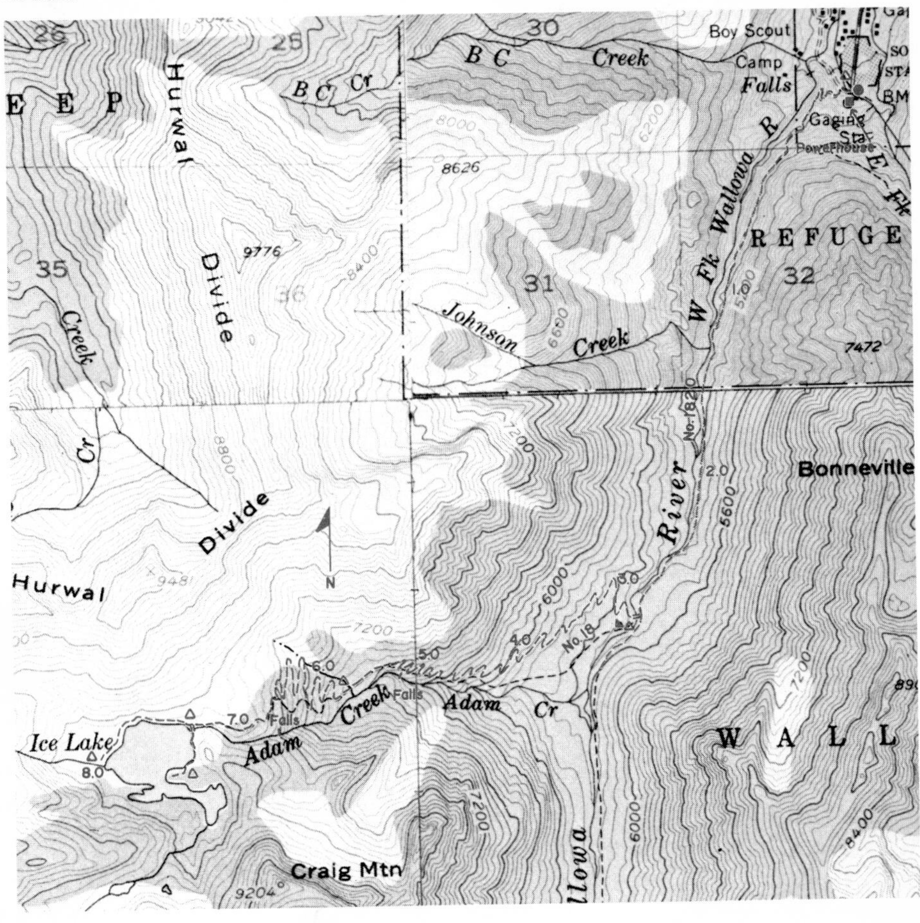

99 ANEROID LAKE NORTHEASTERN OREGON

One day trip or backpack
Distance: 6 miles one way
Elevation gain: 3,054 feet
High point: 7,500 feet
Allow 3½ to 4½ hours one way
Usually open July through October
Topographic maps:
U.S.G.S. Cornucopia, Oreg.
N4500-W11700/15
1954
U.S.G.S. Joseph, Oreg.
N4515-W11700/15
1957

Store at Aneroid Lake

Rustic log buildings and a lake noted for its excellent fishing await the hiker at the end of this trip, which is livened by conies and chipmunks that are seen and heard continually in the rocky areas along the trail.

Take Oregon Highway 82 to Joseph and follow the signs to Wallowa Lake State Park, six miles south of the town. Proceed past the park on the Powerhouse Road. At the fork bear left where a sign points to "Mountain Trails." The road terminates in a large parking area adjacent to well-developed picnic grounds. At the southeast end of the pavement near the powerhouse a large sign reads in part: East Fork of Wallowa Trail, No. 1804 — Aneroid Lake 6 miles. Follow a dirt road a short distance east to where another sign marks the beginning of the trail.

The initial portion of the trail switchbacks up the slope directly above the powerhouse. Wallowa Lake can be seen occasionally to the south. Watch for conies and chipmunks in the rocky areas bordering the trail. (Conies are small, furry creatures that resemble miniature rabbits without the long ears.) The trail moves through the woods and occasional open areas for one and three-quarter miles to an old wooden dam and small reservoir. There the trail continues to climb gradually with a few switchbacks alternating between semi-open slopes and woods. At about three and three-quarter miles it enters a deeply wooded area. Just beyond a small stream crossing is a bench which affords a good spot for a short break. The trail continues climbing through heavy timber, crosses a bridge and eventually enters a large meadow. Shortly after entering this open area, keep to the right where the trail forks.

Just before the six-mile marker you will come to Roger Lake and a sign pointing to Aneroid Lake one-half mile. Continue to the south end of Aneroid Lake and descend to a cluster of buildings. These log structures, which blend well with their surroundings, were built before the turn of the century and are situated on private land — a rarity in a wilderness area. One of the buildings is a small store and cold soft drinks, candies, and sundries may be purchased here. Three cabins are available for overnight use at a very reasonable charge. Campsites are plentiful and the lake is well-stocked with fish.

Aneroid Lake

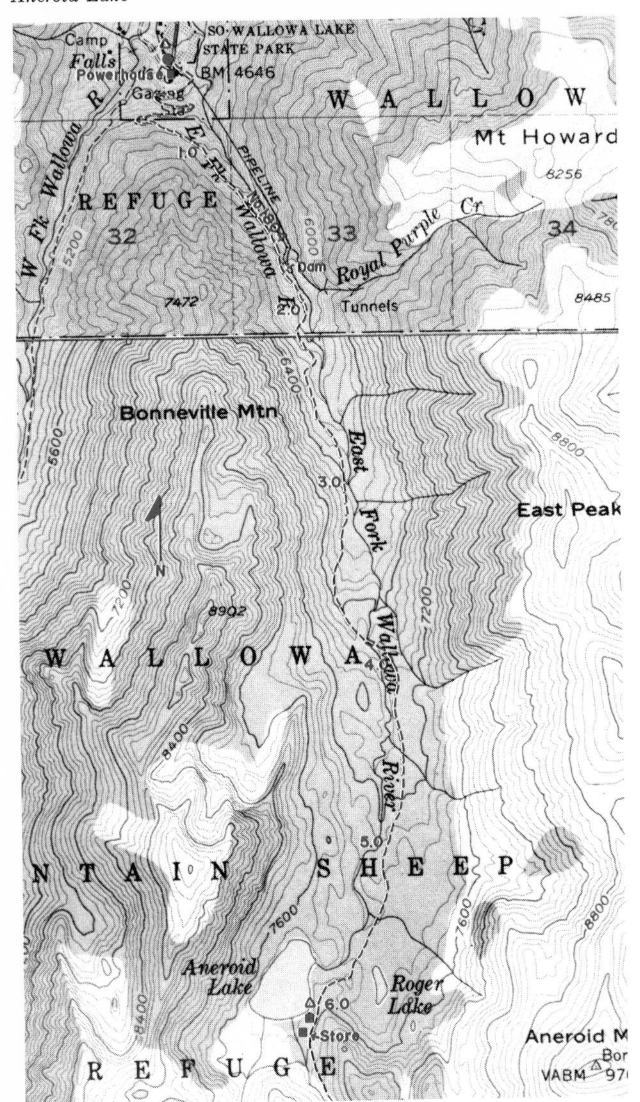

100 PINE LAKES NORTHEASTERN OREGON

One day trip or backpack
Distance: 5 miles one way
Elevation gain: 2,280 feet
High point: 7,540 feet
Allow 3 to 4 hours one way
Usually open July through October
Topographic maps:
U.S.G.S. Cornucopia, Oreg.
N4500-W11700/15
1954
U.S.G.S. Eagle Cap, Oreg.
N4500-W11715/15
1954

Large valleys with meadowed floors, rocky hillsides, and high lakes serve to remind you that you are in typical Wallowa country even though this trail is in the southern part of the range. Although this is a very beautiful trip, the last three miles of road from Cornucopia to the Queen Mine are extremely rough and should not be attempted with vehicles that have inadequate clearance.

Drive on Oregon Highway 86 and turn north at the settlement of Pine, 53 miles east of Baker. Continue north for 11 miles passing through Halfway and Carson to the old ghost town of Cornucopia, once a thriving goldmining center. At Cornucopia, turn right onto Road S-630, and follow the sign to the Pine Lakes Trail, No. 1880. After a few feet keep to the left where a side road curves upslope. Although this three-mile stretch of road is level, it is very rough and the bridges that span several small creeks are in poor condition. The road terminates at the Queen Mine where there is ample parking.

The trail starts at the north end of the turnaround and immediately crosses the west fork of Pine Creek on a footbridge. The buildings of the abandoned Queen Mine, including two tramways, one of which suspends a large bucket high overhead, and a shed far up on the slope to the east, are silent reminders of the frenzied mining activity that occurred in the early part of this century.

Switchback up through brush and woods for about one and one-quarter miles, then traverse across a long, rocky slope where you will enjoy watching for the furry little conies who make their homes in the spaces between the boulders. Then zigzag to the head of the valley and travel on the level through a recently burned area. Climb a short distance further before coming to the upper valley at the three-mile point. Directly below the trail there is a good campsite.

For the next three-quarters mile, hike along the valley floor traveling through woods and stretches of grassy meadow. At three and three-quarter miles, begin switchbacking up the steep slopes on the west side of the valley and continue climbing until reaching the bench and the first of the two Pine Lakes. The trail passes a small concrete dam at the outlet creek from the first lake. Follow the trail around to the north shore of the second and larger lake where you will find good campsites. The remains of old mining machinery can be found scattered around the shores of both lakes.

Hunter's camp near Pine Lakes Trail

Pine Lakes

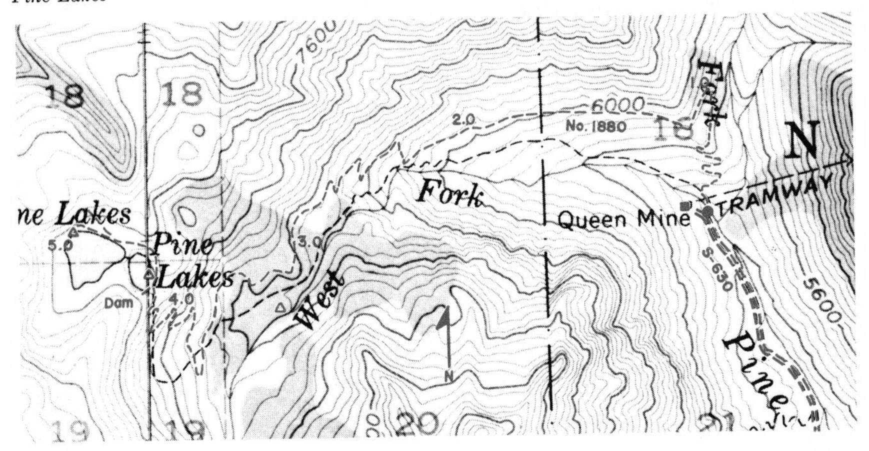

18
18
7600
6000
2.0
No. 1880
Fork
N
Fork
TRAMWAY
ne Lakes
Queen Mine
5.0
Pine
3.0
Lakes
S-630
5600
Dam
4.0
West
N
Pine
19
19
20
21

ALPHABETICAL INDEX OF TRAILS

PHOTOGRAPHIC DATA

Most of the pictures in this book were taken with a Rolleiflex f/3.5 with a medium orange "G" filter. The remainder were photographed with a 4 x 5″ Linhoff III, with Kodak Panatomic X and Plux X film being used in both cameras. In order to obtain the necessary depth of field, a tripod was used for the majority of the pictures with exposure times varying between 1 and 1/5th second from f/11 to f/22. All of the 4 x 5″ negatives were exposed at f/45.

Editor
Thomas K. Worcester

Graphic Design
Robert Reynolds

Typography and Lithography
The Irwin-Hodson Co. - Arcady Press

Lithographic Plates
Pacific Color Plate Co.

Binding
Lincoln & Allen

PHOTOGRAPHS: